OFFENDER ASSESSMENT

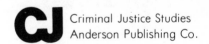

CJ Criminal Justice Studies
Anderson Publishing Co.

CRIMINAL JUSTICE CASEBOOKS

OFFENDER ASSESS- MENT

a casebook in corrections

ROBERT B. MILLS

University of Cincinnati

Table of Contents

Foreword

Robert Mills' *Offender Assessment* is a unique contribution to the training of correctional treatment and supervisory personnel. It does not aim to present a system so much as to define and discuss the interpersonal relationships of interviewer and interviewee in the diagnostic process. His methods are applicable to any correctional setting where there is interaction between two persons in a diagnostic or treatment situation. The assessment methods described would benefit any correctional official attempting to reach an understanding with an offender, whether that official is a pre-service student, a professional social worker, a psychiatrist, a psychologist, an instructor or a guard, and whether the offender is a juvenile or adult, male or female, first offender or recidivist, misdemeanant or felon, a cooperating prisoner or a hard-core, reluctant client. The complete case histories presented in this *Casebook* provide a context for dealing with specific problems encountered in typical cases.

An important feature of the training process is the author's distinction between the quantitative, objective facts and statistics as a basis for decision-making and the subjective, intuitive, clinical approach as the basis for problem-solving. The integration of both approaches may be used as the foundation for both the clinical and actuarial approaches to reducing criminality. Both approaches are aimed at tackling the immediate problems of the offender, which may lead to the discovery of more subtle problems that underlie criminality.

It is essential, however, to recognize the differences between these two objectives: the first deals with determining the cultural competence of the offender without necessarily affecting his criminal predisposition; the second objective, which is more difficult, goes to the heart of the correctional process to locate and treat the significant problems underlying and sustaining individual criminality.

The *Casebook* attempts to meet both objectives, and in so doing moves the correctional worker beyond the formalized fact-gathering that has characterized so much of our pre-sentence investigation and classification. Dr. Mills is concerned with any clues for treatment and supervision that will change the offender and, if possible, completely convert him from crime to a law-abiding life-style.

This text will put meat on the bare bones of traditional case histories as used in corrections. It is a valuable and original contribution, since it refines and extends the use of case studies in the field of correctional education and practice.

Howard B. Gill
Institute of Correctional Administration
Boston, Massachusetts

Introduction

Assessment of cases is essential to criminal corrections. Investigative reports are prepared prior to sentencing, institutional assignment, probation/parole violation adjudication, and release by various corrections specialists in order to guide the flow of offenders through the criminal corrections system. At such crucial choice-points in case disposition, the investigative work of the corrections specialist is influential in the decisionmaking of sentencing judges, correctional institutions, parole boards, halfway houses, or community agencies. Thus, a close examination of case assessment and investigation is an essential tool in education and practice which has seldom been fully developed in the professional corrections field.

The Casebook maps out a skills-training process to introduce diagnostic report-writing, with particular emphasis on the presentence investigation (PSI) conducted by probation officers. Students are guided through a series of graduated steps toward production of full-fledged assessments of offenders. Discussion of guidelines, practice cases with assigned tasks, questions for discussion, comments by supervising officers and the author, and supplementary readings highlight each step of the investigative process.

The skills-practice method involved here begins with concrete situations and issues and generates more general conceptual issues through classroom discussion. Thus, theory is embedded in the context of practical problems to be resolved, inverting the "trickle-down" theoretical emphasis so beloved of academicians. I have found this "clinical" method of teaching more effective with criminal justice students, and have come to believe that skills-practice should be the backbone of most professional instruction. The study of criminal cases serves the same function as the study of a cadaver does for the medical student; i.e., it reminds students of the clients to be served through our skills while minimizing the effects of error. Skills-practice may actually be more demanding on instructors than traditional theory courses, but in my experience, skills-practice produces more spontaneity and two-way communication in classroom or workshop settings.

Furthermore, the Casebook can be used to advantage in the in-service training of neophyte probation/parole officers, or as a useful reference in any probation department, parole agency, juvenile court, halfway house, or correctional institution because of its practical emphasis on the guidelines for report-writing. Corrections officers may also utilize the Casebook for self-study to improve assessment skills. The sequence of chapters moves in a structured manner toward production of completed case reports, and encourages a critical approach toward report-writing.

The task of assembling written assessments on offenders normally falls to probation officers in courts at the time of sentencing (although a team of specialists may be used in some courts to conference a PSI), while within correctional institutions a classification officer normally coordinates information required for placement. The functions of the classification officer may also be assumed by a team, as in reception centers, and a variety of titles are used, including "Case Manager", "Psychologist", "Caseworker", etc. Finally, reports used in parole or other releases are assembled by an institutional parole officer, whose functions may be subsumed under a variety of titles. The common feature of such operations, however, is a concern for the most effective handling of offenders as they progress through various stages of the corrections system, and the monitoring and updating of offender behavior through written assessments guides the overall process.

In the Casebook I have espoused the point of view that, in the interests of reducing duplication of effort and fractionalization of the corrections process, probation officers become concerned with the *total* supervision/treatment process, from sentencing to release, at the "front end", the time the offender is sentenced. I have further recommended that corrections officials involved in assessment activities achieve a broad expertise which will enable them to coordinate and interpret to judges and parole boards the specialized work of psychologists, psychiatrists, social workers, educators, and counselors. It appears to me that the specialist in corrections represents the common pathway through which many recognized professionals must direct their efforts. If the profession of corrections is to achieve its full stature, the investigators must assume more than the clerical function of "passing on" information needed by decisionmakers. While it is not suggested that the corrections specialist should *replace* the services of other professionals, these specialists should be knowledgeable about the diagnosis and treatment afforded by mental health professionals (for example), and be able to work with them in a collaborative manner, as equal partners in a mutual enterprise. The acquisition of such broad expertise is beyond the scope of this Casebook, but should be anticipated in academic training programs and workshops.

The message of the Casebook can be summarized as follows: the corrections report-writer is encouraged to move from *description* of to *prescription* for offenders. In other words, to take the factual life-history of offenders and, through the application of statistical and clinical methods, guide supervision and treatment by constructing the best possible set of predictions about an offender's behavior.

Practice cases utilized in the Casebook have been gathered from a variety of correctional settings to illustrate different formats and styles used in various courts and institutions. Cases have not been chosen as *ideal* or *model* cases, since such models are sometimes discouraging to students. In fact, cases are presented "warts and all", with the omissions, distortions, and weak logic of the original reports retained as a challenge to the student's critical faculties. Questions for discussion and comments from officers are intended to highlight possible issues in the case, and test the ingenuity of the student. Nor are these "exotic" cases. An attempt was made to select run-of-the-mill offenders who best reflect the day-to-day tasks of offender investigation.

Names, events, and circumstances of all practice cases have been altered to protect the individuals involved, while the substance of each case has been retained. It is important to remember that persons described here are still with us (with a few exceptions), together with their relatives and victims. Therefore, the Casebook should be used in a professionally responsible manner, with respect for the teaching purpose for which it was designed.

The author wishes to thank the many criminal justice students in the College of Community Services at The University of Cincinnati, who patiently "road-tested" earlier versions of the Casebook, and whose suggestions and reactions have been incorporated in the final version. The support and assistance of my colleagues in the College is gratefully acknowledged, especially Prof. Carol Harten for arranging time for me to complete the manuscript, and my Chairperson, Prof. Keith Haley, for his patient support. Howard B. Gill's critical reading of the manuscript resulted in many constructive changes. Also, I have received substantial assistance from the late Dr. Samuel Yochelson, Dr. Stanton Samenow, Hon. Gilbert Bettman, Barton Anson, Raymond J. Clark, Dr. Robert Levinson, Philip J. Muldoon, Capt. Jeffrey Butler, William Dallman, Dr. Howard Sokolow, Dorothy Mack, Laura Weinland, Terry Drumm, George Farmer, Ron Darling, and many others. Finally, Editors Rick Adams and Candice Piaget, along with William Simon of the Anderson Publishing Company have provided the patience and expertise to complete this lengthy project.

Robert B. Mills,
Cincinnati, Ohio
October, 1979

Part 1
FORMS AND FUNCTIONS OF OFFENDER EVALUATION

Chapter 1
The Investigative Function in Corrections

"There are many decision points in the system which have implications for resocialization of offenders in the community. If we can improve our classification technology at these crucial points, then our resocialization efforts should improve dramatically. Our failure to 'see' the offender in his community, as processed by the system, has been our major weakness in trying to classify offenders for treatment. . . . We are also beginning to know that classification for resocialization is more socially productive than labeling for punishment."

Thomas G. Eynon

The term "corrections" is often equated with the concept of imprisonment. This association, common as it is, is a perfect example of "tunnel vision" — of a narrow perspective that fails to recognize the broad parameters covered by the field of corrections. The modern student of criminal corrections must be exposed to the holistic character of the criminal justice system in order to develop a critical appreciation of the various roles played by corrections workers. By understanding the variety of professional opportunities open to the future corrections worker, students will be able to see beyond the stereotyped images of jail and prison "duties" — to realize that corrections specialists are located not only in prisons but in probation departments attached to courts, in halfway houses and specialized agencies in the community, and in parole agencies.

Despite the variety of settings in which correctional work occurs, a common bond does exist between corrections workers: All are part of a newly emerging *profession* of corrections. Therefore, the acquisition of appropriate skills which can be utilized across a number of correctional settings is essential in the education of a well-rounded professional in the field of corrections.

Organizational analysis of the corrections field shows that the flow of offenders through the system is guided by diagnostic investigation at certain choice-points. Six major choice-points appear to be salient in the sequence of offender management and supervision, with investigative reports commonly requested to aid in decision making at each of these points:

Sentencing Alternatives by Judges. A pre-sentence investigation (PSI) is prepared by a probation officer to guide the sentencing judge in making disposition of cases following conviction. In some courts, where diversion is contemplated or eligibility for bail questioned, an investigation may be conducted *prior* to conviction.

Supervision/Counseling by Probation Officers. The information and recommendations contained in the pre-sentence investigation are also used for the guidance of the probation officer designated to supervise the case.

Referral to Community Agencies. Where the PSI includes referrals to community service agencies, usually as a part of a probation sentence, the PSI report may be used as an intake summary for the recipient agency. Such community referrals might include halfway houses, drug counseling, employment training or placement, medical or psychiatric treatment, welfare, or other specialized services.

Institutional Classification and Placement. Diagnostic workups within correctional institutions usually include a social, psychological, medical, vocational, and educational evaluation to guide assignment to work units, degree of security, schools, or counseling.

Parole Decisions. Institutional parole officers prepare parole plans utilized for release decisions by parole boards. Such parole plans are later used by parole officers in the community to guide supervision and referral, similar to Steps 2 and 3 above.

Revocation of Probation and Parole. In situations where incarceration is under consideration for an offender on probation or parole, judges typically request reviews of progress, or lack of progress, while under supervision.

In addition to the six types of decisions mentioned above, an important purpose for investigative reports is their use in research. Evaluation of the accuracy of investigative reports in decision making is needed to improve the quality of predictions made about offenders.

Diagnostic investigation of offenders can be seen as one of the key skills commonly possessed by corrections workers in many segments of the corrections system. And one of the most important skills that need to be mastered by students in corrections is investigative report writing.

The general purpose of investigative reports is to guide the orderly, rational processing of offenders through the judicial/corrections system. To some extent, the kinds of decisions to be made about an offender may result in a somewhat different emphasis in reports; for example, prison officials face a different set of dispositional alternatives for a newly sentenced offender than did the judge who passed sentence. Similarly, a probation officer referring an offender for psychiatric counseling may emphasize different factors than those stressed in his PSI report for the sentencing judge.

The sad fact of present-day corrections practice is that separate reports are commonly prepared at most of the decision-points mentioned. Such duplication of effort demonstrates the relative isolation of correctional facilities from each other, and the tragic isolation of probation and parole agencies from the mainstream of community service agencies. Historically, corrections agencies and institutions have developed differing forms, work styles, and personnel to deal with their common need for valid diagnostic information in making predictions about their common clients. The most notable exception to such fragmentation is the Federal Courts/Correction system, which is organized "vertically" so that a basic pre-sentence report, with suitable updates, is sequentially used by sentencing judges, probation officers, institutions, the parole board, and parole officers.

The Nature of Investigation in Corrections

The corrections officer starting an investigation of an offender faces a task basically similar to that of any clinician in a counseling or community services agency. That is, he must project from a limited set of information about an offender a series of behavioral alternatives *for the future.* Such is the definition of criminal correction; to describe a sequence of social remedies tailored to an offender which will attempt to reconcile the safety needs of the community with the personal needs of that offender, and ultimately, to change that offender in a reformative manner. Thus, we are inevitably dealing with behavioral *predictions,* just as in other fields of counseling and other social interventions.

The fact that criminal corrections deals heavily with use of social authority, and often in a punishing context in response to specific anti-social acts, should not blind us to the similarity of the diagnostic investigative process involved; both conventional counseling and criminal corrections deal in behavior predictions in the service of constructive personal change. Both fields require a sophisticated understanding of human nature imbedded in a perspective on society.

Like his clinical cousin, the corrections worker engaged in investigation works from two sets of data: *present functioning* of his client and *past history.* The most important description of an offender's life is *cross-sectional;* the officer reports on the offender's current attitudes, behavior, and functioning at the present time, including a detailed description of his current crimes. Such a cross-sectional account is enriched and deepened by consideration of significant features of past history in the life of the offender. The corrections worker in his investigation searches for patterns of behavior through an interweaving of past and present performance; the existence of such identified patterns gives his recommendations predictive power.

A precautionary note should be sounded here about the cross-sectional nature of investigative reports, such as the PSI. People and situations do tend to change over time. Offenders often complain bitterly about the "paperwork" that trails after them, arguing that they become the victims of their arrest records, and are "frozen" into a negative social image. Even where updating of records is attempted prior to decision-making, offenders believe that past reporting exerts a biasing effect upon their future opportunities.

The most valid response to such comments is to point out that research and human experience suggest that most behavior tends to run in somewhat predictable patterns. The most potent predictor of future behavior is a careful summary of past and present performance. If an offender's past indicates an ingrained propensity for crime, and that tendency is reinforced, criminal acts are likely to be resumed at some future time when the opportunity permits, unless specific interventions are carried out to interrupt that pattern. Whether we are making love, spending money, or heisting service stations, behavior which has been reinforced tends to persist in recognizable patterns.

Since society is based upon a reasonable amount of predictability in the behavior of its members, and since that predictability rests upon the reinforcement of behaviors, there is little reason to believe that criminality should be a general exception to the iron law of reinforcement. If criminal acts have "paid off" in the past for an offender, what evidence can we afford to accept that the offender will be able to refrain from similar acts in tempting situations? What "soft" data can we trust which indicates resistance to criminal temptation? What value can be assigned to expressions of guilt and shame, resolutions of personal change, the impact of supportive families, good prison behavior, religious conversion, or productive work habits? Criminal corrections is a complex calculus of retribution, deterrence, incapacitation, and reformation. We operate in a tangled web of objective facts and "subjective" motives.

Herein lies the crux of a dilemma for the conscientious officer preparing an investigative report; it is a dilemma shared with sentencing judges and parole boards. Is it possible to be governed *solely* by the statistical probabilities generated by arrest records and similar data (which leads to parole prediction tables and other quantified sentencing guides)? If so, in its most extreme (and absurd) form, sentencing and parole could be administered by computer, without the need for intervention by human judgment. Yet, if such a course is regarded as too mechanical, how can offender behavior predictions escape the fallacies inherent in human judgment?

"Computer Justice" denies the complexity of human motivation and behavior, undermines the possibility of change or reformation, and hardly fulfills the requirements of justice as it is ordinarily conceived. At the opposite extreme, each offender can be seen as a totally unique individual caught in a web of his own making, and for whom a unique social remedy should be devised. Such remedies might include relief of intrapsychic conflicts, redesign of the offender's opportunity structure, or application of some *Clockwork Orange* type of aversive behavior modification. Such "clinical" and individualistic approaches to criminal disposition have their appeal, but are hard to implement given the crude social remedies available to our criminal justice system, and enshrined in our criminal laws.

To what extent do we deal with the *offense* as a category with social sanctions already prescribed, or with the *offender* as an individual with a specific "problem"? This dilemma was first described by Paul Meehl years ago in his now classic book, *Statistical Vs. Clinical Prediction*. An "actuarial" approach to justice, assuming a valid data base could be established, might be recommended to segregate the chronic criminal from the rest of society, but probably at the high cost of dehumanizing the judicial process. A "clinical" process of evaluation of each offender's idiosyncratic needs and problems, with behavioral prescriptions for their correction, would require what at this point would be an unrealistic level of resources, and a high degree of sophistication, a sophistication that the corrections field has not yet attained. And in fact, the degree of subjectivity in making such investigations might be considered unacceptable in the long run. The margin for error would always exist, involving possible risks to public safety in the implementation process.

These two alternative methods for evaluating and predicting offender behavior have been described in rather exaggerated form to indicate the necessity for compromise. Each corrections investigator has his personal "computer" consisting of a backlog of experiences with similar cases against which he tests the probable behavior of each offender before him. The officer must weigh and sift each facet of the offender's life, testing the motivation for change and attempting to balance the attitudinal information against the "objective" arrest record. While the officer may not always articulate such deliberations in the terms just described, the process is nonetheless very real.

In an analytic fashion, the officer must resolve the dilemmas of prediction by integrating the "actuarial" probabilities with the unique potentials of each offender. For example, he is responsible for knowing that it would be foolish to overlook the arrest record of a felon who has successfully spent his recent life by burglarizing residences; and he must attempt to strike a balance with the burglar's expressed desire to change his criminal life-style, evaluate the probable impact of a supportive family, etc., in recommending probation vs. incarceration.

Some corrections investigators have dealt with the dilemma of prediction, with all of its implied uncertainties of judgment, by refusing to cope with such complexities. Such officers deal only with "facts," failing to integrate their investigations into sentencing recommendations (predictions). Unfortunately, officers utilizing such strategies pass the dilemma on to the recipients of their reports, either sentencing judges or parole boards. By refusing to deal with the human judgments and recommendations which they are in a good position to offer, such officers fail to operate as full-fledged professionals, and do not contribute to the growth of criminal corrections as a professional discipline.

The narrow "fact-seeking" officer fails to realize that the attitudes and motives of his client are as real and "objective" as his name and occupation, although the description and recording of attitudes may take a high level of skill to describe in a precise and impartial manner. Corrections investigators need to become sensitive to changes, attitudes, and shifts in the lives of their clients and to work with such changes, while simultaneously maintaining a realistic understanding that deeply ingrained patterns of behavior are not easily overcome, despite verbal reassurances of "unconditional good will" by the officers.

Finally, the corrections investigator must attempt to strike a balance between the personal needs of the offender and the safety of the community (or the maintenance of security and order in the correctional institution). However, it is rare that an offender will initially perceive his best interests as coinciding with the recommendations of the officer. Nevertheless, the reconciliation of the offender with the interests of the community (or institution) remains the end goal of corrections. It is a vital first step for an offender to recognize that the sanctions imposed by judges, institutions, or parole boards are a just and fair solution to his transgressions, and that such authorities are taking into account both his interests and those of his community.

Corrections investigators, operating from courts, institutions, and parole agencies, are a major point of contact of offenders with "the system," and the attitude and demeanor of officers is closely studied by offenders for consistency and objectivity. The offender often tends to make an implicit decision on whether to cooperate with a probation officer during pre-sentence investigation, based upon his perception of the understanding and sympathy extended by the officer during such interviews. Naturally, the offender is also "testing" the officer in some instances to determine the potential for manipulating the situation to his advantage.

Summary

Investigative/diagnostic reports serve a crucial role in guiding decision makers at key points of the flow of offenders through the criminal corrections process. The professional skill demonstrated by officials in preparing such reports is a major contribution of the emerging profession of corrections to the efficiency of the correctional system. The assembly of investigative reports is both an art and a science in the attempt to strike a balance between the needs of individual offenders and the safety of the community or institution.

Six points of decision were identified at which investigative reports have proven useful. Correctional investigation was compared to diagnostic reporting in mental health settings; the purpose of such investigations was defined as an attempt to predict future behavior based upon cross-sectional analysis of present functioning enriched by patterns derived from past offender history. Correctional reporting was viewed as a combination of "actuarial" and "clinical" methods of prediction in which the skill and experience of the investigator are tested. The acceptance by the offender of the investigator's work as a valid representation of his situation was deemed to be an important asset to the investigative process.

Discussion Questions

1. To what extent does the work of a modern corrections officer represent a profession? What are some of the implications of criminal corrections as a profession?

2. What are the relative advantages and disadvantages of using the same basic PSI, with suitable updates, for each offender as that offender passes through various stages of the correctional process, as occurs in the Federal corrections system?

3. Would the accuracy of sentencing and parole decisions be improved by complete reliance upon actuarial predictions generated through past results with criminal groups? What are the issues involved in such a strategy?

4. What are the possible shortcomings of limiting PSI reports to verified "facts" (arrest record, employment history, and family members) in sentencing decisions by judges?

Supplementary Reading

Presentence Investigation Report. Division of Probation, Administrative Office of the United States Courts. Washington, D.C. 20544 (January 5, 1978). (U. S. Government Printing Office, Washington, D.C. 20402. Publication 105, Stock Number 028-004-00012-5. Price $2.30)

> This is an excellent monograph on guidelines and procedures to be used in Federal Courts for preparation of presentence reports.

Handbook on Correctional Classification. Committee on Classification and Treatment of American Correctional Association. (Leonard J. Hippchen, Editor) Cincinnati, Ohio: Anderson Publishing Company, 1978.

> An ambitious effort to summarize the "state of the art" in classification and treatment of the offender, with a plea for greater use of community-centered corrections. Thomas Eynon's Chapter 3 on "Classification and Treatment in the Community and the Institution" is especially recommended.

Meehl, Paul E. *Clinical vs. Statistical Prediction.* Minneapolis: University of Minnesota Press, 1954.

Chapter 2

Criteria for the Investigative Report

The preparation of investigative reports is an exacting task because of the significant decisions about offenders which may be based upon such reports. In addition, the written word tends to become relatively permanent, particularly in court and correctional settings, so that care must be exerted in initial case preparation.

The form in which investigations are reported varies from court to court; also, most agencies and correctional institutions have evolved somewhat different reporting forms, as will be noted subsequently. Despite the multiplicity of forms in which the details of cases are to be recorded, it is possible to state a generic set of standards which should guide all reports in correctional settings.

The principles stated in this chapter should be used in the practice cases to follow to test the student's understanding of the application of competent standards to report-writing. These principles are described as follows:

Accuracy. Most representations in offender reports have been obtained through personal interview with an offender, so that the bulk of information in such reports comes from the offender himself. It is essential to cross-check information through relatives, victims, police, employers, schools, and arrest records whenever possible. Discrepancies should be resolved through follow-up interviews before reports are prepared. Statements made by an offender that have not been verified should be labelled "unverified" in most instances. Self-contradictions should be reviewed with the offender if they occur. Careful note-taking (and/or recording) is essential during interview. Some agencies have established a policy of review of written reports by offenders (where no confidential source of information is involved) to minimize misunderstandings.

Example: The client states that he enlisted in the U.S. Marines in 1974 and received an honorable discharge in 1978. However, the client was unable to produce an honorable discharge document, and no military records were obtained, so that his statement remains unverified.

Objectivity. It has proven difficult for investigators to sustain a balanced judgment with some offenders who are uncooperative, defensive, or malingering, or offenders whose crimes are particularly repugnant. Strong emotional reactions, both positive or negative, have a way of creeping into reports, particularly in the choice of factors which are emphasized in evaluative summaries. One's subjective biases have a way of coloring professional judgments, so that even experienced officers should check themselves when they find themselves reacting strongly to a client. Such strong reactions exert what is called a "halo effect" on reporting, which can sometimes be counteracted through consultation with a colleague or supervisor, or even by transferring a case.

Neophytes often err in the direction of positive distortion. Flushed with the idealism of the classroom, the neophyte dons rose-colored glasses to become an advocate for his clients, sometimes omitting damaging details that may discredit his undercover advocacy on behalf of the offender.

Example: A volunteer probation officer presented a PSI to the sentencing judge involving a client who had left the scene of an accident after injuring a pedestrian in a cross-walk. The PSI presented a glowing account of happy family life, steady job advancement, and community activity on the part of his client. The judge noted that the volunteer had failed to contact the injured victim, or to explain why his client had sped from the scene, and had omitted three *driving while intoxicated* convictions on his record, while recommending leniency. The volunteer was highly embarrassed, and found it difficult to explain these omissions. He had, with the best of intentions, become the victim of positive distortion.

On the other hand, experienced officers sometimes become needlessly jaded and pessimistic about their clients. Some resolve the delicate problem of objectivity by reporting "just the facts," so that their reports tend to be lifeless, routine, and not very helpful. Such officers fail to recognize that the more intimate issues of family relationships, attitudes toward their offenses, or receptivity to supervision/counseling can also be described in a relatively "objective" manner.

Feelings, emotions, and attitudes are obviously subjective phenomena; still, such matters are important "facts" in the life of people, and should be reported because they are relevant.

Clarity. Written communication is a difficult art, often subject to misinterpretation. Since most correctional reports may be used for a variety of purposes at different times, it is always good practice to keep them simple, clear, and unambiguous. Avoid a $5 word where a 25¢ word will do the job. Legal and psychiatric jargon are notorious offenders. A corrections investigator who imitates the stilted, formal style and terminology of lawyers is often not communicating clearly to the recipients of his reports.

Similarly, the clinical language of psychiatry and psychology should usually be reduced to more broadly understood English. A good rule of thumb for the officer is, if you are sure you understand a legal or psychiatric report, then you should be able to reduce it to basic English. If you do not understand it, you should be wary about incorporating such information in your report. It may be advisable to check with the source of any reports one does not fully understand. A psychiatric and legal dictionary is also a good investment.

It is always good professional practice to have a colleague or supervisor review reports for clarity before submitting them, and to rewrite sections that appear to be ambiguous. Perhaps the most helpful way to build clarity into report-writing is to routinely check with the recipients of such reports, whether it be judges, parole boards, or outside agencies. Such cross-checking is more than a courtesy; it expresses a professional concern for the impact of one's work.

Completeness. The practical realities of busy work schedules sometimes encourage short-cuts; failure to reinterview offenders to resolve discrepancies, failure to seek records, or the omission of interviews with relatives to cross-check information supplied by an offender. It is important to develop a check-list of sources which satisfy one's professional standards of workmanship, and to deviate from this check-list with caution.

If client-reported facts about arrests, military service, family life, employment, or education are unverified, it is considered more responsible to acknowledge that certain matters are unverified than to leave the issue in doubt. A concern for fairness to clients and to one's responsibility as an officer requires that no potential asset of a client go unrecognized, or that no hidden weakness be omitted.

Example: In completing a PSI on a 28 year-old married client charged with drunkenness and disorderly conduct, the investigator noted that the client was extremely defensive, appeared to have a low self-concept, had dropped out of school in the 8th grade, was chronically under-employed at a series of unskilled jobs, and had a history of episodic drinking. The client was placed on probation with this same officer, and finally revealed months later that he was almost totally illiterate, and that this deficiency had weighed heavily in his job prospects and in his feelings of personal inadequacy. In his initial investigation, it had simply never occurred to this officer that his client might be troubled by the inability to read and write.

Brevity. The previously cited requirements of completeness need not preclude a reasonable brevity in reporting. Every minor fact need not be reported. Many investigative reports roam on page after page in a cut-and-dry fashion to fulfill an outline the officer believes is required by his agency. Such an exhausting ritual is not creative and is seldom helpful to the recipients of reports. Masses of verbiage are just as likely to obscure the employment history of a client, for example, as to reveal the essential work performance involved.

Competent reports are organized around cardinal features in the life of the offender, summarizing and highlighting the uniqueness of that client, while some of the less-important details are left in rough note form.

Knowing the Report Recipients. There is no substitute for knowledge about the decision makers for whom reports are intended, whether it be a sentencing judge, warden of a prison, or a psychiatric counseling agency. The investigative report should be phrased in language that communicates most clearly to those persons who are to receive the report, and contain the information needed to address the decisions to be made about the offender. In some cases, this may mean that revisions in language and emphasis may be necessary. The warden of a prison is concerned with different issues than the intake social worker of a psychiatric counseling center, though both may be dealing with the same offender at different times. Therefore, the notion of an "all-purpose" report may not be viable in some settings, despite the efficiency of such a concept. It may be necessary to excerpt portions of a basic report and to rewrite the evaluative summary and recommendations to be responsive to the needs of a job training center or a family counseling agency, for example, in making such referrals. Such modifications are compatible with the probation/parole officer's role as "broker" between the offender and a range of community service agencies.

However, there is a more subtle and chronic problem faced by report-writers. How does one deal, for example, with a sentencing judge reputed to have strong biases against certain offenses or toward certain offenders? In preparing a PSI for such a judge, the officer is acting as a *consultant* whose credibility and reputation are tested by the acceptance of the report. There may be a subtle temptation to tailor such reports to please the judge, thus confirming his biases. Such temptations may be severe in an inexperienced or insecure officer, who may believe that his tenure in the job may depend upon being politically pliable, for example.

It is probably going to be difficult to adhere to a professional standard of objectivity with so much static in the communications system. The insecure officer who writes reports to confirm the biases of his "employer" is attempting to buy a short-range security for himself, but at a high cost of independence of judgment. In the long run, the officer's credibility is almost certainly impaired.

Ideological differences leading to differential strategies are commonplace in criminal corrections. Even the most conscientious and experienced professionals often arrive at different conclusions about offenders. The chronic advocacy of either a "hard line" or "soft line" may reflect sincere beliefs, but may also indicate some myopia of judgment. In either case, a reduced overall effectiveness is probable. It is considered more professionally mature to strive for a receptive openness, to marshal one's facts and judgments to the best of one's ability, and to be prepared for differences of opinion.

Example: A sentencing judge is staunchly orthodox Roman Catholic and is reputed to be opposed to all forms of contraception. A probation officer is preparing a PSI on a 25 year-old woman convicted of welfare fraud. Among other things, this client is troubled by four out-of-wedlock pregnancies by four different men, the offspring appearing to be mildly mentally retarded. The officer wishes to include a referral to Planned Parenthood for contraceptive advice in his recommendations. However, the officer fears a storm of indignation from the judge, and is tempted to omit this recommendation. Ask yourself, what would *you* do in this situation?

It seems apparent that probation officers need a firm sense of their professional identities in negotiating such touchy situations. Hard-and-fast rules are simply not available to guide officers, since such problems are endemic to the corrections field. However, officers should recognize that, in the long run, their usefulness in investigation rests upon the independence of their judgment, and should strive for an integrity which guides the impartial use of their skills.

Knowing the Resources Available. One of the most indispensable tools of the corrections investigator is a thorough and current knowledge of the options available within the corrections system and of the community resources available to offenders. Sensible recommendations are grounded in the ability of an officer to generate alternative dispositions; that is, to match up the needs of an offender with available resources. Otherwise, investigative reports can become a sterile, academic exercise. It has proven easy to encourage the notion of such matching, but the skills involved are sometimes hard to teach, since such skills depend upon an intimate knowledge of one's work setting and community. Neophytes should consult with more experienced officers for ideas about options available.

The probation/parole officer needs to know the legal penalties available to judges for prescribed offenses, workings of bail or diversion programs (if any), and a working understanding of probation/parole violation procedures. Knowing the capabilities of one's probation/parole agency for supervision, caseloads, and specialized supervision is necessary. Being aware of the availability of work-release programs, job training and placement, and contacts with prospective employers is also essential.

In addition, in order to construct comprehensive planning for offenders, officers should know referral procedures to counseling agencies, schools, halfway houses, medical/dental clinics, welfare, addiction centers, Legal Aid, Alcoholics Anonymous, or other specialized community services.

The institutional classification officer is usually knowledgeable about a more limited set of alternatives, which may include degree of security required for custody, educational placement, shop placement, group or individual counseling, or medical/dental services required by the offender.

PRACTICE CASE 1

Following is the pre-sentence investigation of an actual case prepared by Probation Officer Michael Lovelace. Names of the officer, the judge, and the client have been altered to protect their identities. Certain details of the case have also been changed for the same reasons, but the essence of the case was as reported. Please read this case critically in order to discuss the questions which follow. (Please do *not* read the probation officer's comments or the case commentary until you have completed your review of this practice case.)

Pre-Sentence Investigation

Name Johnson, Kenneth	**Folder No.** 39842
Address 3049 Upshaw Terrace	**Offense** POSSESSION (misdemeanor)
Age (DOB) 9/18/61	**Plea** Guilty
SS No. 293-13-9053	**Judge** O'Flaherty
Date of Report 12/8/79	**P.O.** Michael Lovelace
Arrest Status O/R	**Date Due** 12/10/79

LEGAL RECORD:

A. *Present Offense* — This 18 year-old white single male pleaded guilty to a charge of possession of 161½ grams of a substance established to be marijuana. On 11/30/79 he was stopped for investigation by police while driving his grandfather's pick up truck a few blocks from his home. Search of the truck revealed a quantity of marijuana hidden under the dashboard. Mr. Johnson denies intent to sell this drug, stating that he had recently purchased it for $200 for his own use. He was unable to identify the seller. He claims he smokes marijuana for recreational use only, and denies addiction. His attitude appeared reasonably candid, and he appeared to be frightened about sentencing.

B. *Prior Record* — As a juvenile, defendant reported he was charged with building a campfire in the woods near his home. According to defendant, he was admonished by Juvenile Court, and sent home in custody of grandfather, Marcus Johnson, 3049 Upshaw Terrace. On another occasion two years ago, he paid costs of court for a broken headlight on a borrowed vehicle. Since Juvenile Court records were unavailable, juvenile arrests are unverified. There is no arrest record as an adult.

FAMILY
HISTORY:

The defendant is the oldest of 7 children, and has lived with grandparents at his present address since he was 12 years of age, when his parents became divorced. The defendant's younger siblings remained with mother, who re-married and lives in Los Angeles. He stated that he has no particular problems with his grandparents, and enjoys living with them in their upper middle-class home in Chatham Hills.

EDUCATION:

Mr. Johnson is a senior at Roosevelt High School in Chatham Hills, and receives work-credits for part-time employment as a construction worker in his grandfather's contracting business. He reported himself to be an "average" student, and attempts to avoid bad influences around him at the high school. He states that he is lining up construction jobs for the summer in order to earn enough credits for graduation. He intends to become a carpenter apprentice in the construction business. His family and school were not contacted at the defendant's request.

DRUG USE:

The defendant claims that he uses "1 or 2 joints" each day, and that such recreational use of marijuana makes him sleepy and relaxed. He denies that his use of marijuana interferes with his other activities, and does not regard himself as having a drug problem. He occasionally drinks beer on dates with his friends, but says he does not enjoy drinking. He admits experimentation with "speed" and LSD a few times, but did not enjoy his experiences with these drugs. He denies regular use of hard drugs, noting that "I try to keep away from people who do that" at the high school. He reports his health to be excellent.

EVALUATIVE
SUMMARY:

This 18 year-old white single male pleaded guilty to possession of a quantity of marijuana he had purchased for his own use for $200. He reports light use of this drug for recreational use, and denies addiction. He has no adult arrest record. The defendant appeared quite candid and open in interview, and has never been in serious trouble. He is a senior at Roosevelt High School, and is completing his education by earning work-credit in a part-time construction job with his grandfather's firm. He appears to have a comfortable home which affords him considerable stability. His health is good, his attitude is good, and he appears to have no serious personal problems. He appeared frightened and impressed by his arrest and subsequent court appearance.

RECOMMENDATION:

A fine is recommended. Mr. Johnson is not believed to be in need of probation supervision, or of treatment for drug addiction.

P.O. Lovelace Comments on the Johnson Case:

"I had a positive response to this young man, and I suppose some of that came through in my PSI to the Judge. Johnson seemed like such a clean-cut youngster . . . in a way, he reminded me of some of my son's friends. He struck me as very sincere about not getting into any further trouble with the law. I probably took some shortcuts in my investigation I wouldn't have considered in a more serious case. I should have checked out his school and his family situation more closely, but our caseload here is so heavy already.

"Judge O'Flaherty didn't go along with my recommendations. I think the Judge is very hard on drug cases. He sentenced Johnson to 60 days in jail, but suspended the sentence, and gave him two years on probation. The Judge wanted him checked out for drug treatment, too. Mr. Smith got the case, laid down the law to him, but put him on a minimum reporting basis. The Drug Treatment Center checked him out, but they didn't recommend any treatment. So far he's given us no further problems."

Discussion Questions

1. Does this case meet the standards for a good investigative report? Has adequate cross-checking been done?

2. Does P.O. Lovelace show any biases in his report? If so, what are his possible biases, and at which points are they shown?

3. Do you believe that the defendant has accurately reported his use of drugs?

4. Do you believe that the defendant's attitude toward his arrest should affect his sentence? If so, how do you justify it?

5. What, if anything, would you have added to this report?

6. If you were Judge O'Flaherty, what disposition would you make of this case?

Case Commentary

The probation officer seems to have relaxed his standards considerably in investigating this case. He appears to have made an early decision either that the case did not warrant serious investigation, or that the defendant's reports could be trusted, or both. At any rate, his failure to obtain school background, juvenile arrest records, and to interview the grandfather is rather unusual. Trying to read between the lines, it sounds like young Johnson bought marijuana from a "snitch," which led to an easy arrest. Perhaps someone inferred that Johnson was not very deeply involved in trafficking, but no real information was offered on that aspect of the case. It is possible that Johnson was charged with possession because he refused to cooperate with the police investigation of his supplier; but this is all speculation.

It is easy to agree with Lovelace's admission that he felt a positive response to this young man. A positive bias is clearly expressed in his report and in his recommendation for leniency. Perhaps he felt a fatherly, protective attitude which was inspired by Johnson's fear of the court, his clean-cut appearance, or his upwardly mobile, middle-class background with which Lovelace could identify. Or perhaps he was attempting to over-compensate for Judge O'Flaherty's strict attitude about drug users. It is also possible that Lovelace is not impressed with the evils of marijuana use; after all, the decriminalization of marijuana is an issue of public policy at this time.

One might certainly wonder what officer Lovelace's attitude would be if he discovered that this defendant had told lies about the extent of his involvement in drug sales and use. We simply have no way of knowing if further digging and cross-checking would have shaken the defendant's story about light "recreational" use of marijuana, and his distaste for alcohol or hard drugs. Sometimes we act like benevolent parents who would rather not hear the worst about our children.

Johnson's attitude about his arrest suggests that he desperately wants to maintain a conventional identity untainted by delinquent actions. Mr. Lovelace seemed to respect such motivation in the defendant, and his recommendation of a fine would have processed this young man out of the criminal justice system. Judge O'Flaherty seemingly played it safe by asking for a two-year period of supervision in case Johnson was more drug-involved than the report indicated. The judge's sentence also reinforced his view of the seriousness of marijuana use, and his initial 60-day sentence was designed to further frighten the defendant into a recognition of the heavy penalties which might result from his continued use of illegal substances.

This case was chosen as an introduction because it raised some controversial issues of drug abuse. The case also illustrates the human judgment issues that undergird our use of so-called "facts" in criminal cases, with the necessity to be perceptive about human affairs.

Chapter 3

Outline for Investigative Reports: The Face Sheet

"Get your facts first, then you can distort 'em as much as you please."
Mark Twain

Mark Twain's wry comment reminds us that simply "getting the facts" is no guarantee of an impartial investigative report. Just the opposite can be true. A thin gloss of facts selected to emphasize a biased prior conclusion about an offender is always possible in corrections work. The competent investigator learns to suspend judgment when interviewing an offender for the first time; by remaining receptive and open, he gains a fresh perspective on the offender and is in a position to encourage his client to be candid. The suspension of judgment during the initial phases of information-gathering is part of the officer's commitment to impartiality and fairness in preparation of diagnostic reporting.

It is an idealistic notion to believe that the significance of an offender's life can somehow be squeezed onto a few sheets of paper. Novelists, for example, have taken much more space to teach about aspects of life experience. It seems appropriate, therefore, to approach report-writing with a self-critical sense, recognizing that the assessment of offenders is still partly an art, partly a science, but mostly just common sense.

A careful and skillful approach to offender assessment is critically important because important decisions involving an individual's freedom must be guided by investigative reports. In attempting to respond to the heavy responsibility this represents, most corrections agencies and institutions have designed reporting forms to serve as outlines in assembling reports in order to standardize such reports, thus keeping the investigator on the right track. The use of such standard outlines is almost universal in prisons, courts, probation/parole agencies, and community agencies. Throughout the correctional system, the proliferation of such reporting forms is so diverse that it would serve no useful purpose to describe their infinite variety. Therefore, a few examples of these outlines (face sheets) are reproduced for illustrative purposes (Exhibits 1 and 2), since the types of information requested tend to be similar from agency to agency.

The use of standard forms helps a given court or agency to maintain completeness of record-keeping and to locate information in a familiar location on the forms. The standardization of reporting forms within an agency or systems (such as the Federal probation/parole system) also helps to provide a minimum standard of quality control in information-gathering about offenders.

Outlines are also a kind of "security blanket" for the inexperienced officer who needs structural guides to assist him in making assessments. Unfortunately, standardization is also a trap for the unwary, luring officers into the false belief that by completing the formal requirements of an outline, they have discharged their responsibilities to the offender. Thus, a too-strict adherence to formal reports may lead some officers to a lack of innovation, a staleness of routines, and ultimately, boredom with the tasks of offender assessment.

It is the contention of the author that standard report forms are meant to be guides *only,* and that an attempt to capture the uniqueness of each offender transcends the requirements of formal report forms. By regarding such forms as guidelines only, the corrections officer will be able to maintain the freshness and vitality so important to the work of assessment.

The variations between reporting forms tend to be rather minor, so that it is possible to present a generalized outline of the types of information considered useful in most correctional settings. On the basis of the outlines presented in this Casebook, students should be able to transpose the described methods to the requirements of any specific corrections agency.

A workable compromise between the two extremes of over-standardization and over-individualization is an objective worth striving for. The student is encouraged to adopt the organization of reports suggested here, while at the same time developing variations suitable to his own work-style and the requirements of the agency in which he may be employed. While the methods described in this text may not be perfect for every student or situation, they do provide some standardization with an opportunity to capture the unique individuality of offenders.

Form of Investigative Reports

Normally, investigative reports as used in various corrections settings are divided into two sections: the *face sheet* and the *body* of the report.

Face Sheet. Certain identifying facts regarding offenders are displayed on the front page of reports in a standard form for quick reference, filing, and summarization. A typical format is illustrated by Exhibits 1 and 2, which are used in U.S. Courts and the State of South Carolina respectively.

Body of the Report.   In most cases, the substance of investigative reports is presented in narrative form under various standard headings, organized into a general outline of the areas to be covered, with emphasis on critical points that have developed in the investigation. Often, officers use a work-sheet or check-list to interview the offender. Additional work-sheets are also used for interviews with relatives, police, witnesses, employers, schools, etc. These work-sheets may then be assembled, and a final narrative report written or dictated.

Preparation of the Face Sheet

The format for presenting face sheet information differs from setting to setting, as noted previously. Generally, a typical format is shown as Exhibit 3. This format is suitable for a pre-sentence investigation; modifications would be necessary for a prison, parole, or other type of correctional setting. The following information should be included in the face sheet:

Offender's Name. State the full name of the client, verified from the court docket or appropriate official records. Nicknames, maiden or married names, and aliases should be included.

Reason for Referral. In some instances a separate referral sheet may come from a judge, listing specific questions to be considered.

Address. Present place of residence, including zip code and telephone (if any), or legal address if institutionalized. When appropriate, the name and address of responsible relative may be included. When client is transient, a list of recent addresses may be useful if supervision in the community is anticipated.

Age. Verify stated age of client against stated date of birth, and stated place of birth. Verification by birth certificate may be necessary in some cases, to

Exhibit 1

PROBATION FORM 2
FEB 65

UNITED STATES DISTRICT COURT

PRESENTENCE REPORT

NAME John Jones

ADDRESS 1234 Beach Street
       Detroit, Michigan 48201

LEGAL RESIDENCE Same

AGE 38   DATE OF BIRTH 8-25-26 (ver.)

SEX Male   RACE White

CITIZENSHIP United States

EDUCATION High School

MARITAL STATUS Married

DEPENDENTS Four (wife and
      three children)
SOC. SEC. NO. 000-11-2222

FBI NO. 678910

DETAINERS OR CHARGES PENDING: None

DATE October 14, 1964

DOCKET NO. 56971

OFFENSE Possession of
      Distilled Spirits
      26 U.S.C. 5686(b)

PENALTY $5,000 or 1 year, or both

PLEA Guilty, 2-14-64

VERDICT

CUSTODY Personal Bond

ASST. U.S. ATTY. James E. Carver

DEFENSE COUNSEL Thomas Flanigan
      781 Cadillac Tower
      (Court Appointed)

CODEFENDANTS *(Disposition)* Case of Robert Allen (pending)

DISPOSITION

DATE

SENTENCING JUDGE

Exhibit 2

South Carolina Probation, Parole and Pardon Board

HON. WALTER D. TYLER, JR., CHAIRMAN
DISTRICT SIX
FLORENCE, S. C.

HON. JOHN E. HUSS, D.D.
DISTRICT ONE
CHARLESTON, S. C.

HON. H. L. LACKEY
DISTRICT TWO
COLUMBIA, S. C.

GRADY A. WALLACE
DIRECTOR

HON. CHARLES R. SANDERS, JR.
VICE CHAIRMAN
DISTRICT THREE
GREENWOOD, S. C.

HON. MARION BEASLEY
DISTRICT FOUR
FOUNTAIN INN, S. C.

HON. ELIZABETH M. MYERS
DISTRICT FIVE
CAMDEN, S. C.

OFFICE ADDRESS:
MIDDLEBURG OFFICE PARK
OFF 2700 BLOCK FOREST DRIVE
COLUMBIA, S. C. 29204

MAILING ADDRESS:
P. O. BOX 11368
CAPITOL STATION
COLUMBIA, S. C. 29211

PRESENCE REPORT

Name: Marital Status:

True Name: No. of Dependents:
or Alias

Address: Education:

Age: Offense:

DOB: Detainers or Charges pending:

Sex: County of Trial:

DISPOSITION:

Remarks:

Investigator:_____: Date:_____

Name:_____: Title:_____

determine whether client falls under juvenile or adult jurisdiction.

Race. Self-identification during interview is preferred.

Social Security Number. This important aid to proper identification should be verified by inspection of a Social Security card.

Education. Last grade completed in school, according to client. H.S. or college diploma should be verified, when possible, if graduation is claimed.

Marital Status. Current status of single, married, divorced, separated, widowed, or common law. List prior marriages, if any.

Employment. Current employment, or last job if institutionalized. Verification through pay stub, ID, or phone call to employer may be necessary. Note general type of employment: clerk, warehouseman, laborer, etc. Indicate whether full-time or part-time.

Dependents. Persons for whose support client is legally responsible, either by current or past marriages. Welfare support should be noted, if any.

Current Offense(s). Legal charge(s) from affidavit or court docket. Docket number and date of charge should be included.

Penalty. The statutory penalty for current offense(s) is sometimes included on face sheet. Use appropriate law reference book.

Plea. Did defendant plead guilty, or was defendant convicted, either by judge or jury? Date of plea should be noted.

Prosecutor. Name of prosecutor is included for reference.

Defense Counsel. Name and address of defense counsel should be noted, and whether defense counsel was court-appointed, public defender, or Legal Aid.

Custody Status. Is defendant released on bond, on own recognizance (O/R), or held in custody pending disposition by Court? Dates of custody are important, since judges often recognize period of custody when passing sentence as "time served" on sentence.

Detainers or Charges Pending. This is an important reminder to the court and jail personnel that other jurisdictions may have charges pending against defendant, or that probation/parole violations may be pending.

Codefendants. Is this case tied in with others? If so, what is the status of other defendants? Furnish names and docket numbers for cross-reference.

FBI Number. Certain categories of more serious offenses, including all felonies, are referenced by case number with the Federal Bureau of Investigation for national distribution. Police records should be consulted for the appropriate FBI Number, and reported on the face sheet.

Due Date. Time and place at which PSI is due before sentencing judge for disposition of case.

Name of Judge. This is the person for whom report was prepared, and who referred case for investigation.

Date of Report. Date on which PSI was completed, transcribed, checked for accuracy, and signed by probation officer.

Name of Probation Officer. Persons who conducted investigation and prepared PSI.

Supervisor. Some agencies require that authorized supervisor review report, and approve it by signature before PSI is submitted to sentencing judge.

Disposition. This information is added later, when decision of sentencing judge has been made. This is the final outcome of the investigation and may be useful for research.

PRACTICE CASE 2

This exercise is to be completed using the sample face sheet in Exhibit 3. Student is to interview a "client" who can be a classmate or colleague. The exercise can be conducted either in or outside of class, or by demonstration before a class. The "client" has pleaded guilty to a charge of *driving under the influence* (DUI), and Judge Mergenthaler has accepted the plea, and

Exhibit 3

SAMPLE PRE-SENTENCE REPORT FACE SHEET

Name (incl. nicknames or aliases):	Offense(s):
Addresses:	Docket Nos.:
	Penalty:
Telephone: ( )	
Age, place & date of birth:	Plea:
Sex:	Judge:
Race:	Reason for Referral (optional):
Social Security No.: - -	Prosecutor:
	Defense Counsel:
Education:	
Marital Status:	Custody Status:
Dependents:	Detainers or charge pending:
Current Place of employment:	Codefendants and Dispositions:
FBI No.:	
Date due:	
Report Completed:	
Probation Officer:	
Supervisor:	

Disposition:

referred the case for investigation prior to sentencing. The judge asks, "Is this person in need of alcoholic treatment?" There are no previous criminal or traffic offenses.

The "facts" to be related by the client are that he had a jealous fight with his companion at a house party, became excessively drunk, and drove away from the party in a rage. The erratic driving was noted by police, a breath-alyzer test was administered, and the charge was made. The client is now sober and full of remorse. Drinking history and other details are to be supplied by the "client." Statutory penalty for DUI is a sentence up to 6 months, a fine up to $500, and driving suspension up to three years.

Having interviewed the client, student is to complete the face sheet information (typewritten if possible), and prepare a recommendation on sentence for Judge Mergenthaler on a separate page.

Discussion Questions

1. Did you conclude in your recommendation that a reasonable basis existed for reduction of the maximum penalties prescribed by statute for drunken driving? If so, describe your reasoning which led to reduction of sentence, or recommendation for probation and/or alcoholic counseling.

2. List the points on the face sheet for which you would want verification. How would you set about verifying the information supplied during interview with your "client"?

3. What were the emotional reactions experienced by the "client" to this interview? Or, if *you* became a client during this exercise, what were some of your reactions to the interview?

4. How did your client express remorse? Did you find such expressions convincing? If you used such expressions of remorse in your recommendation to Judge Mergenthaler, how did you justify them to the judge?

Discussion of this exercise in class may be helpful in revealing how other students handled the information, the interview, and the sentencing recommendations. It is especially helpful to role-play presentation of this case to the "Judge" if another student volunteers to role-play Judge Mergenthaler.

Chapter 4

Outline for Investigative Reports: Body of the Report

The content and organization of correctional reports has borrowed heavily from the fields of mental health and social service; these traditional fields have had an obvious influence on the work of corrections. Historically, the social work profession has been extremely influential, especially in juvenile and probation work, contributing its emphasis upon social history-taking and readjustment of offenders in community settings.

The more recent introduction of psychologists has centered most intensively, though not exclusively, on offender classification and placement in institutions. The psychiatric profession has had a long history of involvement with the criminal justice system in determining criminal competency, along with an emphasis on individual treatment and intrapsychic change. Sociologists/criminologists have added important theory and research on social-psychological explanations for criminality which continues to influence investigative reports on offenders.

This brief overview of the contributions of other established professions is intended to highlight the multi-disciplinary nature of the emerging profession of corrections, and to illustrate how the work of investigative officers has been influenced by others. Nevertheless, it is essential to confirm the requirements of corrections as a separate profession in its own right.

In practice, this means that an investigative report in corrections is *not* a social work history, although social history is a prominent part of such reports, and the officer may be trained in social case work. Neither is an investigative report a psychological/psychiatric evaluation, although diagnostic evaluation may be incorporated into a correctional report, and the officer may have psychological training.

The task of communicating the necessary corrections emphasis in PSI reports is complicated by the fact that another established professional usually sits in judgment on the work of the probation officer; that is, the judge, as the representative of the legal profession. The necessity for cross-professional communication places a special responsibility on the probation officer. The probation officer, functioning in the middle of a tangled matrix of professionals from differing backgrounds, must act as a communicator, and as a translator of psychological/social/legal jargon into clearly understood assessments.

Exhibit 4 is a sample outline for pre-sentence investigation. Slight modifications and adjustments may be necessary to adapt this model to parole and institutional settings. Subsequent chapters of this Casebook take up implementation of this sample outline in greater detail. It should be noted that some correctional agencies provide structured work-sheets to guide interviews with offenders, police, relatives, employers, and others. The worksheets used by the Federal Probation system are reproduced as Exhibit 5.

Exhibit 4

Sample Outline for Pre-Sentence Investigation

I.   Current Offense(s)

    A. Official version (verify from court record, police, prosecutor, witnesses)

    B. Defendant's version (attempt to summarize discrepancies if different from official version)

    C. Attitude toward offense, including attitude toward victim, restitution, incarceration, and probation

II.   Prior Arrest Record (from FBI, State, and Local "Rap Sheets")

    Include juvenile record where possible, and all jurisdictions where defendant is known to have traveled or resided. Review record in detail with defendant, identify discrepancies, and probe attitude toward previous offenses, as with current offense. Probe for undiscovered crimes. Summarize pattern of criminality (if any), and summarize multiple offenses in narrative form, noting disposition of charges.

III. Family History

    Birthplace, early years, place in sibline, attitude of parents, family climate, early misbehavior, main influences on client

IV.   Marital History

    Early heterosexual behavior, marriages, sexual adjustment, children, attitudes toward family life and child support

V.   Home and Neighborhood

    Present and past living situations, peer influences, and socioeconomic level, social mobility

VI.   Education

    Early school years, highest grade completed, school adjustment, truancy or other misbehavior, results of achievement tests

VII. Employment

> History of employment from present position back to first work experience, reasons for leaving, patterns and trends, periods of unemployment, work skills and training, work attitudes and aspirations, relationship to criminal behavior

VIII. Religion

> Early influences and church memberships, current participation, significance of religious/personal values for client

IX. Military Service

> Draft or volunteer, length of service and assignment, advancement in rank, reaction to conditions of military life, combat record, decorations and awards, disciplinary actions, type of discharge, use of veteran's benefits, service-connected disabilities, and post-military adjustment

X. Hobbies and Use of Leisure Time

XI. Physical Health

> Early childhood diseases, disabilities and injuries, physical abnormalities, dental problems, venereal disease, hospitalizations, general health, attitudes toward health problems, personal grooming, and nutrition

XII. Personal Adjustment

> Use of alcohol and drugs, mental breakdowns, periods of treatment/hospitalization, abnormal ways of relating, bad habits, communications skills, personal problems

XIII. Evaluative Summary

> Summary of most significant factors from investigation, including factors contributing to criminality. Potentials and strengths from personal history. No new material is to be included in the evaluative summary.

XIV. Recommendations (optional in some settings)

> Present recommendations for disposition of case, developed in logical way from preceding Evaluative Summary. Justify each recommendation from information in report. If probation is recommended, present proposals for residence, employment, type of supervision required, treatment, training, education, or other options as appropriate. Try to be specific. If confinement is recommended, note special problems and needs of offender while in custody, if any. Try to include the probable response of the offender to the various alternatives recommended.

Note: Some of these categories may be omitted in brief reports. If verification of information is not feasible, such as military service, that should be acknowledged.

Exhibit 5 (Page 1)

WORKSHEET FOR PROBATION INVESTIGATION

PROBATION FORM (SHORT FORM) MARCH 1960 **1a** WORKSHEET	UNITED STATES DISTRICT COURT FEDERAL PROBATION SYSTEM	DISTRICT	DIVISION	DOCKET NUMBER

COURT NAME *(last - first - middle)*	DATE INTERVIEWED	REPORT DUE	RECORDED BY

TRUE NAME *(last - first - middle)*	SENTENCING DATE	SENTENCING JUDGE

ALSO KNOWN AS:	DATE OF CONVICTION OR PLEA	CONSENT FORM SIGNED? ☐ YES ☐ NO

PRESENT ADDRESS *(number, street, city, state, zip code)*	GIVE SPECIFIC DIRECTIONS	LENGTH OF TIME AT THIS RESIDENCE
		TELEPHONE NO.

LEGAL ADDRESS *(if different)*

IDENTIFYING DATA

AGE	DATE OF BIRTH	PLACE OF BIRTH *(city & state or foreign country)*	SEX	RACE	CITIZENSHIP	EDUCATION

MARITAL STATUS	NO. OF DEPEN-DENTS	SOCIAL SECURITY NUMBER	FBI NUMBER	OTHER IDENTIFYING NUMBERS

OFFENSE

OFFENSE	PENALTY

PLEA	VERDICT	WHERE COMMITTED	WHEN COMMITTED

WHERE ARRESTED	WHEN ARRESTED	ARRESTING AGENCY

NAME OF AGENT RESPONSIBLE FOR CASE	DATE OF COMMISSIONER'S HEARING	AMOUNT OF BOND	CUSTODY

IF DETAINED, WHERE	DAYS IN CUSTODY	NAME OF U.S. ATTORNEY

NAME OF DEFENDANT'S ATTORNEY	ADDRESS OF DEFENDANT'S ATTORNEY	TELEPHONE NO.

NAMES OF CODEFENDANTS *(present status)*

DEFENDANT'S VERSION

PRIOR RECORD — List below all other arrests whether convicted or not *(include juvenile court and military)*

DATE	COURT	LOCAL ARREST NUMBER	OFFENSE	DISPOSITION

Exhibit 5 (Page 2)

FAMILY HISTORY

NAMES OF IMMEDIATE FAMILY *(list spouse and children under MARITAL HISTORY)*

NAME *(Place a check mark √ beside name if person has ever been arrested)*	RELATION-SHIP	BIRTHDATE OR AGE	PRESENT ADDRESS	OCCUPATION OR SCHOOL STATUS

MARITAL HISTORY — Present and previous marriages, including common-law

NAME OF SPOUSE	AGE	PLACE AND DATE OF MARRIAGE	NUMBER OF CHILDREN	OUTCOME OF MARRIAGE

NAMES OF CHILDREN *(include those from previous marriages)*	BIRTHDATE OR AGE	ADDRESS, SCHOOL, CUSTODY, SUPPORT

HOME AND NEIGHBORHOOD

TYPE OF NEIGHBORHOOD	TYPE OF DWELLING	CHECK ONE ☐ RENTING ☐ OWNED	MONTHLY PAYMENT	NO. OF ROOMS OCCUPIED	NO. OF PERSONS LIVING WITH DEFENDANT

Exhibit 5 (Page 3)

LIST PREVIOUS ADDRESSES *(start with most recent address)*	CITY OR COUNTY	STATE	DATES	
			FROM	TO

EDUCATION

HIGHEST GRADE COMPLETED	AGE LEFT SCHOOL	REASONS FOR LEAVING

OTHER TRAINING RECEIVED *(business or trades)*

NAME OF SCHOOL *(list schools attended - start with last school)*	LOCATION	DATES ATTENDED	
		FROM	TO

RESULTS OF PSYCHOLOGICAL TESTS *(IQ, aptitude, achievement),* SPECIFY TEST AND DATE. ALSO GIVE CITIZENSHIP AND ACADEMIC RATINGS

RELIGION

RELIGIOUS PREFERENCE	ATTENDANCE ☐ FREQUENTLY ☐ OCCASIONALLY ☐ NEVER
NAME AND ADDRESS OF CHURCH	NAME AND ADDRESS OF PASTOR

INTERESTS AND LEISURE-TIME ACTIVITIES *(sports, hobbies, creative work, organizations, reading, talents, and accomplishments)*

HEALTH
CHARACTERISTICS

PHYSICAL *(explain poor health, previous illnesses, surgery, injuries, handicaps, addictions)*

MENTAL AND EMOTIONAL *(general social adjustment, personality traits, mental disorders, hospitals and treatment, self-evaluation)*

Exhibit 5 (Page 4)

EMPLOYMENT — List jobs held during past 10 years

DATES	NAME AND ADDRESS OF EMPLOYER	NATURE OF WORK, WEEKLY WAGE, REASON FOR LEAVING, EMPLOYER'S EVALUATION
STARTED		
ENDED		
STARTED		
ENDED		
STARTED		
ENDED		
STARTED		
ENDED		

OCCUPATIONAL SKILLS, INTERESTS, AND AMBITIONS, REASONS FOR EXTENDED PERIODS OF UNEMPLOYMENT

MILITARY SERVICE

SERVICE NUMBER	BRANCH OF SERVICE	DATE OF ENTRY	DATE DISCHARGED	TYPE OF DISCHARGE
HIGHEST RANK HELD	RANK AT SEPARATION	DECORATIONS AND AWARDS		VA CLAIM NUMBER C-

CAMPAIGNS, PREVIOUS ENLISTMENTS, OVERSEAS DUTIES, COURTS MARTIAL, ATTITUDE TOWARD MILITARY EXPERIENCE

IF MILITARY OBLIGATION HAS NOT BEEN COMPLETED GIVE:	SELECTIVE SERVICE BOARD AND ADDRESS OR RESERVE STATUS	ORDER NUMBER	CLASSIFICATION

FINANCIAL CONDITION

LIST FINANCIAL ASSETS (real estate, insurance, real and personal property, stocks, bonds, checking and savings accounts, income from pensions and compensation, rentals, boarders, and family income).	LIST FINANCIAL OBLIGATIONS, INCLUDING BALANCE DUE AND MONTHLY PAYMENTS (name mortgage, rent, utilities, medical, personal property, home repairs, charge accounts, loans, fines, restitution).

EVALUATIVE SUMMARY

ANALYSIS OF HIGHLIGHTS OF BODY OF THE REPORT FACTORS CONTRIBUTING TO PRESENT OFFENSE AND PRIOR CONVICTIONS	DEFENDANT'S ATTITUDE TOWARD OFFENSE EVALUATION OF DEFENDANT'S PERSONALITY, PROBLEMS AND NEEDS, POTENTIAL FOR GROWTH, AND FUTURE PLANS

RECOMMENDATION (include basis for recommendation)

PRACTICE CASE 3

Conduct a pre-sentence investigation by interviewing a classmate or friend, using the sample outline presented as Exhibit 4 as the basis for interview. While a more detailed description of the topics to be investigated is covered in subsequent chapters of this Casebook, it should be possible to prepare a written report on your "client."

Your client should be prepared to describe his own background accurately, and use imagination in supplying details of the offense. Your client has been caught in a local supermarket shoplifting a number of gourmet food items valued at $21.75. These items were concealed on his person while going through the checkout. There is no previous arrest record on this client. The statutory penalty for this misdemeanor is up to 90 days in jail, up to $500 fine, or both. The client appeared in court without an attorney, and was defended by the public defender. Judge Mergenthaler found the defendant guilty on the evidence, referred the case to you for PSI, asking, "What is going on with this person?"

You are to prepare a pre-sentence investigation report based upon your interview with the "client," and construct a recommendation for Judge Mergenthaler. Be ready to discuss and defend your recommendation in class.

Discussion Questions

1. If this were a real case, what resources would you consult to verify some of the background information supplied to you? Be specific.

2. What were the mitigating and aggravating circumstances in the life of your client that influenced your recommendations?

3. Were you able to maintain a reasonable freedom from personal bias in your summary of the case? At what points do you believe your personal value system may have influenced your judgments?

4. What were your client's feelings about revealing personal information to you? For instance, did you note defensiveness or evasiveness? If you had played the client, what would your reactions to the interview have been?

5. Attempt to rank in order of importance the kinds of information which you believe would influence the decision of Judge Mergenthaler in passing sentence, from most important to least important. Compare and discuss your rankings with other class members.

Chapter 5
Evaluative Summary and Recommendations

A discussion of the issues around summary and recommendations is presented at this point because subsequent student assignments are based upon the writing of such summaries in response to the practice cases presented. In this way, the student amasses practice in what is recognized as the most demanding part of investigative reporting.

The distilled wisdom of the investigator is displayed in the evaluative summary and recommendations. The decision maker, whether it be the sentencing judge, correctional institution, parole board, or community service agency, is provided in the summary with a brief overview of the results of the investigation. In practice, many judges are able to read only the PSI summary and recommendations to capture the essence of the case.

Evaluative Summaries

Normally, an evaluative summary consists of only a few narrative paragraphs. Summarizing requires the investigator to compress hundreds of facts and impressions about an offender into a few well-chosen and accurate statements. No new information should be presented in a summary. The summary should consist solely of information previously covered in the body of the report, so that the reader can consult the body of the report for further details.

The prefix "evaluative" has been chosen to signify that *acts of judgment* are required in preparing summaries. Significant facts must be sifted from merely routine information; a judgment must be made regarding information that can safely be omitted. Categories of information must be combined into brief characterizations, such as employment history and prior criminal convictions. Both positive and negative features of an offender's life history must be weighed, and a balanced account of strengths and weaknesses presented that is relevant to the sentencing decisions to be made (or for later use by institutions and parole boards).

The preparation of evaluative summaries separates the experienced from the inexperienced, and the professional from the "hack." The decision to omit certain material in favor of something else, to compress a long work history into a few statements, or to emphasize certain facts ahead of other facts, requires sophisticated judgment. Such skills are not produced overnight, nor do such skills automatically transfer from related professional fields to corrections. Thus, a skilled mental health professional may show inappropriate judgments in recommending for offenders.

The kinds of integrative statements made in summaries are necessarily more subjective in nature as the officer moves further away from the factual information base he has gathered. The freshly appointed officer should not be dismayed that judgments are requested of him; judgments are in the nature of corrections work. The student/neophyte has to learn to live with his limitations, applying himself seriously to the task.

It should be apparent that as facts and impressions are synthesized into summary statements, an enhanced opportunity arises to inject personal biases and "halo effects" into the report. To some extent, personal bias is inevitable. Each person's life experience has resulted in personal convictions and values that are reflected in the ways we describe the lives of offenders, despite our best efforts to be "objective." Some officers have a reduced tolerance for alcoholics as a result of personal experience, others feel a generalized hostility toward young delinquents, while another may find it difficult to be charitable toward college students! As professionals, we have an obligation to become acquainted with our "hang-ups," and to tread carefully when writing summaries on offenders whose activities have triggered a heavy personal response.

One check on the quality of judgments made in evaluative summaries is to review the information base from which summary statements have been made. Is the summary really supported by facts in the body of the report? In the field, officers find the comments of supervisors and colleagues valuable in checking the internal consistency of their conclusions and the possibility of bias. The presence of highly charged descriptive adjectives is often a clue to strong emotional reactions in the report-writer. Adjectives like "worthless," "no-good," "moronic," or "hopeless" have no place in professional writing.

Rating Scales and Prediction Tables

The struggle to maintain objectivity in investigative reports and to promote equitable decisions on dispositions can be aided by statistical tables of past performances by various offenders. Such tables can be consulted by sentencing judges or parole boards to estimate probability of offender outcomes, or refined into rating scales of "risk factors" involved in various dispositions. Use of such tables is claimed to minimize personal bias and lead to a more scientific and equitable processing of offenders.

Typical rating scales are shown in Exhibit 6 (Dept. of Parole and Probation, State of Nevada) and Exhibit 7 (Dallas Adult Probation Dept.). Each offender to be rated collects a series of "points" according to such factors as *no prior convictions, use of a weapon, age, violation of probation or parole, employment*, etc. The degree of risk to the safety of the community associated with probation or parole can thus be quantified into a single number, and applied to the offender by the decision maker. In Exhibit 7, a "clinical override" is provided (Section F) to take account of factors not covered in the scale. If such scales and prediction tables are based upon competent empirical research, a more equitable and efficient disposition of offenders should be possible. The use of such instruments is another check against biased reporting and quixotic sentencing practices.

A price must be paid, however, for the "standardization" of correctional penalties. Standardization tends to de-emphasize consideration of individuals in the process, unless careful consideration is given to overriding the statistical predictions when special factors exist that were not taken into account in the rating scales. As stated in Chapter 1, the too-literal use of scales and prediction tables also tends to "freeze" correctional practices into patterns based upon past performance of offenders. This, of course, can impede innovation in the system.

Guidelines for Preparing Evaluative Summaries

While it is not always possible to prescribe a general format for evaluative summaries because of the variety of situations for which reports are written, a typical summary might address the following considerations:

Offense(s). Is the current offense situational, or does it indicate more chronic criminality? What is the background of criminal involvement? Was violence threatened or used? Was offender armed? What was motive for offense? What is the relative culpability of defendant, if others were involved? Is shame and guilt present? Does offender acknowledge responsibility?

Exhibit 6

OFFENDER CHARACTERISTICS AND RISK FACTOR TABLE

LOW 10-8	MODERATE 7-6	HIGH 5-4	VERY HIGH 3-0

Offender's Name _____ Case No. _____

1) No prior convictions   = 2 points
   One prior conviction   = 1 point
   Two or more prior convictions   = 0 points   _____

2) No prior incarcerations   = 2 points
   One prior incarceration   = 1 point
   Two or more prior incarcerations   = 0 points   _____
      a) If previously incarcerated, offender has
         remained in free community for 3 or more
         years continuously since last incarceration = 1 point

3) Age at first commitment 18 years or older   = 1 point
   Otherwise   = 0 points   _____

4) Offense did not involve personal injury
   to victim   = 1 point
   Otherwise   = 0 points   _____

5) Offense did not involve use of weapon   = 1 point
   Otherwise   = 0 points   _____

6) Verified employment or full-time school
   attendance for 6 months or more prior to offense = 1 point
   Otherwise   = 0 points   _____

7) Offender has not been previously convicted
   of same offense   = 1 point
   Otherwise   = 0 points   _____

8) Never had probation or parole revoked or been
   committed for new offense while on probation
   or parole   = 1 point
   Otherwise   = 0 points   _____

TOTAL POINTS   _____

RISK FACTOR RATING   _____

Exhibit 7

PROBATION EVALUATION SCORE SHEET

Dallas Adult Probation Dept.

Complete this form prior to the Probation Date so that it accompanies the Probation Papers which are presented to the Judge. If a person does not qualify in a particular item, a zero should be entered opposite that item in the score column.

NAME: _____ CASE NO.: _____

OFFENSE: _____ DATE: _____

	WEIGHT	SCORE
A. PRIOR CRIMINAL HISTORY		
1. No prior arrest (other than present offense)	5	_____
2. No arrest in past 5 years (other than present offense)	4	_____
3. No felony convictions, felony probation or misdemeanor probation	4	_____
4. No arrest for automobile theft	4	_____
5. Present offense not for checks, burglary, robbery, theft, or DWI	3	_____
6. No aliases or tattoos	3	_____
7. No more than 2 prior arrests	4	_____
8. Has not been to a juvenile training school	3	_____
9. Has not had prior jail commitments	3	_____
10. No assaultiveness in prior criminal history	3	_____
11. First arrest did not occur prior to age 20	2	_____
TOTAL: PRIOR CRIMINAL HISTORY	38	_____

	WEIGHT	SCORE
B. NARCOTICS, DRUGS AND ALCOHOL		
1. No history of opiate use (opium, codeine, morphine, heroin)	5	_____
2. No history of heroin or cocaine use	5	_____
3. No history of marijuana, amphetamines, demerol, LSD, or barbiturate use	3	_____
4. No history of alcohol involvement in this or prior arrests	4	_____
TOTAL: NARCOTICS, DRUGS AND ALCOHOL	17	_____

	WEIGHT	SCORE
C. EMOTIONAL AND PHYSICAL		
1. No history of psychiatric or psychological disorders	3	_____
2. No sex offense attributed to personality or emotional disorders	3	_____
3. Sexual adjustment appears normal	2	_____
4. Favorable physical condition (health)	2	_____
5. Favorable physical appearance	1	_____
6. Delinquent behavior not attributed to associates .	4	_____
7. Has favorable attitude toward probation and future	2	_____
TOTAL: EMOTIONAL AND PHYSICAL	17	_____

D. EMPLOYMENT AND EDUCATION
   1. Employed at present (if housewife give credit
      same as employed) .... 3 _____
   2. Has held present job six months or more .... 3 _____
   3. Has a vocational skill .... 2 _____
   4. Attending school, receiving a pension, social
      security, unemployment compensation or un-
      employed due to medical disability .... 2 _____
   5. Veteran with Honorable Discharge .... 1 _____
   6. Completed high school or has GED .... 2 _____
   7. Has a job commitment (give credit if employed) .. 1 _____
   8. If children involved, is suitable care arranged ... 2 _____
   9. Has a favorable attitude toward work .... 1 _____
              TOTAL: EMPLOYMENT AND EDUCATION .. 17 _____
                                                       _____

E. FAMILY TIES
   1. No family criminal record .... 4 _____
   2. Lives with spouse or family .... 2 _____
   3. Parents neither separated nor divorced .... 2 _____
   4. Supports spouse and children or self, if single ... 2 _____
   5. Marital stability—no divorces or separations
      (give credit if single) .... 1 _____
              TOTAL: FAMILY TIES .... 11 _____
                                   TOTAL RATING: _____

F. SCALE: Chance of successfully completing probation.
          Circle the number you feel is the appropriate
          rating in this case.

0 5 10 15 20 25 30 35 40 45 50 55 60 65 70 75 80 85 90 95 100
        Very Poor | Poor | Average | Good |Very Good

                                                    WEIGHT   SCORE

Community. How serious a threat is offender to safety and welfare of others? Does offender commit offenses while drinking or using drugs? Would a disposition other than incarceration depreciate the seriousness of the offense in the community? Is probation a sufficient deterrent? What are the relative risks/benefits of working with the offender in the community? Is offender employable?

Offender's background. What strengths/weaknesses are present in terms of family/work/education/military service? Is client motivated to change? Has behavioral change taken place since arrest? Has client made any efforts at self-correction for existing problems?

The guidelines just described establish the basis for the final section of the report, *recommendations*. It can be seen that there is a steady progression throughout the report from *description* of the offense and the offender toward *prescription* of disposition for the case.

Recommendations

Recommendations are the action plans suggested by the investigative officer, and are thus the real end product of the report. If the proper ground-work has preceded the recommendations, this final section should flow easily from the evaluative summary of the case. In any event, recommendations should never come as a surprise to the reader, as a course of action not foreshadowed by the preceding material.

Recommendations must be written with some restraint, since the corrections investigator is acting as a consulting resource to the judge or parole board, and not as an arbiter. The sentencing judge, for example, should not be "boxed in" by the recommendation; the legal options open to the court should be handled with respect as alternatives. One probation officer wrote, "No one who really knows this offender could possibly consider him for less than a maximum sentence." It does not take much imagination to see why the judge was irritated with this recommendation!

One method for preparing recommendations is to examine several alternatives, while pointing out the probable outcomes of each alternative disposition, based upon your investigation. In this way, the judge is able to select the sentencing alternative which seems most likely to satisfy his sentencing objectives.

In some jurisdictions, judges do not desire probation officers to make recommendations, believing that PSI recommendations are an intrusion upon the legal prerogatives of the judiciary. In other cases, judges believe that sentencing decisions should be reached independently, so that PSIs should stop short of recommendations. In either case, the procedures of the court must be observed. In some jurisdictions, PSIs are supplied to the prosecutor and defense counsel prior to sentencing, but without the recommendations attached. In these cases, recommendations are prepared on a separate page.

Because of the importance of sentencing recommendations in the life of offenders, it has become common practice to have recommendations reviewed by a supervisor, or by a staff conference in the probation agency. Recommendations make stringent demands upon officers for a working knowledge of legal penalties, the sentencing habits of judges, community alternatives, caseload information, and specialized capabilities for supervision of offenders. Corrections investigators must also be skilled in predicting case outcomes.

A recommendation is a *prognosis,* a set of predictions of an offender's response to various dispositions. Since the officer is no longer dealing with facts, but with probabilities, some humility is appropriate. Characteristically, recommendations are hedged with "weasel words" — "*In my opinion,* this offender . . .," or "While chances of success in treatment may seem slight, *I believe* . . . ." Any recommendations should be accompanied by a supporting rationale consistent with the body of the report.

The construction of sensible recommendations is the point at which experience weighs most heavily. Again, as stated in Chapter One, the mind of an experienced officer may be visualized as a computer that evaluates a particular offender against countless other offenders of a similar type. In this capacity, the officer is seeking an optimum solution that will provide correctional impact on the offender with acceptable levels of risk to the community. Statistical tables of risk factors provide an important check-point. Another valuable addition to the final recommendations is the experience of other colleagues, each of whom may add a valuable idea to the overall recommendation.

To the extent that an officer can be specific in his recommendations, weight is added to his suggestions. If probation is contemplated, the length of supervision should be specified, the intensity of supervision indicated, and a time-table established to achieve the objectives of supervision. If a period of incarceration is recommended, the degree of security necessary for the offender should be indicated if possible, together with any suggestions for institutional placement. If medical, psychiatric, dental, or drug treatment is needed, a referral plan indicating the agencies or clinics to be involved should be included. A blue-print for supervision, either on probation or parole, should anticipate the problems to be encountered, and specifics on family, residence, employment, or education spelled out in advance.

In all such planning, the main criterion is *practicality;* no decision maker can afford to trust a plan of supervision anchored in mid-air. Practical planning for an offender means that contingency referrals to halfway houses, schools, employers, treatment agencies, and families need to be worked out in advance. If release plans are centered around a community agency that happens to have a lengthy waiting list or time-consuming intake process, and no prior commitments have been made, the offender may become frustrated, and this alone can jeopardize the success of the entire rehabilitation plan.

Communication Feedback

It is always good professional practice to seek conferences with diagnostic report recipients, whether it be in a judge's chambers, with the staff of a prison, a parole board, or a community mental health center. Despite our best efforts, the written word does not always communicate the subtleties of our thoughts, or permit the two-way exchange of viewpoints which is so helpful to professional growth.

Any investigator builds confidence in his judgment by seeing his investigations accepted and implemented, and by sharing with judges and others one's innermost impressions of offenders. Corrections investigators also learn by seeing their recommendations rejected in favor of other alternatives; it is very important for the officer to understand the points at which his impressions of an offender may have diverged from a judge or colleague, and to be able to discuss such differences of opinion in a non-defensive way. Such differences occur frequently in any professional setting where complex decisions about people are at stake, and should not be taken personally. The best way to promote new learning is to seek feedback at every opportunity from instructors, colleagues, and officials.

PRACTICE CASE 4

This pre-sentence investigation of Harry Love was conducted by Probation Officer Cyril Saylor for Judge Hardcase. Names and certain details have been altered, but otherwise the PSI is reproduced as presented to the judge. Note that the recommendation has been deleted, and that the format does not exactly follow the outline recommended in this Casebook.

You are to construct a recommendation, using the report as the basis of justification. You are to answer the questions for discussion following the case. Avoid reading comments by the probation officer and the case commentary until you have completed this assignment.

PRE-SENTENCE INVESTIGATION

Name: Harry Love

Aliases: None

Age: 27

DOB: 10/10/51

Sex: Male

Race: Negro

Marital Status: Single

Address: Various

Charge: Burglary

Docket Nos.: 32895

Penalty: 1-20 yrs.

Plea: Not Guilty

Finding: Guilty as Charged (5/3/78)

Prosecutor: Ben Coors

Defense Counsel: Public Defender

Custody Status: County Jail

CURRENT OFFENSE:
On 4/1/78, at approximately 11 PM, South Bend Police were summoned to Jake's Food Shop, 1222 W. McMicken Avenue, to investigate an alleged burglary, The glass in the front door had been smashed and a witness, a waitress in a tavern across the street, observed the defendant leaving the premises. Using her description, the defendant was apprehended one block away, but denied the accusation. He objected to being returned to the scene for identification by the witness, and in a struggle a bottle of wine fell from his pocket, and was broken. Judge Hardcase found him guilty as charged, and the defendant was remanded to the County Jail pending pre-sentence investigation.

ATTITUDE OF COMPLAINANT:
Jake Somers, owner of the store, related that several packs of cigarettes, a roll of pennies, and some loose change found on the person of the defendant, were his property. The loss of merchandise was about $5. Replacement of the glass amounted to $50. The owner does not believe that leniency for the defendant would serve any useful purpose. He explained that the neighborhood is practically ruled by hoodlums who steal merchandise and commit vandalism almost at will. Such conditions have prevailed for a long time, with the result that Mr. Somers is contemplating selling the store, since he can no longer cope with the delinquency.

PRIOR RECORD:

5/11/69 Auto Larceny Counsel & Guidance	Juvenile Court
6/1/73 Non-Support Ordered to pay $10 wk.	South Bend, Ind.
11/15/73 Drunkenness $10 & Costs	South Bend, Ind.
1/26/74 Disorderly Conduct Costs	South Bend, Ind.

6/8/74   Disorderly Conduct   South Bend, Ind.
$10 & Costs

9/24/74   Burglary   South Bend, Ind.
2 yrs. Probation

12/31/74   DUI & Reckless   South Bend, Ind.
5 days jail, $111 fine, 1 yr. Suspension

1/15/76   Drunkenness   South Bend, Ind.
Referred to State Mental Hosp. for Evaluation

4/15/76   Burglary   South Bend, Ind.
Ref. to State Hosp., returned & sentenced to
Pendleton State Reformatory. Paroled 7/28/77

11/24/77   Assault & Battery   South Bend, Ind.
Dismissed.

A detainer has been filed for violation of parole
at the County Jail.

MITIGATING AND AGGRAVATING CIRCUMSTANCES:

Despite the fact that the glass on the defendant's shoes matched the structure of the broken glass in the burglarized store, and the cigarettes found on his person matched the serial numbers of missing cartons, the defendant claims he was the victim of mistaken identification. The witness described the defendant's clothing, but he claims he had attempted to cash a check in that tavern earlier that evening without success. He also denies a bottle of wine was taken from the premises or that he attempted to escape. Since he is a parolee, he is forbidden on the street at that hour. Mr. Love retains a "chip on the shoulder" attitude in spite of the fact that he had only been released a few days earlier from jail for non-compliance with parole regulations. Although assault and battery charges were dismissed, he was cautioned by his parole officer against exploiting middle-aged women who apparently enjoy his attentions and support him. Although Mr. Love is believed to be an alcoholic, he has attended only one A.A. meeting, and refused to return. Further, employment was obtained for him at McDonald's restaurant, but he did not see fit to cooperate. Not only is the defendant manipulative and evasive concerning his behavior, but he demonstrates attributes of a sociopathic personality and might be returned to the Indiana State Reformatory, according to his parole officer.

EDUCATION: AND EARLY LIFE:

The defendant is a native of Selma, Alabama, but was reared in South Bend, where he achieved an 8th grade education with a largely inadequate school performance. Several elementary grades were repeated, even in slow learner classes. During formative years, he resided primarily with relatives, which may have sown the seeds of anxiety and resentment manifested later in antisocial activity.

FAMILY AND NEIGHBORHOOD: The defendant's 50 year-old father, Morris Love, is a native of Mississippi who has been engaged in productive work with the U.S. Post Office. His wife, Nellie Lou, died during childbirth of their 3rd offspring. The father resides in a modern apartment building in a suburban neighborhood, but will not tolerate the defendant's presence because of his excessive drinking and inability to hold a job. The defendant's paternal grandparents will provide a home for him, but he refuses to stay with them because of the rigid discipline imposed. He prefers to run the streets with his drinking cronies.

The defendant asserts that he formerly maintained a common-law relationship with a 16-year old woman, Molly Ann, who bore a son by him in 1972. He states he was ordered to pay $10 week for child support by the County Welfare Dept., but has never paid. He admits to living with various women on Welfare in the past few years, and that he was stabbed by a female "acquaintance," which resulted in his arrest for Assault and Battery after he beat her up. She declined to prosecute.

INDUSTRIAL HISTORY: For approximately 3 months he worked for Dave's Sunoco Station earning $65 week. The owner relates that he was a fairly competent employee, but that finally his drinking, absenteeism, and petty thefts forced him to discharge Love. In former years, he worked at Dynamite's Car Wash as a wiper earning $2.25 an hour, but was not considered reliable and drank too much wine to keep the job. He worked briefly for Lenox Chevrolet as a car-washer, but drinking and "laying off" resulted in his discharge. Since he has never adjusted to any employment situation, his work history is deemed unsatisfactory.

PHYSICAL AND MENTAL: Mr. Love is a 27 year-old single Negro who was born 10/10/51. He is of slight physical stature, and weighs 135 pounds. When examined by the Jail physician, he was found to be in satisfactory condition with no venereal infection. However, in the past he has contracted gonorrhea for which he was treated at the South Bend Clinic. In January, 1975, he was probated by his father to the State Hospital for evaluation of alcoholism. He was diagnosed as suffering from neurotic anxiety, and escaped the hospital five times. He suffered hallucinations, heard voices, and exhibited behavior symptomatic of *delirium tremens*. He was committed to Indiana State Hospital for the Criminally Insane on 4/15/76 for evaluation. On the Wechsler Adult Intelligence Test, he measured a Verbal IQ score of 74, indicating a "borderline" intelligence. After a period of observation, he was diagnosed *"Passive-*

Aggressive Personality with history of alcoholism" and returned for trial to South Bend, following which he was sentenced to Indiana State Reformatory.

CHARACTER AND CONDUCT:

Alcoholic indulgence, usually in the form of wine, is apparently such a deeply entrenched facet of the defendant's social functioning that his entire value structure is negatively affected. Although promiscuity has been a factor in his antisocial activity, his sexual expression is within normal range. Habitual gambling and narcotic addiction are denied. Positive leisure-time pursuits are unknown to him, and presumably the majority of his time is spent socializing in taverns. Avocationally, he enjoys fishing, and during adolescence he was interested in boxing. Although he was exposed to the Baptist faith, religious activity has been ignored. An examination of the defendant's adjustment shows no strengths in any area.

He demonstrates a sociopathic attitude, and pursues the satisfaction of his creature wants without regard to consequences. Clinical evaluation showed him to be evasive, untruthful, hedonistic, and supremely unimpressed with the advantages of positive moral behavior.

Summarily, alcoholism has brought Mr. Love to the brink of complete degradation and personality disintegration. If this individual's life is to be salvaged, the reasons for his alcoholism must be diagnosed, so that his condition may be dealt with effectively. However, the defendant's extremely limited intellectual endowment must be taken into consideration in any realistic rehabilitative program.

Probation Officer Saylor Comments on This Case:

"Judge Hardcase sentenced Harry Love to a term of 1-15 years in the Indiana State Reformatory. I don't think anybody here was surprised by the sentence, and certainly not me. If I had been the Judge, I would have hit him with the maximum. After talking with the parole officer about the grief he got from this guy, I can't see anybody wasting his time with him. He'll do better in prison. Maybe when he comes out, he'll be ready to act a little more reasonable. I don't see the parole board giving him much of a break either, not with his record and the fact he's already a parole violator."

Discussion Questions

1. Was this case presented in an objective manner? What statements might reflect some loss of objectivity by Mr. Saylor?

2. What would you guess was the relationship between the defendant's drinking and his criminality, if any?

3. Harry Love was sentenced to 1-15 years in the Indiana State Reformatory by Judge Hardcase. Did your recommendations coincide with the judge? Discuss the basis for agreement or disagreement with the sentence.

4. Judge Hardcase has proudly boasted at Rotary Club luncheons, "I have a 97% success rate in my court with probation!" While citizens applaud such statements, the probation staff is silent about such claims. What are the implications of the Judge's statement, in terms of probation risk-taking and use of probation supervision?

5. To what extent are Mr. Saylor's references to the defendant's "sociopathic personality" justified, in your opinion? Is this condition treatable through mental health facilities?

Case Commentary

Harry Love is a small-time street hustler, but not a very good one, judging by the amount of trouble he has made for himself. To Judge Hardcase, Love must represent some kind of nether world with which he has had little contact, except through the filter of a criminology textbook. To his former parole officer, Love was apparently a frustration in his persistent attempt to elude supervision. Mr. Saylor's summary of this man is certainly not objective; Saylor appears unsympathetic and unsentimental; with the social pragmatism so typical of probation officers, he concludes, "I can't see anybody wasting their time with him." Saylor's report also has a detached quality, almost as if Harry Love had not been really interviewed. The reader gets almost nothing about Love's feelings and aspirations; there is very little of a personal nature in the report. We learn that he likes fishing, and enjoyed boxing as an adolescent, but then Saylor concludes: "An examination of the defendant's adjustment shows no strengths in any area." Thus, any potential in this man is written off.

It is also possible to see Harry Love as the product of institutional racism, a social victim of a system in which he was denied legitimate opportunities, and turned to the streets to survive. Love fits the abstractions of criminological theory very well. However, such labels are not very helpful when the judge has before him a convicted man facing some type of immediate disposition.

To Harry Love's father, who spent most of his working life with the Post Office, his son must be a painful reminder of the family's failure. Did the school system fail Harry Love when he finally left after 8 grades of poor adjustment and misery? What about the prison and mental hospitals which managed to put a label on him, but were unable to re-direct the course of his life?

Such explanations of family, school, and institutional failure would imply that Harry Love was a passive victim of forces he did not understand, and could not control. The studies of Drs. Yochelson and Samenow with chronic criminals point to a different scenario; they would insist that for many criminals like Harry Love, it was the child rejecting the parental discipline during the formative years that was the genesis of the criminality. That it was the young delinquent fighting the values and the discipline of the school system which caused the poor adjustment and eventual drop-off. And finally, that it is the exploitive and manipulative search for short-term gratification which fuels the criminal life-style, and ultimately makes social segregation in prisons necessary. These doctors would insist that Harry Love may be a victim, but is also a victimizer of society. Hence, there may be justification in Mr. Saylor's description of "sociopathic attitudes" in this offender.

The case of Harry Love is troubling and, unfortunately, not uncommon in the corrections system. The ideological squabbles over causes of criminality and the inferred impact of criminal dispositions are endless, and are well-reported in criminology textbooks.

Supplementary Reading

Yochelson, Samuel & Samenow, Stanton. *The Criminal Personality*. (Vols. I-II) New York: Jason Aronson, 1976-77. The authors, a psychiatrist and clinical psychologist, report on 17 years of intensive study and treatment with hard-core criminals. They describe a plan for criminal treatment based upon total responsibility, phenomenononological reporting, and group therapy somewhat similar to Synanon.

Chapter 6
The Art of Interviewing Offenders

"Man is the only animal that blushes. Or needs to."

Mark Twain

The effective use of interviewing skills in offender assessment is an essential prerequisite to the professional practice of corrections. While the correctional setting imposes some modifications of technique, the interviewing and counseling skills used by the investigating officer are similar to those practiced by the other helping professions. Therefore, an acquaintance with literature and coursework in counseling should properly be included in the preparation for corrections work. Like other counseling clients, the offender is a person in trouble (with the law), and requires the same consideration of his situation as a voluntary client in a family counseling agency.

The non-voluntary quality of correctional evaluation probably places a premium on the skills of the corrections officer, who must counter resistance with patience, persistence, and good will. Vriend and Dyer (1973), in commenting on the counseling process with reluctant clients, noted the following typical client reactions:

Silence.

Verbalized hostility toward counselor.

Overcompliance.

Counselor hero worship.

Grandiose expectations.

"Putting the counselor on."

Excessive agreeableness.

Insignificant content.

Denial of need for counseling.

Retreating into humor.

The kinds of reactions noted by Vriend and Dyer are routine occurrences in the interviewing of offenders. The first struggle of the neophyte encountering offenders for the first time is with his own feelings and attitudes; there is always the temptation to counter an offender's hostility and non-cooperation by a counter-rejection of that offender.

In counseling agencies where most clients are eager for assistance, the reluctant offender strikes a sour note. The insecure counselor who expects to derive personal gratification from the appreciation of his clients often finds corrections work too tough. The personal satisfactions of the corrections officer are dearly bought from his clients; it takes hard work and perseverance to see results which are more easily obtained in other counseling settings.

The sum of all the negative feelings and retaliatory actions projected on the offender by a frustrated officer is referred to as *counter-transference*. Counter-transference is the irrational and destructive response of the counselor to a client whom he/she deems to be insufficiently appreciative of the counselor's efforts. Counter-transference is a chronic problem in many corrections officers who have not completely worked out their professional identities and their role-taking functions with clients. Counter-transference is, by definition, over-reactive and irrational, and should not be confused with firmness in handling confrontations with offenders when required. The point of this discussion is the necessity for corrections counselors to constantly examine their values and commitments so that they are guided rationally in their supervision of their clients, and are contaminated by counter-transference attitudes as little as possible.

It takes a certain amount of self-confidence, a resilient ego, and an openness to new experience to avoid the pitfalls just described. Hence, as stated earlier, the first struggle of the neophyte is with his own feelings and attitudes, which is needed to maintain a positive and balanced approach to each offender being evaluated. The techniques described in this chapter involve *simulating* the desired behaviors and attitudes in a self-conscious fashion until through skills practice these interviewing methods become second nature and routine to the student or officer.

"The Big Stick"

The distinguishing feature of corrections that differentiates it from other helping professions is the large amount of socially sanctioned authority, both actual and delegated, carried by the corrections official. An officer can deprive an offender of his liberty, and the officer's recommendations on investigative reports may be influential in depriving the offender of his freedom for long periods of time. Recognition of such authority by the offender may profoundly influence the character of an interview, and of the correctional counseling process. The officer must learn to become comfortable with his authority, and to use it with restraint in the service of the officer and client's objectives.

The reaction of some inexperienced officers is to banish the "big stick," and go hide it in the judge's chambers or in the warden's office. Such officers seem to believe that social casework and counseling can proceed in corrections on the same basis as in an outpatient clinic, that their "good guy in the white hat" image is somehow tarnished by the possession of so much power over their clients. Officers who conduct investigations and counseling while denying their own authority are usually perceived as being weak, and are subject to easy manipulation by their clients.

So, the first struggle of the corrections officer is an unseen one within himself, to determine whether he can adjust to his correctional responsibilities without violating personal values and commitments. As in the law enforcement field, power "comes with the territory." In the police field, officers are trained to use the least possible amount of force necessary to accomplish their job. The officer in corrections might well borrow that concept in the interviewing/counseling of offenders. The cultivation of empathy and concern is facilitated in an atmosphere where coercion is kept in the background as much as circumstances permit. The unnecessary exercise of threats has a chilling and brutalizing effect on offenders, and may drive him into further defensiveness and covert resistance.

Some critics of corrections maintain that the authority role of the corrections officer is so incompatible with the practice of counseling that the effectiveness of correctional counseling becomes moot, because the client is stripped of self-determination in the process. The resolution of these issues is an empirical question beyond the scope of this Casebook; however, it should be noted that parents socializing their offspring retain a considerable power over their children which is gradually relinquished as the children demonstrate a capacity for responsible choices. The power of the corrections worker should be viewed in that context; the effective officer relaxes his authority as the client is able to demonstrate competence and judgment for self-decision on a responsible basis.

Extending Yourself to the Offender

If the officer has overcome the pitfalls of counter-transference and is comfortable with his own authority, he is ready to confront the needs of the offender in the initial investigative interviews. The offender is a person in trouble, and is usually fearful and apprehensive with good reason. The interviewing skills of the officer are crucial at this point to lay the groundwork for a possible supervisory/counseling relationship at a later point. The most effective way to begin the investigation is to extend yourself totally to the offender. This means empathizing with his situation, being a good listener, suspending judgment, and showing a non-possessive warmth, among other things.

Empathy. Empathy is the capacity to stand in another person's shoes, and to temporarily perceive the world from that person's point of view. Empathy involves sensitivity to elicit the thoughts and feelings of another person, and the ability to accurately communicate that understanding to them. Empathy means paraphrasing statements made by an offender, and feeding such statements back in an accurate manner. Empathy also includes the verbalization of feelings and emotions experienced by offenders, with communicative feedback to that client. The test of empathy is the acceptance by the client of the investigator's responses to the client's thoughts and feelings.

Empathy does *not* involve a premature reassurance by the officer that "everything is going to be all right" in order to allay anxiety in an offender. Such statements imply a judgment that the officer is not prepared to make, and which can detract from the authenticity of the relationship.

Suspending Judgment. An important aspect of an investigating officer's objectivity is the ability to refrain from making judgments about the offender's behavior. The aggravated nature of some criminal offenses tempts the officer to make moralizing statements or to communicate his disgust in some manner. The objective of the officer is to obtain a complete and accurate account of events and feelings, and the premature communication of moral judgments has an inhibiting effect on communication. The officer must practice a neutral but persistent curiosity in obtaining a crime history. However, the morally neutral attitude of the officer does not preclude attempting to elicit statements from the offender about his own behavior. Such inquiries can be handled through open-ended questions: "How did you feel after you left the scene of the accident?" "What feelings do you have now about what you did?"

Being A Good Listener.   Most corrections officers conducting investigations talk entirely too much, ask too many questions, and fail to listen closely to their clients. The interview setting should be quiet, and as private as possible. No telephone calls or other interruptions should be permitted. The officer should devote his attention totally to the offender. He can communicate his interest by leaning slightly forward in his chair, by meeting the gaze of his client from time to time (without excessive staring!), and by keeping his note-taking to the minimum required for accurate reporting. The officer facilitates the flow of information non-verbally by nodding occasionally, keeping his expression neutral and attentive, perhaps adding a non-commital "uh-huh" or "I see" to indicate his interest.

Showing a Non-possessive Warmth. "Non-possessive warmth" is a term used in counseling to describe a positive and encouraging attitude toward clients, a climate in which constructive change and growth can more readily occur. As used in corrections, non-possessive warmth refers to an attitude through which the officer is able to seek the positive attributes of offenders so that he is capable of describing the strengths as well as the weaknesses of his clients. The demonstration of warmth and concern can be disarming, if not surprising, to offenders. Expressions of concern are needed to counteract the pessimism, the suspicion, and the punitive expectations with which an offender initiates a relationship with corrections personnel. However, warmth must be an *authentic* expression of the officer's attitude.

Questioning Use of the Question

In completing a correctional investigation, it is convenient to assume that the officer's job is to ask questions, and the offender's responsibility to answer them, since an outsider observing the investigative process would usually note the monotonous repetition of the question/answer, question/answer routine. To the extent that correctional reports are believed to be an accumulation of facts in neat boxes on printed forms, there is some justification for this unimaginative approach to investigation.

However, the effects of the question-dominated interview must be mentioned. In the first place, although constant questions keep the interviewer firmly in control and tend to place the question-answerer in a subordinate position (as if to say, "I am the expert, and you must give up the answers I demand"), this format also tends to make the respondent more passive, and more like an object to be manipulated; the offender is robbed of his identity as a participant in the process. Finally, the question/answer method allows the offender to expect results without any real "soul-searching" efforts on his part; "If I answer all these questions, something will, or will *not*, happen to me."

If corrections is to advance beyond a routine and perfunctory type of investigative reporting, alternative methods of interviewing must be encouraged. One alternative interviewing technique is described as the "open funnel" method, in which the interviewer, by open-ended questions and minimal encouragement, permits the client to explore the problems and main features of his life in his own way, and at his own pace. The assumption is that the client, permitted such freedom, will identify his problem areas more directly and significantly than through a more structured inquiry approach. As the interview progresses (toward the narrow end of the funnel), inquiries about key problems can become more focussed and penetrating, but the climate of the interview will remain on a participatory level.

With the open funnel method, omissions and loose ends must eventually be tied up in order to satisfy a comprehensive investigation. The open funnel method also gives an offender more opportunity to play defensive games with the interviewer and to attempt to manipulate the interview, if that is in fact his goal. The intent of the offender to play games becomes more obvious with the open funnel method, and may lead the interviewer to shift his strategy to more confrontation and direct inquiry if misleading information is being offered. Serious distortions or omissions introduced by an offender during investigative interviews often portend similar difficulties in probation/parole supervision, so that the open-ended type of interview can be seen as a "test" of the client's sincerity. Whether the open-ended interview is more time-consuming than the straightforward question/answer format is a matter of conjecture and personal preference in interviewing style.

Is it possible to eliminate use of questions altogether? Probably not, considering the volume of factual information needed in reports. However, an officer can become more aware of questions used in interviews, and attempt to reduce their volume by shifting to more open-ended types of inquiries. An *open-ended question* gives the client some options, and permits the client to expand upon his thinking in responding.

Examples:

"You say you left school after the 8th grade. Can you remember what your thinking was at that time?"

"When you told me you felt angry enough with your mother to kill her, can you tell me more about what brought on that feeling?"

The *closed question* can usually be answered with a simple Yes or No, so that further inquiries are necessary to amplify the response.

"Did you love your mother?"

"Have you ever smoked marijuana?"

The *loaded question,* which carries the implied threat, "You better answer the right way, or else" is also seen in investigations.

"You wouldn't steal if you weren't prepared to take the consequences, would you?"

"Would you rather go to work and support your family, or would you rather go to jail? It's up to you."

The bombardment of questions is a technique to intimidate or beat down defenses. This technique is sometimes seen in corrections investigations and may have been borrowed from police interrogation. The bombardment strategy may be used as a last resort with recalcitrant clients, but its use seems to lead to conclusions already established by the interviewer. It is the most extreme example of "leading the witness," and its use is discouraged.

The single word question, "Why?" has to be the most overworked question in corrections. While in its literal meaning it symbolizes a search for information about causes, in daily practice the question of *why* has become so overloaded with negative moral judgment that it can no longer be recommended, and its use should be avoided.

"Why can't you stop drinking, and live like other people?"

"Why can't you control yourself? Why do you go on exhibiting yourself in the park?"

To summarize the use of questions, they should be used as little as possible, and open-ended questions should be resorted to whenever possible. Loaded questions, closed questions, or *why* questions should be eliminated. If questions are asked, they should be necessary, and the response should be listened to.

PRACTICE EXERCISE 5

This exercise is to be conducted by a trio of colleagues or fellow-students. One person is to serve as interviewer, one as client, and one as observer. The interviewer is to conduct a mini-investigation of a misdemeanor committed by the client. The client and interviewer are to choose the "crime" prior to the exercise, and role-play the interview, in view of the observer. The objective of the exercise is to gain as much information as possible with the fewest possible questions. The questions that are necessary, however, should be predominately of the open-ended type. The observer is to note use of each question, and what type. This information is then to be discussed with the interviewer following "investigation." Roles of interviewer, client, and observer are then rotated, so that each person gets an opportunity to play all three roles. Discussion questions are then to be answered.

Discussion Questions

1. As interviewer, how many questions did you ask, and what type? In your review with the observer, were you able to find alternatives to the questions you asked?

2. Do you really believe it is possible for a probation/parole officer to be the "good guy" and advocate for his clients while jailing clients who do not conform to the rules of probation/parole?

3. How difficult would it be for you to show a non-possessive warmth and to suspend judgment when conducting an investigation with a convicted child-molester who had murdered his victim? Can you think of other examples of cases you might have difficulty with?

Supplementary Reading

Benjamin, Alfred. *The Helping Interview.* (2nd edition). Boston: Houghton Mifflin Company, 1974.

Carkhuff, Robert R. *Helping and Human Relations.* New York: Holt, Rinehart and Winston, 1969.

Ivey, Allen E. and Gluckstern, Norma B. *Basic Attending Skills: Participant Manual.* North Amherst, Mass.: Microtraining Associates, 1974.

Kleinke, Chris L. *First Impressions: The Psychology of Encountering Others.* Englewood Cliffs, New Jersey: Prentice-Hall, Inc., 1975.

Vriend, John and Dyer, Wayne W. Counseling the reluctant client. *Journal of Counseling Psychology,* 20 (1973), 240-246.

Chapter 7
Ethical Guidelines in Corrections

Code of Ethics
Federal Probation Officer's Association

As a Federal Probation Officer, I am dedicated to rendering professional service to the courts, the parole authorities, and the community at large in effecting the social adjustment of the offender.

I will conduct my personal life with decorum, will neither accept nor grant favors in connection with my office, and will put loyalty to moral principles above personal considerations.

I will uphold the law with dignity and with complete awareness of the prestige and stature of the judicial system of which I am a part.

I will be ever cognizant of my responsibility to the community which I serve.

I will strive to be objective in the performance of my duties; respect the inalienable rights of all persons; appreciate the inherent worth of the individual, and hold inviolate those confidences which can be reposed in me.

I will cooperate with my fellow workers and related agencies and will continually attempt to improve my professional standards through the seeking of knowledge and understanding.

I recognize my office as a symbol of public faith and I accept it as a public trust to be held as long as I am true to the ethics of the Federal Probation Service. I will constantly strive to achieve these objectives and ideals, dedicating myself to my chosen profession.

(September 12, 1960)

The Federal Probation and Parole Service sets a high standard of performance that has long been a source of guidance and inspiration for other corrections agencies. Their Code of Ethics is a typical statement of the formalized general principles which are presumed to guide professional practice in the field. Most corrections personnel subscribe to a similar set of standards in their respective agencies. As corrections becomes more professionalized, official committees of corrections organizations are delegated the responsibility of policing ethical practices of their members, following similar procedures in medicine, law, psychology, and social work.

When one considers that corrections personnel have more close, continuing contact with criminals than any other segment of the criminal justice system, it seems remarkable that so little public revelation of ethical violations by such officers has occurred. To the extent that officers are underpaid and largely invisible to the public, they would seem to be likely targets for corruption by offenders. Yet few instances of corruption have been reported; if violations have occurred, they have generally not reached the media. Partially this may be because internal investigation of ethical breaches in corrections has not reached the developed state of the art seen in law enforcement, and also because corrections seldom operates in the "fishbowl" atmosphere that characterizes much of public policing.

Nevertheless, substantial ethical risks do exist in corrections, which are likely to come under increasing scrutiny in the future. The ethical concerns in this Casebook are limited to investigative reports, where performance failure may indicate good-faith errors of judgment by officers, rather than willful violations of ethical procedures. Thus, the acceptance of a bribe from a defense attorney to favorably influence the PSI on an offender about to be sentenced is a clear-cut violation of ethical practices, while acceptance of a hard-luck story from a glib sociopathic criminal might not be seen as an ethical violation at all. In the bribe situation, the officer may be subject to dismissal, while becoming the victim of a sociopathic story-teller may call for further training and closer supervision. The more subtle errors of judgment in the latter case are the main concern of this chapter.

As stated earlier, the investigating officer must attempt to balance the protection of the community, the protection of the legal/human rights of the offender, and the protection of the integrity of the judicial/corrections system. The major problem faced by the correctional investigator is the restriction of confidential information about offenders to the channels where such information is needed for decision making. The discussion of cases in the hallways of courthouses and public restaurants is rather commonly observed, and is a violation of good ethical practices. The "leakage" of information on offenders beyond official channels is a perennial problem in prisons.

The practices of courts vary with respect to distribution of pre-sentence investigations. Some instances have been reported in which judges have read portions of PSIs in open court in the presence of families and news reporters; such instances can be embarrassing to the offender and the probation officer, although the officer can hardly be held accountable for a breach of confidentiality in such cases. Some courts furnish copies of the PSI to defendants and defense counsel prior to sentencing, excluding the sentencing recommendations. Local practices should be known to probation officers, and carefully explained to defendants, including written consent by the defendant when appropriate.

The procedures of the Federal courts provide that certain information can be excluded from review by the defendant or his counsel. Diagnostic information supplied by counseling agencies or private professionals can be excluded if such disclosure might disrupt a therapeutic program. Information given by families or informants can be excluded if such information was supplied with a promise of confidentiality. The relevant section is reproduced below from Rule 32, Federal Rules of Criminal Procedure (*The Presentence Investigation Report, 1978, P. 20-21*):

> Before imposing sentence the court shall upon request permit the defendant, or his counsel if he is so represented, to read the report of the presentence investigation exclusive of any recommendations as to sentence, but not to the extent that in the opinion of the court the report contains diagnostic opinion which might seriously disrupt a program of rehabilitation, sources of information obtained upon a promise of confidentiality, or any other information which, if disclosed, might result in harm, physical or otherwise, to the defendant

or other persons; and the court shall afford the defendant or his counsel an opportunity to comment thereon and, at the discretion of the court, to introduce testimony or other information relating to any alleged factual inaccuracy contained in the presentence report.

The portion of Rule 32 providing for possible exclusion of "diagnostic opinion" from review by defendants should be useful to investigators seeking reports from private practitioners and agencies. Many psychiatrists, psychologists, and physicians are wary about giving privileged information to an agency of the court because of the risks to confidentiality which they believe may be involved. There are cases in which a psychiatrist has had his own opinions about a former patient quoted back to him by that patient, which can be an embarrassing situation.

Another type of risk to confidentiality is becoming more common with the advent of copying machines in most offices. A probation officer makes a referral to Agency A, and sends along relevant portions of his PSI; later, Agency B requests information about the same client, and the PSI information is duplicated, and sent along to that agency. In a later investigation, the probation officer requests a report from Agency B about that client, and soon finds himself staring at copies of his original report on that client, which had been copied again. The degree of responsibility for confidentiality assumed by third or fourth parties seems to become less and less as the distance from the originating agency increases. This type of round-robin can only be halted if the originating agency insists that no reports be passed on without written consent of the client.

While the general principles of ethical practice are codified and rather easily understood, the kinds of day-to-day decisions in response to situations which arise in practice are not so easily resolved, nor is there always unanimous agreement on the ethical choices to be made. Hence, the cases seen in Practice Case 6 may illustrate some of the complexities involved.

PRACTICE CASE 6

Situation A. Mr. Jones is conducting a PSI on Roosevelt Hensley, who has been convicted of burglary of an inhabited dwelling. Mr. Hensley seems fully cooperative in the investigation; in fact, almost talkative. At some point in the interview, he leans forward, and says to Mr. Jones: "You know, Mr. Jones, I'd like to tell you something, if it can be 'off the record.'"

What are Mr. Jones' options? Should he (1) make the promise, and keep anything told to him out of his PSI? (2) make the promise, and then make up his own mind whether that information should be included, depending upon what information was divulged? (3) inform the client that he might not be able to keep the information out of his report, depending upon what was divulged? (4) inform the client that nothing was "off the record," and that he was not able to withhold secrets because of his official position? What ethical position should be adopted in such circumstances? Justify your response.

Situation B. Mr. Smith has been assigned a PSI on Jerry Dowling, who has pleaded guilty to a charge of *sexual imposition,* which involves sexual overtures to a 12 year-old boy in a city park. He has no prior record. Mr. Smith immediately realizes that the defendant is a close neighbor with whom he is acquainted, and remembers the defendant as a high school music teacher who lives quietly on his street with his wife and two young children.

Ethical decision #1. How should he handle this case?

(a) Should he interview this neighbor routinely, explaining that such situations are part of his responsibility?

(b) Interview Mr. Dowling, explaining that the fact that they are neighbors may actually help to give the judge a better perspective on the case?

(c) Ask to transfer the case to another officer?

Ethical decision #2. How should he handle his subsequent relationships with this neighbor, who knows he works as a probation officer?

(a) He should ignore the episode and pretend he knows nothing about it, unless Mr. Dowling insists upon talking about it (this assumes he got the case transferred to another officer).

(b) He should confront Mr. Dowling with his knowledge of the arrest, pointing out his responsibility to keep surveillance on offenders, and request that no similar episode happen in the neighborhood.

(c) He should inform Mr. Dowling that his knowledge of the arrest was professionally confidential, and would not be divulged to anyone.

Ethical decision #3. Should he privately warn his wife and two children about the possible danger from this neighbor, and swear them to secrecy?

Mr. Jones Comments on Situation A:

"I hesitated, because I thought Hensley was about to reveal something important, and I didn't want to turn off what seemed to be developing into a good relationship with this man. I was tempted to agree to keep it off the record, then argue with him later when I found out what was on his mind. However, I finally explained to him that before he told me anything, he would have to trust my judgment about what went into the report, and I really couldn't make any promises in advance. It turned out he told me anyway about some girl-friend he had stashed away that he didn't want his wife to find out about. She was holding a lot of the stuff he had stolen, and the police got to her in a few days without my help. I included this information in my PSI, and I was glad I hadn't promised to keep anything "off the record." I have Hensley on probation now, and he doesn't seem to hold it against me, although he tells me he would have if I had lied to him about keeping it off the record, and then gone ahead and told anyway. I guess I really believe you have to be straight with these fellows when you do an investigation."

Mr. Smith Comments on Situation B:

"I chose to give this case to another officer for investigation. I think I wanted to spare both of us the embarrassment about telling so much about his personal life, with him being a neighbor and all. Also, I wasn't sure how objective I could be, since I have two young boys that play on the street all the time. I think what really convinced me, though, was what the Judge might think when he found out we were neighbors . . . you know, how much credibility could he give my report?

"I decided to go to Jerry immediately to reassure him that my knowledge of the offense would stay confidential. I told him it was up to the court what would happen, and I didn't see much sense in ruining his reputation in the neighborhood.

"The toughest part for me was keeping quiet around my wife. I was really tempted to warn her about him because I thought it might help protect my boys. I have a very negative feeling about this kind of behavior with children, it gives me the creeps to think about it. But I had promised Dowling, and I knew if I told my wife it might get out somehow. So the only person I discussed the case with was my colleague, who wrote the PSI and who ended up supervising him.

"As it turned out, I believe I made the right decision. He (Jerry) went into psychotherapy briefly, and there were no further incidents with young boys. Jerry was plenty scared by his arrest, you can bet. He was eventually discharged from probation. As you can imagine, he kept out of my way on the street, but we keep up appearances, and he is still living there."

Part 2
CONTENT OF OFFENDER ASSESSMENT REPORTS

Chapter 8
The Reporting of Offenses: Current and Past Crimes

"The broad effects which can be obtained by punishment in man and animals are the increase of fear, the sharpening of the sense of cunning, the mastery of the desires; so it is that punishment tames the man, but does not make him 'better.' "

Friedrich Wilhelm Nietzsche

If the student has examined the outline for a pre-sentence investigation in Chapter 4, he should now be prepared to undertake a more detailed examination of the component parts of a PSI in these subsequent chapters. The first and most important section of the PSI deals- with the *current offense,* since the sentencing of the offender for a current crime is the presumed reason for conducting the pre-sentence investigation. The details of the current offense will also affect prison classification and placement and parole planning, if the offender is to be processed through these channels later.

In counseling agencies, most diagnostic reports start with a description of the "presenting problem." Recommendations for counseling are proposed in relation to a so-called "presenting problem." In the field of corrections, the current offense *is* the "presenting problem" and all background information and recommendations *refer back to the solution of that act of criminal behavior,* in the same way that counseling recommendations in a social agency attempt to resolve a "presenting problem."

Counseling agencies, however, are in the enviable position of being able to consider the perceived self-interest of the client as the *primary focus* of treatment. Probation officers must satisfy the more complex task of balancing the safety of the community against the needs of the offender in seeking some resolution of the current offense. The complexities involved stem from the fact that counseling clients are self-motivated while correctional clients participate in a socially coerced process. Therefore, the task of the probation officer is inherently more difficult, strewn with paradoxes and compromises.

The dual responsibilities of probation/parole officers both to their clients *and* to community safety have tended to set them apart from other helping professions. The public responsibilities of probation and parole officers and their unique standards of client confidentiality have often led to misunderstandings with social workers, psychologists, physicians, and private practitioners. The neophyte officer should not be frustrated by the occasional reluctance of the prestigious mental health professionals to cooperate with him; he should recognize that a difference in mission is involved, that in criminal corrections social accountability must usually take precedence over client self-interest. This is not to say that the helping professions are insensitive to their social responsibilities, but that the traditions and work-habits of the mental health professions, particularly in the area of private practice, have tended to exclude corrections as one of the "helping professions."

Mitigating and Aggravating Circumstances

In practice, the description of crimes, both past and present, by probation officers comes down to a search for mitigating and aggravating circumstances surrounding these crimes that may affect sentencing. Often the public, encouraged by the media, appears to assume that a pre-sentence investigation always means some mitigation of sentence. Such assumptions should never go unchallenged. Any worker who fails to set a standard of balanced objectivity reduces his credibility. A pre-sentence investigation is not a new trial; the question of guilt has been settled. Advocacy, either for or against legal penalties for an offense, should be approached with some caution.

In the investigation of circumstances surrounding crimes, it is sensible for the officer to make a working assumption, subject to modification, that offenders will attempt to color the circumstances surrounding their crime in hopes of receiving lenient sentences. Thus, the offender "loads the dice" in his own favor by blaming others, omitting significant details, and failing to report undiscovered crimes. An inexperienced officer (or one deeply committed to psychiatric or sociological explanations for crime) may be too quick to accept such rationalizations uncritically, thus becoming an inadvertent (and uninformed) advocate for the offender at the time of sentencing.

Probation officers trained in the ideology of the "medical model" seem to be particularly prone to exploitation by offenders in this fashion. For example, if most crimes are perceived as a "symptom" of an underlying "illness," or the product of a "sick society," then all remedies must start in the psychotherapist's office or within a totally restructured society. In the meantime, such officers may be tempted to gloss over detailed and complete descriptions of actual criminal acts. In fact, students or neophyte officers are occasionally not adverse to ignoring current offenses totally in their haste to recommend social work treatment or other high-flown ameliorations for the offender!

Having warned readers of the pitfalls attendant to obtaining criminal histories, we shall proceed to the methodology for investigating current offenses.

Official Version of Offense.   It is usually desirable to obtain the facts of the offense prior to interview with the offender in order to prepare oneself to question details of the offense or reconcile discrepancies between the defendant's version and the official version, if that becomes necessary. It is essential to be thorough in this part of the investigation, since the sentencing judge may not have heard the evidence if a guilty plea has been accepted. Also, the formal charge may not be descriptive of the offenses if a lesser charge has been accepted through plea bargaining.

The probation officer may wish to consult police reports, informally interview arresting officers, interview witnesses or victims, and consult the court record and the prosecutor in order to obtain a complete and accurate picture of the offense.

Defendant's Version of Offense.   Since most defendants are likely to be quite defensive in discussing details of their offenses, it is often useful to initiate interviews with more neutral background information. In that way, the client gets a chance to "settle down," and a basis for some trust in the relationship can be established prior to handling more sensitive areas. On some occasions a defendant may be freshly referred from trial, and may be emotionally aroused and full of grievances. The officer may decide to "hear him out" by listening carefully and sympathetically, and postpone definitive interviews about the offense to a later time.

Whatever the attitude of the defendant may be, the officer should maintain a matter-of-fact, non-judgmental attitude toward the offender, and seek a complete and accurate record of the circumstances of the offense. Since accuracy is important, unobstrusive note-taking is usually necessary; the officer may wish to quote key phrases verbatim for inclusion in the PSI. While the use of a recorder assists accuracy, such devices increase defensiveness on the part of the offender in what is already a tense situation.

Privacy is essential. Interviews should be conducted away from staff, witnesses, or other probationers. No interruptions by telephone should be permitted. If an offender is to be interviewed in custody, it should be kept in mind that the jail setting is not conducive to candor or privacy; however, such interviews are often unavoidable. Through gentle persistence the officer attempts to obtain a chronology of the current offense. Features of that chronology might include the following:

> *Events preceding the offense.*
> *Planning involved in the offense, if any.*
> *Purpose of the offense; what gains were anticipated.*
> *Condition of the defendant at time of the offense;*
>   *drunk, on drugs, emotionally aroused, etc.*
> *Chronological description of the defendant's behavior*
>   *before, during, and after the offense.*
> *Companions involved, if any, and their participation*
>   *in the offense.*
> *Attitudes and behavior of victims, if any, and injuries*
>   *inflicted.*
> *Description of property stolen or destroyed, if any.*
> *Use of weapons or threats by everyone involved in the offense.*
> *Method of arrest, and reactions of defendant to arrest;*
>   *flight, resistance, relief, voluntary surrender, etc.*
> *Attitude and concern of defendant toward victims, property*
>   *misappropriated or destroyed, etc.*
> *Attitude of defendant toward trial, confinement, and*
>   *anticipation of punishment.*

Reconciliation of Official Version with Offender's Version.   Having done his best to establish an interview climate where candor and accuracy are stressed, an officer is often confronted with a series of discrepancies which should be resolved before concluding the investigation. The officer may elect to confront such discrepancies as they arise in the interview, or wait until the offender has concluded his description of the offense. In one case where major discrepancies developed, the officer patiently recorded the offender's description of events, then looked the offender in the eye, stating: "OK, I've heard your account. Now let's start over, and this time tell me what really happened!"

The simplest type of distortion is the *omission* of damaging facts from the offender's account; such a defense places a premium on the officer doing his homework prior to interviewing the offender. Unless key omissions are challenged during the PSI, the credibility of the officer can be in jeopardy with the offender and the sentencing judge. Omissions can be a type of primitive denial, placing the whole burden of forcing self-disclosures upon the officer. Child-molesters are particularly prone to such massive "loss of memory." A typical statement by a child-molester (pedophile) was: "Well, if she says I did that, maybe I could have . . . but I don't remember nothing, I was drinking at the time." Such vague statements are very hard to crack. In general, the drinking excuse is a trap for the unwary, since it may divert discussion into drinking habits and away from the criminal actions.

It is important to attempt to get around the rationalizations used by offenders in self-justification, if the real feelings and motives are to be revealed. For example, an offender in a maiming case said: "Well, he made me mad . . . and I don't take that off nobody!" The reasoning here seems to be that, having aroused anger in the offender, he is no longer responsible for his own behavior, so that the victim has precipitated his own injuries, in effect. The shifting of blame to the victim is extremely common among forcible rapists, who express their conviction that the victim's mere availability on the scene, at a time when the offender was drinking and felt an urge to overpower a woman, provides sufficient justification for the rape.

There can be honest differences of perception between offenders and their victims in feelings and motives that help to explain conflict between husbands and wives, for example. It is up to the officer to make a serious attempt to present a balanced perspective on such tangled conflict situations. Presenting human conflicts in an accurate and impartial manner goes beyond the usual narrow conception of "getting the facts." Feelings and motives *are* facts in the context of a PSI, and should be reported along with the concrete circumstances of a case.

If a point-by-point examination of discrepancies between the offender's account and what the officer believes to be the true facts from the official version cannot be resolved, the offender should be informed of the areas of discrepancy, and such unresolved differences reported in the PSI. If the officer believes that lying, deliberate omissions, or shifting of blame are significant factors, he should report this conclusion, and his rationale for making that statement. Major differences in the factual basis for an offense can have important implications for sentencing, probation/parole supervision, and treatment potential.

Experienced investigators almost universally report they have been "burned" by wily offenders from time to time, who either withheld significant information during investigation, or falsely appealed to the humanitarian side of the officer to the officer's disadvantage. Such experiences with offenders are part of a painful learning process, and should not provoke premature cynicism in the officer.

Reporting of Prior Offenses

The criminal histories of offenders are an indispensable part of their social history which should be developed with the same attention shown to work or family histories in a social service agency.

The first step is a search for arrest records. "Rap sheets" are requested at a national, state, or local level as appropriate. Felonies, sex crimes, and thefts are routinely reported to the FBI in Washington, which assigns a permanent number to each offender for easy identification, so that a current file of major offenses is available on a national geographic basis (FBI Number). Fingerprint and photo identification is also included in this file.

Most states now maintain a similar file of major offenses for their jurisdiction. Most communities of any size maintain a local file of all offenses charged within their jurisdiction, which is available to investigating officers.

Computerization of arrest records has simplified access in some cases. Unfortunately, court dispositions of offenses are sometimes not maintained, so that further checks of court records are occasionally necessary.

It should be noted that arrest records of most misdemeanors are ordinarily maintained only on a local basis. Because of the mobility of many people today, records of prior arrests may be scattered in several parts of the country, if only misdemeanors are involved. Therefore, it may be important to check police records in all locations where the offender is known to have resided or traveled.

Having gathered suitable arrest records, the next step is to chronologically review past offenses with the offender, probing for the same description of circumstances as with the current offense, although perhaps not with the same intensity. The interviewer should be aware that the bare listing of an offense on a "rap sheet" sometimes does not convey the significance of the arrest. An episode of sexual exhibitionism, for example, may be listed as "disorderly conduct." Again, the distortions and omissions attempted by the offender may be most revealing of his attitudes. The defendant who "forgets" most of his previous record may require some prompting to assure that the investigator has a complete record.

A recent study of the 20-year crime careers of 49 robbers in a California prison by Petersilia, Greenwood, and Lavin (1978) criticized heavily the inadequacy of conventional "rap sheets" for identifying the potential of offenders to commit future serious crimes. In their sample, they were able to distinguish *intensives,* whose self-reported offense rate was 50.8 offenses per year, from *intermittents* ("losers"), whose self-reported offenses averaged 5.2 per year. Despite this differential of committed crimes of more than 10 to 1, the lesser intermittent group had served twice as much jail time, on the average! Yet, when their prior records were examined, no significant differences between these groups could be identified, on the basis of "rap sheets."

Petersilia *et al.* recommended that prosecutors and judges be furnished with more complete police records, including multiple clearances of crimes not sent forward for prosecution. Further, that complete records of juvenile offenses and institutional commitments were essential in early identification of the crime-intensive offender who accounts for a disproportionate amount of crime in his community. Their research indicated that by the time adult offenders had been recognized as chronic and intensive, they were often already on the way to "burnout," so that a long sentence might be counterproductive at that late date. They recommended earlier identification of the chronic offender and a long period of incapacitation through sentencing, if such *intensives* could be carefully identified by police, prosecutors, and presentence investigators "with reasonable confidence."

The goal of the investigator is to identify *patterns* of criminal behavior. Criminality, like all forms of behavior, tends to run in somewhat predictable pathways, and the extent and direction of these pathways is a most valuable contribution to prediction of future behavior. The analysis of criminal patterns from past arrests serves to confirm (or negate) the existence of a continuing pattern in relation to the current offense for which sentencing is anticipated.

While a chronological listing of arrests and court dispositions is commonly included in PSIs, it is usually more helpful to make a narrative summary of arrests, in which the arrests are interpreted and trends of illegal activity can be described, if present. For example, it serves little purpose to reproduce a dreary list of 145 misdemeanors over a period of years, all of which involve excessive public drinking. It is much more useful to summarize such information, attempting to characterize trends in alcoholism, periods of sobriety (if any), and the impact of correctional efforts (if any).

Prior Evaluations.

A great deal of time and effort may be saved if prior PSIs, institutional reports, or parole evaluations can be located. If such reports are complete, a review and update may be all that is necessary. Previous reports should be procured and reviewed in advance of interview if possible. Do not count on the offender to provide knowledge of the existence of prior reports, since many offenders do not believe that review of previous evaluations is in their best interest. If probation/parole supervision has been used previously, a review of the offender's response to supervision can be very useful. When possible, an interview with previous supervisors should be conducted to obtain a more detailed account of their experience with the offender.

The First Offender.

Special attention is always accorded offenders for whom no previous record of crimes can be found. There is a widespread assumption (usually accurate) that judicial leniency is justified with first offenders, based upon the belief that no entrenched criminal pattern has been identified. In many cases, investigation will confirm this situation to be true. Further, sentencing judges may be reluctant to label the first offender as a criminal, or to subject that person to the crime-encouraging influences inside prisons alongside more hardened offenders.

Some observers of crime, however, have characterized "first offender" as a legal fiction to justify leniency, a fiction that is not always justified by the facts. Most of us have been "first offenders" at some time in our lives, but have never been caught. It seems unlikely that the so-called "first offender" has really been convicted for the first occurrence of a criminal violation, when the enormous volume of undiscovered crime is considered.

For example, Drs. Yochelson and Samenow, in their previously cited study of hard-core criminals, were able to document a continuing stream of criminality in their offenders dating back to early grade-school years. The number of arrests by police was miniscule in relation to the volume of depredations committed. In one noteworthy case, an offender estimated that he had committed 3,000 rapes before his first arrest. As a "first offender," this man was then treated leniently by the court. The psychological processes of the criminal as he carries out criminal acts are excerpted in Exhibit 8 from Vol. 1 of *The Criminal Personality.*

Exhibit 8

THINKING PATTERNS OF CRIMINALS WHILE PLANNING AND EXECUTING CRIMINAL ACTS

(Excerpted from *The Criminal Personality* (Vol. I) by Samuel Yochelson and Stanton Samenow, with permission of the authors)

"Sometimes a criminal is evaluated in light of the details of a single crime that are brought out by an investigation. But one crime for which a criminal is apprehended does not tell the whole story. He has usually committed many undetected crimes, and there is invariably a tremendous amount of criminal thinking that he has never acted on; therefore, others never know of it . . . Criminal thoughts pass through his mind in a steady stream, with some dropping out simply because of the limit on the mind's capacity to process them.

. . . When a criminal enters a store merely to purchase cigarettes, possible crimes immediately begin to run through his mind. He views the merchandise, the customers, the salesmen, the cash register, purses, and credit cards all in terms of crimes he could commit. This kind of thinking occurs repeatedly, wherever he goes. . . . The criminal mind is a reservoir of criminal ideas. One of these ideas may be activated solely as a consequence of a desire to stir up excitement. But the valves of the idea reservoir may also be opened up by a triggering external stimulus. Certainly when the criminal thinks that he has been put down, the increase in criminal thinking is enormous.''

". . . the criminal does have a conscience. However, it is usually not operational. Committing some types of crimes constitutes a putdown, in that the criminal has "standards" of what is personally offensive to him. . . . "Corrosion" is our designation for a mental process in which external or internal deterrents are slowly eliminated until the desire to commit an act outweighs the fears to the point where the desire is implemented. This is not a process of rationalizing; the criminal does not believe that he has to justify anything to himself. . . . The gradual process of corrosion occurs up to a point, and then a mental process that we call "cutoff" comes into play. Cutoff allows the criminal instantly to dispose of deterrents, both internal and external, freeing him to act. . . . It is not conscience that restrains him from violation as much as it is fear of apprehension. It could be said that corrosion is a gradual cutoff, giving way to an abrupt final cutoff before violation.''

"Cutoff is a learned mental process; it is discipline to eliminate fear, and the criminal child begins to practice it early in life. The criminal makes the cutoff of fear a cornerstone of his life. It allows him to do as he wants. In search of triumph and conquest, he cuts off deterrents, including experience. . . . When the criminal employs the cutoff, much that he appears to value is eliminated. It is a mental process that operates with surgical precision in getting rid of internal deterrents. Thus, the criminal may serve Mass at nine o'clock in the morning and steal at ten . . . although cutoff becomes habitual, the invoking of cutoff is still an act of choice. The criminal always has control over his own thinking.''

"The closer he gets to committing the crime, the more sure he becomes that all will go as planned . . . most important is his rising certainty that he will not get caught. This "superoptimism" increases with the cutoff of deterrents. This extreme certainty is absolutely necessary for a crime. . . . In a superoptimistic state, the criminal views the crime as a *fait accompli*. He has already spent the proceeds in his thinking. Indicative of this is the criminal who, contemplating the robbery of a particular bank, thought, "I hope they keep my money safe." It was as though the money in that bank already belongs to him. . . . Just before the crime, the criminal is in a state that perhaps can be attributed to the excitement from the power thrust that accompanies the commission of any crime. But another aspect is a rise in the fear that he might get caught. . . . If things do not go according to schedule, the fear of detection once again emerges, and appropriate steps must be taken. . . The most tragic consequences of the return of fear is injury to a victim beyond what had been planned. The criminal's mind is so programmed that, if he is faced with the unexpected—being reported or in any way opposed at the time of the crime— a homicide or serious injury may result.''

"Most criminals experience a return of the fear of apprehension after a crime—not panic, but fear that is sometimes as intense as that experienced just before the crime. . . However, unless there is an immediate danger, this fear gives way to a tremendous sense of triumph in having succeeded. . . . After the commission of a crime, the criminal is still psychologically "amphetamized.''

His energy output remains high. There is no letdown after the big event; instead, he goes on to more activity, some of which is arrestable but a great deal of which affords him a power thrust as the "big shot." . . . The criminal celebrates after a crime. . . . They drink or use drugs, or both, to eliminate fears and to seek new excitements, often sexual, after a crime. . . . The talk itself is very exciting. He may also flash a roll of money and try to impress others with the size of his "haul."

". . . the conquest and triumph are far more important than the proceeds. In an assault, success is overpowering the victim and escaping outweighs in importance what the criminal took from him. In a sexual crime, the conquest is far more exciting than the sexual act. In fact, it is not sex that the criminal is after; he often rejects consenting sexual relationships because they are not exciting and there is no challenge . . . he places little value on money itself; its value lies in what it will accomplish in terms of further power thrusts for criminal ends. The more money the criminal has, the quicker he spends it . . . after the commission of an offense, the female is what one criminal called his "psychological Rolls Royce." He does not consider himself a "man" unless at least one woman is available to him."

"When the criminal is arrested, he protests the arrest if there are grounds . . . the prevailing theme in his mind still is the injustice of getting caught. He does not realize that he should have to be accountable to anyone. This belief may be obscured by a barrage of other issues that the criminal raises, which have to do with his present circumstances and life history. That is, he goes through a list of other injustices—"others do it," he was led into it, he associated with the wrong people, he was born into the ghetto, he never had a chance in life, he needed the money, and so forth. The sociologic and psychologic excuses may camouflage what to him is the basic injustice—being apprehended and confined. A small number of criminals voice their indignation less and experience transient depression, with some suicidal thinking that comes and goes. . . . Except in the event of psychosis, the scheming to get out persists."

Undetected crimes have been treated very lightly in corrections. Certainly serious legal and civil rights questions are involved if confessions to undiscovered crimes were to be included in corrections investigations. The almost universal practice is to go "by the record" in conducting investigations.

Nevertheless, common sense suggests that some attention should be paid to criminal violations that are believed to be continuing, even when charges are not contemplated for lack of evidence. Questions about protection of community safety, the effectiveness of probation and parole supervision, and the responsibilities of corrections officials are involved here. It is therefore recommended that investigating officers probe for undetected crimes in their investigative interviewing.

PRACTICE CASE 7

This practice case is an excerpt from the PSI of Jack Compton, a 30 year-old separated laborer with a 6th grade education who is self-employed. He is facing sentence from Judge Cuthbert in the City Court of Goldsboro, South Carolina on two charges, driving under suspension (D.U.S.) and driving under the influence (D.U.I.). You are to interview Jack Compton, and prepare a narrative report on his current and past offenses for Judge Cuthbert. Another student or colleague is to role-play Jack Compton by studying the "rap sheet" in advance, and trying to convince the investigator of his good driving habits and sterling character, in order to avoid further penalties. You are then to answer the discussion questions, and be prepared to justify your responses in class.

Pre-Sentence Report

Name: Jack Compton

Judge: Cuthbert

Report Due: 12/2/78

Offense: 1) Driving Under Suspension
2) Driving Under Influence

Plea: 1) Plea of Guilt
2) Finding of Guilt

Official Version:

(1) On November 25, 1978 one Jack Compton did on secondary Road #33, six miles out of Goldsboro, operate a motor vehicle while his license to do so was under suspension.

(2) On November 25, 1978 one Jack Compton did on secondary Road #33, six miles out of Goldsboro, operate a vehicle while being under the influence of intoxicating liquor, alcohol, or drugs.

Defendant's Version:

(1) The defendant states that he is guilty of driving under suspension.

(2) The defendant states that he is not guilty of the driving under the influence charge.

Prior Record:

Date of sentence	Court	Offense	Disposition
5/5/68	Goldsboro City Court	D.U.S.	$100 fine
12/18/69	Goldsboro City Court	Grand Larceny	10 days or $25 fine
9/9/70	Goldsboro City Court	D.U.S.	$100 fine
12/2/71	Goldsboro City Court	D.U.I.	3 yrs. Susp. or $2,000; or 90 days Jail upon payment of $500 and 3 yrs. Probation
12/2/71	Goldsboro City Court	D.U.S.	45 days Jail concurrent to above
10/19/72	Goldsboro City Court	D.U.S.	45 days Jail
9/21/74	Goldsboro City Court	D.U.S.	Fine
9/21/74	Goldsboro City Court	Assault & Battery of High & Aggravated Nature	3 yrs. Jail
9/18/75	Goldsboro City Court	Escape	4 Months consecutive to any other sentence
11/1/78	Goldsboro City	No Vehicle License Oper. Unsafe Vehicle	$153 or 6 days Jail

Discussion Questions

1. Do the prior offenses seem to form a pattern? If so, how is that pattern related to the current offenses?

2. Would you be able to recommend disposition to Judge Cuthbert on the basis of your investigation? What other information would you require, if any?

3. Prior to your interview with your "client," what was your impression based upon the prior record and current offenses? Did your impression change after interview? If so, in what way?

4. To what extent do you think of Jack Compton as a "criminal"? What forces are operating, in your opinion, which may be causing him to continue to violate traffic laws?

Case Commentary

The probation officer could not be located to comment on this case. However, in reviewing the PSI, it was noted that Jack Compton was a local resident who lived in a trailer outside of Goldsboro. His wife had left him many years ago because of his drinking, and there was nothing in his trailer but empty bottles and a pack of dogs he kept around. He tried to scratch out a living by keeping a battered pickup truck, doing hauling and casual laboring jobs when he could find work. He seemed to have a running argument with the Goldsboro Police for the last 10 years about driving under suspension, and when he was "loaded," which was most of the time. He always claimed he had to drive to make a living, and he was probably right.

Mr. Compton was neither too bright, nor too lucky, in his dealings with the police and the Judge. His assault and battery involved beating up one of the Goldsboro Police one night outside a tavern when the officer was off-duty. Jack Compton would probably not be considered a serious "criminal" by most standards, yet his violations of law and public behavior are chronic and show no signs of abating. His attitude toward the local police and court could charitably be described as "casual." It could be inferred that he continues to drink and drive under suspension, and that the fines and jail sentences he has received seem to provide only brief interruptions to this pattern. The legal penalties he has suffered do not appear to have made much of an impression upon him, a common problem faced by many communities with drunken drivers.

To the extent that this lonely man is wedded to the bottle, he presents a tough challenge to the court. If an adequate program of probation supervision is available to the court, and an alcoholic treatment center or A.A. program is also available, a period of probation might be prescribed with a mandatory referral for alcoholism. In the absence of such services, judges sometimes prescribe long jail sentences both as a "life-saving" measure for the drinker and a contribution to public safety. An additional problem is that Mr. Compton requires a vehicle to make a living, and probably cannot afford to maintain such vehicles in a safe roadworthy condition. If his drinking pattern could be interrupted, his probation officer might assist in finding employment which would not require driving. The ability of courts to consider these interventions depends upon an adequate staff of probation officers, backed up by community facilities.

Supplementary Reading

Petersilia, Joan, Greenwood, Peter W., & Lavin, Marvin. *Criminal Careers of Habitual Felons*. Washington, D.C.: National Institute of Law Enforcement and Criminal Justice, Law Enforcement Assistance Administration, U.S. Department of Justice, 1978 (U.S. Government Printing Office, Washington, D.C. 20402 — Stock No. 027-000-00696-5). This highly readable and pertinent study contains many valuable tips on the relative ineffectiveness of parole supervision, the motivations of the chronic criminal, crime-switching, violence, and family-social backgrounds of the chronic offender. As the authors repeatedly warn, their findings probably do not generalize to the larger group of more casual offenders.

Chapter 9
The Reporting of Offenses: Attitude of the Offender

"Frequently parents under investigation (for child abuse) have admitted that they were mistreated as children. It never occurred to them that this is wrong. Even after the Judge has found them guilty and is ready to sentence them, they still feel deep down they didn't do wrong. They're not lying to themselves. They just don't know any better."

Sgt. Patrick Curran, Cincinnati Police
Youth Aid Bureau

Sergeant Curran has perceptively pointed out a dilemma of the corrections system; the sentences prescribed by law fail to correct because the offenders fail to respond in the anticipated fashion. The abusive parents do not accept their mistakes with their children, and hence, cannot accept the punishments inflicted as just and valid. Countless similar examples are seen in our courts. The frustration in corrections is especially keen with repeat offenders who typically receive ever-heavier doses of punishment, fail to accept the social censure implied, are not corrected, and sometimes emerge from prisons more defiant and embittered than ever.

One expression of the dilemma of corrections is the old adage, "There are no guilty men in prison." The conditions of jail life seem to encourage a self-protective shield of rationalizations and half-truths that are mutually reinforced by other prisoners, and seldom challenged by corrections officials.

The author has encountered groups of fathers serving 6-month sentences for failure to support their families. Some local jails place the "non-supporters" together on work details, where close association permits these men to reinforce each other's excuses: "The old lady wanted me out of the way, so she could step out with some other guy"; "The welfare worker had it in for me"; "The Judge hates blacks"; "My attorney railroaded me." By the time the "non-supporters" complete their sentences, such excuses have congealed into seeming truths, and the men emerge angry, suspicious, and full of revenge against their wives, welfare, or whomever they believe has "conspired" against them.

To the extent that these men have managed to displace blame to others, the corrective value of their sentences has been wasted. A more promising strategy might have been to mobilize guilt in these men with regard to their failure to be responsible for their families, and to promote family care as a positive part of their self-esteem.

The Carrot and the Stick in Corrections

Perhaps the most basic difference between corrections and the helping professions is the extensive use of *negative sanctions* (i.e., punishment) in the corrections field. The heart of the criminal justice system is a carefully graduated series of punishments prescribed for violation of society's laws. A criminal trial can be seen as the symbolic acting-out of an ancient morality play, as old as civilized mankind, wherein the transgressor is punished in proportion to the seriousness of his violations. The court hopes for a *special deterrent* effect on the offender that will inhibit future violations, as well as a *general deterrent* effect on would-be offenders who witness the punishment.

A cynical observer, Friedrich Wilhelm Nietzsche, once wrote:

> The broad effects which can be obtained by punishment in man and beast are the increase of fear, the sharpening of the sense of cunning, the mastery of the desires; so it is that punishment tames man, but does not make him 'better'.

While few modern authorities would dispute the increase of cunning in the criminal, there is considerable dispute over the "taming" or the intimidation of the criminal as a result of prison experiences. But a review of the debates over "just deserts" for the criminal is beyond the scope of this Casebook. The student in corrections must come to grips within himself regarding the use of socially sanctioned authority to deprive others of their liberty.

In the meantime, the correctional worker must work with the realities of the corrections system; he cannot hand the "big stick" of authority over to someone else while he deals only in "carrots." An increasing number of idealistic young corrections workers seem to be "carrot-holders" who keep their "stick" well-concealed. In some cases, judges are transformed by these workers into the "bad guys" who deal in jail sentences while they (the corrections workers) maintain the purity of their "treatment" approach. Such a viewpoint is ultimately self-defeating, as well as unconvincing to an offender. A corrections worker, like a good parent, is both supportive and restrictive, as the needs of his client require.

A thoughtful analysis of the probable impact of punishment, or the anticipation of punishment, is a crucial piece of information for a sentencing judge, and much underestimated by probation officers. The effectiveness of "shock probation" in Ohio is a good and practical example of the value of short periods of incarceration for selected offenders. The corrective effect of a short sentence, followed by community supervision, has been more beneficial for certain offenders than longer sentences.

Guilt v. Shame in Offenders

In everyday usage, the terms *shame* and *guilt* are used almost interchangeably. However, shame and guilt, as described in psychological literature, can be differentiated in ways which have important implications for correctional investigators.

Guilt

Guilt is the painful recognition of having violated one's own code of values. The guilty person has acted against his conscience (or *superego*). The roots of conscience are laid down in early childhood when a set of rules and acceptable behaviors were internalized (*introjected*) into the value structure of the child. As an adult, each person acts on a code of behavior he considers his own, often unable to verbalize the sources of such values. When this code is violated, he experiences guilt. The Biblical saying "The wicked flee when no man pursueth; but the righteous are bold as a lion" expresses the inner conflict involved in guilt. Guilt requires no witnesses, and it cannot be imposed upon another person; it must arise from within that person. The operations of conscience (through avoiding guilt) are seen as the basis for personal autonomy and self-discipline.

Shame

Shame is the painful experience of "losing face" before another person. Shame is a *social* experience, it requires witnesses. Some people may cheat on their income taxes without guilt, but experience shame when challenged by IRS. Shame can be imposed upon us by others, and may be external to our value system.

It should be obvious that shame and guilt can occur together, or in a sequence with each other. The seeds of guilt can be implanted and nourished by shame experiences. For example, we may feel shame when arrested by police for drunken driving, shamed when we stand up in court for sentencing, but guilty when we come to realize the risks caused to others because of our irresponsibility. Thus, a social shame imposed upon us by police and court is followed by an inner response of guilt triggered by that shame, since the act that evoked the social response was a violation of our inner value system.

One of the most memorable examples in literature of the workings of guilt and shame is seen in the agonies of poor Stephen Dedalus, as described in James Joyce's *Portrait Of The Artist As A Young Man*. Dedalus, troubled by guilt over masturbation, is driven to confess to expiate his "sins." The shame he felt at sharing his awful burden with a priest was described. Unfortunately, like most young men, he again fell into "sin," and must repeat the cycle:

"Could it be that he, Stephen Dedalus, had done those things? His conscience sighed in answer. Yes, he had done them, secretly, filthily, time after time and, hardened in sinful impenitence, he had dared to wear the mask of holiness before the tabernacle itself while his soul within him was a living mass of corruption.

"How came it that God had not struck him dead? The leprous company of his sins closed about him, breathing upon him, bending over him from all sides. He strove to forget them in an act of prayer, huddling his limbs closer together and binding down his eyelids: but the senses of his soul would not be bound and, though his eyes were shut fast, he saw the places he had sinned and, though his ears were tightly covered, he heard. He desired with all his will not to hear nor see. He desired till his frame shook under the strain of his desire and until the senses of his soul closed. They closed for an instant and then opened. He saw.

". . . He sprang from the bed, the reeking odor pouring down his throat, clogging and revolting his entrails. Air! The air of Heaven! He stumbled toward the window, groaning and almost fainting with sickness. At the washstand a convulsion seized him within; and, clasping his cold forehead wildly, he vomited profusely in agony.

". . . His eyes dimmed with tears and, looking humbly up to heaven, he wept for the innocence he had lost . . . Confess! He had to confess every sin. How could he utter in words to the priest what he had done? Must, must. Or how could he have done such things without shame? A madman! . . . Little fiery flakes fell and touched him at all points, shameful thoughts, shameful words, shameful acts. Shame covered him wholly like fine glowing ashes falling continually. To say it in words! His soul, stifling and helpless, would cease to be.

"... His sins trickled from his lips, one by one, trickled in shameful drops from his soul festering and oozing like a sore, a squalid stream of vice. The last sins oozed forth, sluggish, filthy. There was no more to tell. He bowed his head, overcome."

From *Portrait Of The Artist As A Young Man*
by James Joyce

The behavior of the fully socialized person is self-limiting because of conscience; the socialized person moderates his behavior because his internalized values do not permit him to recklessly intrude upon the rights of others. The social fabric of society depends upon most people automatically observing the rights of others. Thus, the operation of guilt as a check-point has a functioning relationship to the safety of the community.

Shame is likewise a powerful motive for many people, and a shaming experience can quickly produce altered or inhibited behavior. Schneider (1977) proposes that shame has "two faces"; shame as *discretion*, a kind of restraint exercised to avoid a possible shaming experience; and shame as *disgrace*, the familiar experience of being caught and punished for unacceptable behavior.

Reckless and his associates (1967) have dealt with shame and guilt through what is known as the "crime containment" theory. They propose that the restraint to refrain from criminality arises from two general sources: *outer* containment, or social pressures, and *inner* containment, or self-control. Outer containment is the result of development of role training to obey the norms of one's group through a sense of "identity or belonging." Inner containment is manifested through the workings of conscience, an internalization of the rules of society. There seems to be a clear implication in Reckless' theory that the violation of outer containment results in shame, while violation of inner containment is punished by guilt.

In examining the criminal, it is important to assess their vulnerability to outer controls through shame, and inner controls through guilt. Both features may be operating, or neither. Piers and Singer, in their classic monograph on shame and guilt, caution that guilt and shame often co-exist in a typical cycle:

> It is an almost universal occurrence in our culture that impulses (or acts) of aggression generate a sense of guilt which results in their inhibition. . . . The resulting passivity brings about a conflict accompanied by the anxiety signal of shame. Shame in turn might lead to overcompensatory aggressive fantasies or behavior, setting off the alarm signal of guilt. Thus, a vicious cycle is established: Aggression → guilt → inhibition → passivity → shame → overcompensatory aggressiveness → guilt.

Application to the Criminal

From this discussion it should be apparent that most criminals are characterized by various degrees of defective socialization, with the result that guilt operates sporadically, if at all. The absence of guilt when committing rapes, homicides, beatings, and other gross crimes is often quite marked. The inhibitions imposed by a normal conscience do not seem to be in operation. The absence of guilt is one of the prime criteria for diagnosis of the *sociopathic personality*, regarded as one of the great reservoirs of criminality. The sociopathic criminal is seldom concerned with the damage inflicted on his victims, and views the whole process of punishment as something externally (and unjustly) imposed upon him.

By the same token, many criminals seem mobilized to resist the impact of shame and punishment as a social learning experience. The legal penalties imposed upon such criminals are rationalized as "a bad break," "I got unlucky," "part of the costs of my trade," — as a personal vendetta, a pseudo-masculine badge of rebellion, or as evidence of racial prejudice. While even hardened offenders may develop considerable anxiety in anticipation of punishment, the lessons to be learned are often lost in a welter of resistance and rationalization.

A refreshing exception to the tiresome litany of excuses made by offenders was a recent confession by David Berkowitz, the "Son of Sam" killer. In an interview from Attica Prison in New York, he stated:

> There were no real demons, no talking dogs, no satanic henchmen. I made it all up via my wild imagination so as to find some form of justification for my criminal acts against society. . . . (My) invented tale about demons was an effort to cover up a guilty conscience. I attached a cause to my actions in order to condone them . . . I feel at peace with myself. (Associated Press, 2/22/79.)

A judge, in passing sentence, is committing a misnomer. He pronounces the offender "guilty." Actually, guilt is an inner response to violation of conscience, and it cannot be imposed. Judges in reality are proclaiming a public shame against the offender, and their finding may or may not result in guilt on the part of the offender.

The corrections investigator, in assessing an offender, may find convincing evidence of remorse or contrition with regard to the violation committed. To the extent that such self-punishing, self-limiting attitudes are demonstrated, logical conditions for mitigation of sentence are created. An offender who genuinely regrets his crimes lessens the social need for external penalties. His behavior is self-correcting; his punishment is already built-in. In some cases, the guilt-driven offender seems to welcome the judge's sentence, using the sentence as a penance or expiation, in the same way that a parishioner accepts the penance from a priest during confession.

Identification of Shame. The officer should be alert to some of the clues that may indicate shame. These include:

(1) Fear of consequences emphasized by client. Over-concern with imprisonment, public exposure, media coverage, confidentiality (or lack of it) of the facts about himself and his offense.

(2) Blushing or sighing when details of crime are discussed.

(3) Attempting to avoid embarrassing aspects of the offense.

(4) Some disorientation, confusion, or anxiety in discussing aspects of the crime, as opposed to evasiveness.

(5) Avoidance of eye contact with interviewer.

(6) Responsiveness to reassurance by the interviewer, since a central fear is rejection or contempt of others, and at a deeper level, abandonment.

(7) Spontaneous desire to provide restitution to victim.

(8) Tendency to accept blame, rather than displacing to others.

(9) Withdrawal from friends and relatives, reluctance to discuss case with others.

(10) Possible suicide attempts.

Identification of Guilt. While some overlap with shame is present, the following features may be noted:

(1) Tendency toward voluntary confessions, surrender to police, report crimes beyond current offenses.

(2) Tends to dwell on details of offense, and personal motives ("Why did I do it?")

(3) Usually has high personal standards.

(4) Needs to accept responsibility, provide restitution to victim, replace damages through "good works."

(5) Occasionally appears to be seeking punishment; does not defend himself adequately in legal actions.

(6) Inclined to depressive states.

(7) May make planned suicide attempt, or self-maiming (intropunitive).

It should be pointed out that the identification of guilt and shame attributes in an offender is *not* an attempt to establish psychopathology, although excessive guilt and shame may be indices of personal maladjustment. The presence of guilt and shame following commission of crimes is characteristic of normal persons, and should be anticipated during investigations. The presence of guilt and shame are *positive* qualities that can be utilized by probation/parole officers or treatment facilities to help contain criminal temptations.

PRACTICE CASE 8

The following is excerpted from the PSI of Hilda Jones, a rather plain-looking 18 year-old single white female, oldest in a family of five children residing with her parents in a modest suburban neighborhood. Hilda has been unemployed for the past 6 months, having left school at age 16 to help support the family. Her father has been unemployed for the past year, having been laid off, and his unemployment benefits have recently run out.

Instructions: For cases 8 and 9, select one of the recommendations from the list that follows each PSI or Offense Record, justify your choices, noting with particular attention the attitudes of the defendants toward his or her offenses.

Pre-Sentence Report

CURRENT OFFENSE: *Larceny by Trick* (3 charges, each under $50)

On December 20, 1978, defendant entered _____, _____, and _____ department stores, purchased miscellaneous merchandise, paying for same by signing the name of Geraldine Summers, rightful owner of a Visa charge card. Defendant stated that she "borrowed" the card without permission from Mrs. Summers, who is a neighbor, during a visit to the Summers home, where she is apparently a frequent visitor. The department stores made the complaint, but have no recommendations for disposition.

Merchandise was recovered from the defendant's home by police. It consisted of two women's coats, a scarf, 2 prs. gloves, a doll, and various toys which the defendant stated were intended as Christmas gifts for her family. Mrs. Summers was contacted, and said she was satisfied that the merchandise was returned. She knew of no other misbehavior by the defendant, and was "very disturbed" by the case.

Defendant pleaded guilty, and was referred for PSI. She was tearful during interview, and denied previous thefts or misuse of credit. She volunteered to make restitution. She noted that she had shamed her family, deserved to be punished, and that her arrest record would now make it more difficult for her to obtain employment. She was accompanied by her father, Hector, age 45, who stated that he was unaware of her larceny, and had never known her to act in an unlawful manner previously.

PRIOR RECORD: No juvenile record.

Recommendations: (Choose one)

1. Fine, with lecture from Judge.
2. One year of probation supervision. P.O. should attempt job placement for defendant, and referral to social agency for family.
3. Suspended sentence, with one year of probation supervision, which is to include restitution, job placement, and social agency referral.
4. 60-day sentence on each charge with "shock probation" to follow, probation to include restitution, job placement, and family referral.
5. 60-day sentence on each charge, to run concurrently.
6. 60-day sentence on each charge, to run consecutively.

PRACTICE CASE 9

The following is excerpted from the PSI of Harry Johnson, a 28 year-old warehouseman who is currently unemployed following a dispute with his former foreman over excessive absenteeism. The defendant's 2nd wife, Imogene, age 32, has applied to the Welfare Dept. for support of herself and their two children, age 1½ and 3 yrs. Mrs. Johnson stated that the couple separated two months ago after quarreling over his weekend drinking, which has provoked abuse of family charges against him. Her statement was: "He can be the sweetest man alive when he is sober, but we always fight when he's drunk."

CURRENT OFFENSE: *Assault & Battery* (misdemeanor)

Defendant was arrested by police at 2:00 A.M. on March 3, 1979 in an alley adjoining Wild Bill's Cafe on Main St. He was engaged in a fight with Opie Gully, who was also charged. Both men appeared somewhat intoxicated, but were not charged by police with public intoxication. Defendant stated that the fight involved a bet over a football game, and that he became enraged when the co-defendant, Mr. Gully, refused to pay him. Both men were treated for bruises at General Hospital, and released. Mr. Gully also reported that this defendant threatened to "whip my ass" if he testified against him in court. Defendant was convicted of A & B, and referred for PSI.

During interview, defendant explained that Mr. Gully had made him angry by refusing to pay off on a football bet while the pair were drinking at Wild Bill's Cafe. He also stated: "I never back down from a fight." He insisted that his co-defendant was responsible for the fight "because he made me mad." He denied any problems with alcohol, and denied that he had threatened Gully if this co-defendant testified against him.

PRIOR RECORD:

Within the past six years, this defendant has been charged four times with Assault & Battery. In each case, the charge was dismissed for want of prosecution because complainants did not appear at the trial. In addition, two Disorderly Conduct charges were Costs Remitted. Five years ago he served 3 days on a Public Intoxication charge.

During this six-year period, his wife, Imogene, has charged him with Abuse of Family twice. Both charges were dismissed at her request. According to her statement, she "wants Harry to straighten up," but did not wish to cause him to lose his job, which at those times provided family support.

Recommendations: (Choose one)

1. Fine, with stern lecture from Judge and referral to A.A.
2. One year of probation supervision, with referral to alcoholic program as condition of probation.
3. Suspended sentence, with one year of probation supervision, including job placement and referral to alcoholic program.
4. 60-day sentence, with "shock probation" following, including referral to alcoholic program and job placement.
5. 60-day sentence.

Discussion Questions

1. To what extent were your recommendations influenced by the attitudes of these defendants? Were you able to justify your recommendations on the basis of the defendants' attitudes?

2. Were you able to differentiate between guilt and shame, if these attributes were present in either case?

3. Could you rank the goals of sentencing, from most important to least important, for these two cases? The goals of sentencing are said to be *punishment, deterrence,* and *treatment.*

4. (For Class Discussion — Optional) Did differences appear in sentencing alternatives between members of the class? In discussing such differences, could you define them as personal biases?

Case Commentary

The cases of Hilda Jones and Harry Johnson were selected because of the contrast in attitudes these two defendants show toward their offenses. Hilda is regarded as a situational offender who, out of a desire to provide her brothers and sisters with Christmas gifts, was tempted into fraudulent behavior which was an apparent violation of her moral beliefs. Harry's reaction is typical of most violent persons; he blames the victim for precipitating violence, and invokes his sacred right to punish others who arouse his anger. In fact, he even threatens further violence if his drinking buddy testifies against him, a maneuver which may have proven successful in previous assault charges (inferred).

Therefore, Harry has violated no internalized norms, feels no guilt, and social remedies must be externally applied to inhibit him. Hilda, on the other hand, seems to feel keenly the shame she has brought upon herself and her family, and invites retaliation by the Court in order to expiate her guilty conscience.

Most corrections students, in selecting recommendations, seem to sense the sharp attitudinal differences between these two defendants. With rare exceptions, students making recommendations on Hilda have chosen one of the three probation alternatives, citing Hilda's need for guidance and social assistance, and predicting her positive response to such measures. As a sentencing alternative, treatment is emphasized over punishment and deterrence.

In the case of Harry Johnson, students predominantly select the 60-day "shock probation" alternative. Students cite the need for both punishment and treatment of his alcohol abuse as sentencing objectives, with punishment taking precedence. The need for strict probation supervision to curb Harry's violent tendencies while drinking is usually also mentioned.

Chapter 10
Family and Marital History

"Experience is the child of Thought, and Thought is the child of Action. We cannot learn men from books."

Benjamin Disraeli

Disraeli's comment has special significance for the corrections specialist who must, if he is to be responsible to his client and his profession, determine why offenders end up the way they do. An individual's experience is often an elusive realm that defies pat explanations as to why an offender has chosen deviant paths. Yet the study of men and women and the reasons why they are in trouble is a true requirement of the corrections field. It has become a traditional practice of the helping professions to obtain a life history of individuals being considered for treatment intervention on the assumption that such histories will contribute to an overall understanding of those persons, and add some predictability to their current behavior. Corrections, as a primary helping profession, follows that tradition.

The corrections investigator needs to keep in mind that social history taking is not a mere recital of facts, but a search for strengths and liabilities in the personality of an offender that can be utilized in sentencing/supervision/treatment decisions about that offender. Like a prospector panning for gold, the officer may sift a quantity of routine information, searching for nuggets that may illuminate the life of an offender more clearly. Like the prospector, he must sometimes be prepared to be disappointed when nothing but dross appears in his investigation.

Cohn (1976) analyzed the common belief in corrections that "broken homes cause delinquency." As a former psychiatric social worker himself, Cohn reasoned that even when a *relationship* between broken homes and delinquency could be demonstrated, it was still necessary to prove that the broken home *caused* the delinquency, because of the multitude of other factors that might be causing that relationship to occur. He cited the example of a Midwestern city where a research study established a relationship between sale of ice cream and rape. Thus, it might be possible to conclude that increased sale of ice cream was causing more rape; an alarming prospect, especially for ice cream salesmen. As a matter of fact, it was the presence of warm weather which brought more people out into the streets, which caused both ice cream sales and rape to increase at the same time.

In their study of hard-core criminals, Yochelson and Samenow (1976) also noted the prevalence of broken homes, poverty, and truly adverse circumstances in the life-histories of their subjects. However, upon closer examination, they concluded:

Over half the criminals come from stable families in which the parents have lived together, have raised the children, and have experienced the usual tensions in living . . . As we probed beyond the fact that a home was broken, we found that the breaking of the home in some cases helped to stabilize life for the children, because what remained was a cohesive concerned family unit; for if the father left, mother, grandparents, uncles and aunts still remained. In fact, every home we looked into had some stabilizing influence, with caring, responsible people stepping in to assume parental roles. When called to account, however, the criminals have attributed their violating patterns to the tensions of family life, exaggerating them or citing them out of context.

As a result of their investigations, Yochelson and Samenow determined that criminal outcomes could not be predicted from early deprivation. In some homes where both parents were irresponsible, many children did not turn out to be criminals.

The interpretation of family histories, therefore, needs to be approached with some caution. Even under ideal circumstances, a person's recollections of early life are often colored by wishful thoughts and fantasies, with a repression of the unacceptable events. A rejected child, for example, may recall his mother in rosy, idealized terms in what has been called the "family romance." Such retrospective distortions are difficult to sort out in a brief family history, although they can be illuminating when detected.

In one instance reported by Yochelson and Samenow, an offender reported an idealized relationship with his mother; he "would never do anything to hurt her." However, an interview with the mother revealed that her son, using information about his mother's employment as a domestic, had burglarized the employer's home, thus jeopardizing a long-term trust relationship between his mother and her employer. Far from being a victim of circumstances, as he claimed, this offender had consistently been a *victimizer* of others whenever the opportunity presented itself since his earliest years.

A serious problem for the investigator can be caused by those offenders clever enough to play into the pre-conceptions of the officer about causes of criminality. Many experienced offenders, veterans of multiple reports by corrections officials, often "coach" the inexperienced officer with convincing reports of broken homes, bad companions, racial oppression, lack of employment, and mental problems. Such tales fit into popular (and scholarly) rationales as causes of crime, and may be duly reported by the investigator as mitigating circumstances for current offenses. Such misconceptions, even when partially true, should not be allowed to mask an offender's pattern of criminal activities, if such a pattern can be identified.

The careful investigating officer cultivates a degree of skepticism regarding glib recitals of background information that fit too neatly into psychological/ sociological explanations for criminality. The officer needs specifics; he looks for internal contradictions in the facts supplied by offenders, seeks cross-checks through relatives, victims, and records, and attempts to resolve discrepancies through confrontation of the offender during interview. Finally, in sifting the mass of information obtained through these sources, he checks himself for stereotypes and biases that may be influencing his reporting.

Generalized Goals of History Taking

As the investigator probes into chronologically remote areas of the offender's life, the accuracy of the information he obtains tends to diminish, as well as its application to correctional decisions to be made about the offender. Hence, some information may simply be collected "for the record," a procedure questioned by some authorities as a needless waste of time and energy, particularly when only a brief report would suffice. An effort should be made to stress only those items that appear to have some connection with the offender's current or potential situation, and the officer should make that connection as clearly as possible.

The generalized goal of history taking can be seen as an attempt to present a balanced account of *ego-strengths* and *ego-deficiencies* that have clearly characterized the life-style of the offender. Such qualities affect decisions about *amenability to supervision or counseling, ability to initiate and maintain pro-social activities,* and the *ability to withstand delay of gratification in the pursuit of objectives.* Contributing factors for this information may include strong family ties, past achievements, or influential parental surrogates, such as teachers, coaches, or clergymen. Past hopes and aspirations may be strengths that can be re-mobilized to replace criminal temptations. The investigator must be open to such possibilities in his assessment, attempting to get a "reading" of the personal resources available from within the offender himself.

Family History Taking

Highlights of family history include the following; the information should be amplified in more detail whenever significant anecdotes or themes are obtained:

Birthplace. Geographical location of birthplace, verified by birth certificate, if available. Any unusual circumstances of pre-natal conditions, birth, illegitimacy, or other family problems should be included. Was pregnancy planned?

Childhood Years. Did discontinuities or deprivations of maternal care occur during infancy? Was client placed in boarding homes, adopted, or placed with relatives? How was support provided during early years? Was father continuously present in home? What is offender's recollection of family climate during early years? Repression of early life is sometimes seen when childhood was traumatic.

Siblings. What was offender's place in sibline, and what were the ages of brothers and sisters in relation to offender? Was client perceived in any special way by family as the "darling of family," the "black sheep," or "troublemaker"? With which sibling does client identify most closely?

Parents. What was attitude of parents toward client? Which parental figure (if any) was the role model for client? Which parent was disciplinarian, affectionate, or uncaring? Was client favored by either parental figure? What crises occurred at home: separations, unemployment, deaths, poor health, drinking, etc.?

Early Misbehavior. Was client in trouble in early years? Describe episodes of misbehavior. Was client rebellious, a dare-devil, excitement-seeking, impulsive, or prankster? Was counseling advised for client, and with what result (verify)?

Major Influences on Client. Who were important role models for offender: parent, relative, brother or sister, companions, neighbor, teacher, coach, clergyman, Boy Scout leader, or others (if any)?

Marital History Taking

The detailing of sexual history depends upon the purpose of the report.

Sex offenders require an extensive review of their patterns because of the connections with current problems; referral to an appropriate professional for such evaluation is common, unless the officer has experience in dealing with sex offenders. For other offenders, an overview may be sufficient, recognizing that sexual exploitation may represent one phase of a general criminal exploitation of others.

Early Sex Behavior. At what age did early sex play begin, and what forms did it take? Who were partners: neighbors, siblings, strangers, and what were the ages of partners? Was early sex play discovered, and what disposition, if any, was made? Was early sex heterosexual, homosexual, or both? At what age did masturbation start? At what age did sexual intercourse commence, with what partners, and what frequency? What is attitude of client toward early sexual behavior?

Adult Sex Patterns. At what age did regular dating commence, with what partners, and what frequency? List marriages, both formal and common-law. Describe marital adjustment and unusual features, if present. Are homosexual involvements present, including prison and military life? Are sexual variations present, including use of prostitutes, extramarital affairs, exhibitionism, Peeping Tom activities, sadomasochism, and impotence. What form of contraceptives are used, if any?

Family Life. Do both partners describe marriage as mutually satisfactory? What social, financial, or personal problems are present, if any? Were children, if any, planned? Obtain age, social background, and date of marriage. Obtain ages of children and developmental history. Is client the parent of any out-of-wedlock children? What are support arrangements for family? How does client react to intimacy of family life?

PRACTICE CASE 10

A pre-sentence investigation has been prepared on Wally Ames to guide Judge Rudin in passing sentence. You are to prepare an evaluative summary and recommendation on the case from the information provided, with particular emphasis on the family history. Finally, answer the discussion questions following the case.

United States District Court
Pre-Sentence Investigative Report

Name: Wally Ames	Judge: Rudin
Charge: Interstate Transportation of Stolen Motor Vehicle	PSI Due: 1/20/79
	Co-defendant: Chester Loser (at large)
Plea: Guilty	Defense Counsel: Public Defender
Penalty: 1-5 yrs. and $5000 fine	Prosecutor: Whalen

CURRENT OFFENSE: Defendant is a 23 year-old white married male referred 12/21/78 for pre-sentence investigation. He entered a plea of guilty upon advice of counsel, the Public Defender assigned to the case. Investigation revealed that while living at a Salvation Army shelter in Phoenix, Arizona, the defendant met Chester Loser, a 26 year-old derelict with an extensive criminal record. Mr. Loser offered the defendant a ride to the Midwest in a car he claimed was borrowed. However, the defendant admits he watched Mr. Loser steal license plates from another vehicle and place them on the stolen vehicle without raising objections. At the apparent instigation of the co-defendant, Mr. Ames says he stole a small amount of money and beer from the pony keg where he was employed in Phoenix.

While the pair was on the way to Cincinnati, a number of minor burglaries were committed, and stolen goods were pawned for food and gasoline. Mr. Ames says he participated in the burglaries only as a lookout under instructions from the co-defendant. In Cincinnati, the pair ran out of money, and Mr. Loser proposed a hold-up of the Midwest savings and loan. Mr. Ames refused, and the pair separated. Mr. Loser was said to be hitch-hiking to Chicago, and is still at large. Mr. Ames went to his oldest brother's home (Donald Ames, age 27, 515 Marburg Avenue), driving the stolen vehicle, and was subsequently arrested at that location. He gave no resistance, and has been fully cooperative with the investigation. No other charges are pending at this time.

PRIOR RECORD:

No FBI record. The defendant leads a very nomadic life, and reported minor arrests for loitering, blocking sidewalk, and panhandling in various cities. None of these charges amounted to more than a fine, according to the defendant. Phoenix PD reports no outstanding warrants against him, and have no record on the defendant. Other jurisdictions were not contacted. There is no local record.

INTERVIEW DATA:

Mr. Ames presents himself as a quiet-spoken, docile, and introverted individual. He speaks in a whisper, and is sometimes hard to understand. He was estimated to be of "average" intelligence. He presents his life history in a matter-of-fact monotone, with little or no attempt to excuse his behavior. He described himself as a criminal, a bum, and in his words, "a queer."

FAMILY HISTORY:

Mr. Ames is the youngest of three brothers, born in Chicago. The oldest, Donald, age 28, is actually a half-brother, the product of an early indiscretion by the mother. Both Donald and the second brother, Victor, age 25, had extensive juvenile records, had been classified "incorrigible," and wandered about the country quite a bit. Donald Ames has shown quite an interest in the defendant, and has visited the investigator repeatedly to give information. Donald is currently employed as a truck-loader for the Kroger Company, where he appears to have a good work record. He is buying a home with his wife on Marburg

Avenue. The defendant continues to live with this couple while awaiting sentence. Whereabouts of Victor, middle brother, is unknown to the family.

The defendant's mother, Flora, died, apparently of natural causes, when Wally was three years of age. He was placed in a foster home for a year before being reclaimed by his father, Daniel. Daniel was a truck driver who spent much time on the road. He was described by both brothers as a cruel, tyrannical man who took out his hostility on the children, especially while drinking, which was continual. He lived with several women for brief periods, none of whom exerted much care for the three children. Wally was quiet, and would not retaliate against his father; instead, he bore the brunt of the father's anger. The older brothers frequently ran away from home. Wally was 16 years old when his father was killed in a road accident, and he went to live with his uncle, Jason Ames, for the next four years. This uncle did not like Wally, but he says, "I stuck it out anyway."

At age 20, Wally was hospitalized at Longview State Hospital following erratic behavior at his uncle's home in Sedamsville. The following is excerpted from his psychiatric report at that institution:

"At the time of admission he was quite seclusive and withdrawn, and seemed to have marginal contact with reality. He reported thoughts about suicide, and his behavior was occasionally bizarre. He was diagnosed as a *"Schizophrenic reaction, chronic undifferentiated type."* After treatment was initiated, his functioning improved, so that he was released for home visit two months after admission. He eloped from home visit to enlist in the military service. Final diagnosis: *"Schizophrenic reaction, chronic undifferentiated type, improved."*

His military service record indicates that he made a fair adjustment for 10 months. Then he was charged with theft of another soldier's camera, and given a court-martial. At this time, he disclosed his psychiatric record, and was given a medical discharge from the Army.

After leaving the Army, Wally's nomadic pattern resumed. Usually, he would return to his brother's home periodically, never holding a job for more than a few weeks. A check with several former employers indicated that Wally was considered a good worker, but restless. He made few friends, and usually walked off jobs without notice.

PRESENT
SITUATION: For the past month, while awaiting sentence, the defendant has been employed at the Slabside Manufacturing Company as an assembly-line paint sprayer, making $168 a week take-home. While employed, there, he met and married Mary Greer a 21 year-old

woman employed as a clerk at the Slabside plant. She appears to be very involved with him, and has stopped in to talk with the investigator twice. The couple appears to be compatible, and Wally has now moved into her apartment at 2122 Whiteside Avenue, for which she pays $125 month.

Discussion Questions

1. In recommending disposition of the Wally Ames case, were you able to justify your recommendations to your own satisfaction? Do you believe that your logic would persuade Judge Rudin? Why or why not? Be specific.

2. What information did you select as the most significant features in the life of Wally Ames to construct a summary? What was the reasoning behind your selection? Compare your emphasis with that of other students.

Case Commentary

Since Wally Ames is currently under supervision, the probation officer did not feel it was appropriate to talk about the case. However, the Judge did sentence this man to three years of probation supervision, and it is known that Ames continues to be employed regularly and lives with his new wife, and that no further offenses have occurred.

This case was selected because of the amorphous quality of Wally's personality; he seems to take whatever shape he is pressed into. Accommodation appears to be the principle that governs his life. Can he then be seen as a situational offender who happened to team up with the wrong person? Without Chester Loser around to lead him into criminal exploits, is he really criminally inclined? If one follows this line of reasoning, is it not reasonable to believe that his new wife, his older brother, and his probation officer together can keep Wally from straying into further criminal behavior?

The examination of Wally's personal history is consistent with that prediction. As the youngest of three brothers, Wally must have been deeply traumatized by the death of his mother when he was 3 years of age. This tragedy was followed by foster home placement, and only grudging recognition of paternal responsibility by his brutal alcoholic father, who was away from home most of the time. Wally must have learned to cope by being unobtrusive and acquiescent. While his older brothers' rebellion took them away from this desperate family scene, Wally was only capable of hanging around, and picking up whatever crumbs of recognition he might get by being pleasant and accommodating.

Such passivity as a coping mechanism must have resulted in an identity crisis of delayed adolescence at age 20, when his adolescent strivings were interpreted as a schizophrenic breakdown. In characteristic fashion, Wally probably found it easy to accept the self-definition of a "mentally disturbed" person. After being sent on a home visit to the indifferent uncle who had him committed to Longview State Hospital, Wally eloped to the Army. As before, he sought a structured system where he would be told what to do and where he would be supplied with an identity that he could not define for himself.

The encounter with Chester Loser was a disaster for Wally because of the casual expediency with which he was exploited by this sociopathic drifter. His older brother, Donald, has provided one of the few reliable anchors in Wally's life, and with his help, Wally has apparently found a wife and job that may meet some of his needs with lasting effects. There are many rocky paths ahead for Wally, but with the combination of circumstances working for him at this time, he may begin to achieve that sense of selfhood and confidence which has been denied to him during his earlier life history.

Supplementary Reading

Cohn, Alvin W. *Crime and Justice Administration.* Philadelphia: J. B. Lippincott Company, 1976.

Chapter 11

Home, Neighborhood, and Education

"For de little stealin' dey gits you in jail soon or late. For de big stealin' dey makes you emperor and puts you in de Hall of Fame when you croaks. If dey's one thing I learns in ten years on de Pullman cars listenin' to de white quality talk, it's dat same fact."

Eugene O'Neill in THE EMPEROR JONES

Eugene O'Neill's 1920 play is a reminder that the poor and disadvantaged of our society often perceive a double injustice in that they are considered both the major perpetrators and the victims of crime, while the so-called white-collar criminal is seldom punished. A voluminous literature in criminology supports the view that the social circumstances into which one happens to be born may determine whether one is prosecuted as a criminal. The President's Commission on Law Enforcement and Administration of Justice (1967) sums up the argument for social deprivation:

> From arrest records, probation reports, and prison statistics a "portrait" of the offender emerges that progressively highlights the disadvantaged character of his life. The offender at the end of the road in prison is likely to be a member of the lowest social and economic groups in the country, poorly educated and perhaps unemployed, unmarried, reared in a broken home, and to have a prior criminal record.

A number of social welfare programs have evolved in the U.S. that are aimed at reducing poverty, increasing employment opportunities, providing compensatory education, and increasing access to the opportunity structure of our society for "protected classes." A derivative benefit from all of these welfare programs is believed to be reduced temptation to criminality, and the actual prevention of crime. A sensitive and compassionate corrections worker can hardly work without a sympathetic interest in such programs, since many of his clients are direct beneficiaries of social welfare programs. The ultimate effect of social benefit programs on the crime rate is a controversial subject that is beyond the scope of this Casebook.

However, the working officer needs to keep several points in mind. The officer does not work with abstractions or statistics, but with individual criminals on a one-by-one basis. Individuals differ in their response to conditions of social deprivation; the vast majority of disadvantaged persons remain law-abiding and responsible, even though they are most often the victims of criminal depredation by their own neighbors. Poor social conditions do not automatically create criminality on a uniform basis. As early as 1915, Healy noted:

> Poverty, and crowded houses, and so on, by themselves alone, are not productive of criminalism . . . The knowledge that 60% of all repeaters come from bad homes does not prove that any particular repeater comes from a bad home, nor does it prove that a bad home in any given case produced the delinquency. There should be evaluation of the personal traits of a bad young man from a bad home, as well as a bad young man from a good home.

The conscientious officer in corrections must protect the non-criminal person from the blanket indictments encouraged by popular stereotypes about race, poverty, and deprivation as crime-inducing influences. At the same time, he must challenge the criminal offender who seeks to use social deprivation and oppression as a shield and excuse for continued illegality. As noted previously, sociological inequities in society have led some offenders to an epidemic volume of rationalizations to excuse continued crime sprees. Blame can be directed everywhere except where it belongs, on the shoulders of the violator. The well-known psychologist, Hobart Mowrer, (1964) noted what he called a "psychiatric folksong" to describe this flight from personal responsibility:

> "At three I had a feeling of ambivalence toward my brothers
> And so it follows naturally I poisoned all my lovers.
> And now I'm happy, I have learned the lesson this has taught:
> That everything I do that's wrong is *someone else's fault.*"

The task of the investigator is to accurately describe the home, neighborhood, and schooling of the offender, especially with reference to criminal influences that the person may have been exposed to. Next, the investigator should assess the reaction of the offender to such influences. If the offender was a "street hustler" from an early age, that fact should be documented. However, if the offender, surrounded by criminal influences, managed to *resist* some of these inducements to crime, that fact could become a crucial feature of his report. To simply characterize a lower class ghetto environment in which an offender was raised, without commenting on that person's response to his surroundings, is to invite the report-reader to make a stereotyped negative judgment on that offender.

Socioeconomic Status

Descriptions of home, neighborhood, and schooling have been grouped by sociologists into social class categories. These categories define one's socioeconomic status (SES). Correctional reports could be improved by understanding the criteria that go into social class assignment, and by using those categories accurately. A typical set of criteria used in classifying socioeconomic status might include:

> *Occupation of head of household.*
> *Income level of subject, or parental family.*
> *Occupation of subject.*
> *Years of education of subject.*
> *Home and neighborhood of subject.*

While researchers, such as Lloyd Warner (1963), have developed weighted scores to assign subjects to six levels of SES, such refinements may be beyond the needs of a correctional investigator. While SES scores are related to income levels, types of occupations, and neighborhoods, there is also a less easily defined *life-style* which accompanies each SES level. Such matters as child-rearing practices, spending patterns, reading habits, drinking habits, sports and hobby preferences, religious preferences, political attitudes, eating habits, and even choice of automobiles have been defined by some observers as class linked. Thus, an individual's SES can be seen as a long-term assignment to a complete life-style.

For purposes of easy reference, the simplified scheme adopted by Hollingshead and Redlich (1958) in their landmark study, *Social Class and Mental Illness* may be useful:

Class I — Wealthy, high-society professionals
Class II — Managers, paraprofessionals
Class III — Small businessmen, skilled and white-collar workers
Class IV — Semi-skilled workers
Class V — Unskilled workers and laborers

In this widely used classification system, Class I persons would be characterized as *upper class,* with inherited wealth, "aristocrats," usually influential as leaders in business, society, and government, and ordinarily with advanced education. Class II has been described as *"lower upper class,"* newly rich, prominent as managers in business and government, normally with college degrees. Class III is the *middle class,* which includes small businessmen and proprietors, middle management, skilled trades and white-collar positions (including civil service), with a strong trend toward college degrees as a condition of employment. Class IV is the *working class,* characterized by blue-collar jobs in construction, factories, trades, and semi-skilled work in restaurants and clerk positions. Typically high school graduates. Class V is the *lower class,* which includes all unskilled laboring jobs, casual employment, and public welfare recipients. Class V has not usually completed high school.

(Note: While Hollingshead and Redlich's classifications suggest that police and corrections officers should be included in Class II as "paraprofessionals," this author is of the opinion that these two groups are firmly wedded to the ideology and life-style of the middle class, along with nurses, social workers, and teachers, as part of the "aspiring" professions. Probably only the traditional professions of law, medicine, and theology should be classified as Class I.)

Upward and Downward Mobility

The movement up and down the SES scales has assumed greater significance in recent years, since the U.S. is usually regarded as a fairly "open" society where such shifts are commonplace. Both upward mobility and downward drifts appear to be associated with increased rates of mental disorder. The pressures and strain of striving for upward mobility are believed to cause increased anxiety, psychosomatic complaints, and need for counseling. The downward drift of persons into the lower class has been seen as the result of prolonged mental disorder, loss of hope, physical disability, and social incompetence, among other things. The descent of a middle-class male into Class V because of chronic alcoholism is a typical example. Thus, the Skid Rows of our cities inflate both the numbers and the social pathology found in Class V.

The "downward drift" theory holds that the disproportionate amount of mental and social disorganization found in Class V is the result of the collection of persons at the bottom of society who have drifted down from higher levels. A complementary factor may be the migration of more enterprising and competent persons to higher SES levels. For example, Harrison Salisbury (1958) was one of the first writers to deplore the forced exclusion of "natural leaders" from public housing developments as such persons were able to achieve higher incomes, and moved away from public housing projects. The loss of such natural leaders deprived the remaining residents of adequate role models, and accentuated the hopeless condition of people left in the projects.

Langner's analysis of the Midtown Manhattan study (1963) found that increases in mental disorders corresponded to increases associated with the stress conditions of lower class life, such as poverty, lack of opportunity, oppression, overcrowding, and loss of hope. Landmark sociological studies (Shaw, 1929; Shaw and McKay, 1931; Thrasher, 1927) point out the concentration of adolescent crime in urban slum neighborhoods with the highest poverty rates. It would seem that the combination of downward drift from upper classes plus the uncertain conditions of life already existing in Class V result in a concentration of social pathology manifested both by high crime rates and mental breakdown.

On the basis of the preceding information, it may be realistic for the corrections specialist to assume a higher probability of delinquent behavior by an offender from such noxious backgrounds than by a similar offender from a middle-class background. Similarly, an offender being considered for return from a correctional institution could be exposed to more criminal temptation in a Class V setting. But probabilities are not *facts;* the investigating officer must check out the offender and the supportive influences that may "immunize" that offender from criminal temptations.

For example, the insulating value of attachment to family and other anti-criminal persons was illustrated in a study by Glaser, Lander, and Abbott (1971), who found that the greatest difference between addicted and non-addicted siblings from the same family was the non-addicts' greater attachment to home, work, and school, and lesser participation in street life. Our slums are a battleground between pro- and anti-criminal values, and no assumptions should be made without checking.

The Middle-Class Corrections Officer v. The Lower-Class Offender

The encounter between some officers and their clients can become a real exercise in non-communication, because of the life-style differences that often go unrecognized. Street language is seldom the language of the officer. The casual opportunism of the offender is often inscrutable, if not downright immoral, in the eyes of the organized middle-class officer. The sexual practices of the offender are often repugnant to the officer, and the offender's loose spending may appear to be careless and thoughtless. The bursts of aggressiveness, particularly while drinking, can be disturbing to the officer. The various stigmata of poverty, including the dirt, the disease, and the untidiness, are repelling to many compulsively neat officers. Such feelings are often particularly acute in an officer who only recently may have exchanged his own poverty for the frail security of a job in corrections. Such reactions are sometimes present even when crime is not the subject of discussion, in social work or mental health agencies.

Niederhoffer (1967) has documented the protective cynicism adopted by police officers after years of such bruising encounters with the seamier side

of human nature. It requires little imagination to predict a similar development in corrections workers. The doe-eyed neophyte in corrections soon learns
the boundaries of what is possible and realistic in dealing with the lives of
offenders whose values and aspirations may differ sharply from his own
values. And the developing professional will also have to learn to keep his
feelings tightly reined and to eventually transcend his ingrained attitudes.

It is hardly surprising that the corrections officer may react positively (or
even overreact) to the occasional offender who demonstrates upward mobility.
The desire for upward mobility demonstrated by the offender is something
an officer can appreciate, and with which he can identify. The desire to aspire
to middle-class standards — to pursue education, to seek job training, to
work steadily, to budget money, to value self-improvement, or even to model
oneself after the probation officer — is welcomed as a sign of a willingness
to live a crime-free life.

There have been many philosophical arguments about whether the adop-
tion of a middle-class life-style represents a desirable or attainable objective
for most offenders. Nevertheless, such a goal seems implicit in the demands
made by many corrections workers on their clients. The investigating officer
needs to look carefully at the recommendations he makes to ensure that
the changes he anticipates through case supervision can be attained by the
offender. It is not proven yet that middle-class status is a panacea for crime
containment, or a realistic goal for the lower-class offender.

Having taken an overview of the complex issues raised by socioeconomic
status, and some of the implications of social mobility, let us look at some
of the specific information to be gathered and summarized:

Description of Home and Neighborhood. In describing the residence of an
offender, the officer should note whether the location is the current residence,
a previous residence, or whether the location is the anticipated residence
of an offender returning on parole, shock probation, etc. He may wish to
note the following:

Location of Home. Describe neighborhood, condition of buildings, residential or inner-city, presence of bars, indigents, drug users, or high-crime area.
What is proximity of public transportation, parks, stores, and other amenities?

Description of Home. How long has client lived there? How many rooms,
bathrooms, garage, etc.? Description of furnishings, and their condition. Who
resides with offender? Will offender have own room, or share? Apartment or
single dwelling, condition of interior and exterior. Owned or rented, amount
of mortgage or rent, and utilities. Estimate value, if owned.

Description of Friends or Relatives in Neighborhood. In his summary, the off
gives an overall impression of the suitability of the home and neighborhood,
based upon his information.

Description of Education. The response to education is an important index
to the offender's social adjustment, as well as providing some guidance to
job training and placement. A successful school adjustment is a strength
that suggests other potentials. A poor reaction to schooling represents a major
failure experience which may have encouraged criminality. Careful interviewing of the client through various phases of his school career is essential,
verified by school records and achievement tests. Features to be included are:

Names of schools attended, locations, and dates attended. Verify.
Attendance record. Verify.
School performance. Summarize.
Favorite subjects? Difficult subjects?
Disciplinary actions taken. Verify.

Achievement or intelligence tests. Note special conditions or remarks, names and dates of tests, scores.

Diplomas granted. Rank in graduating class. Verify. If client dropped out, Last year completed, and circumstances for leaving school. Verify.

Interpretation of Educational Tests

Investigators should be able to accurately report the significance of school achievement tests in their report, since such tests are a valuable resource for assessing both the achieved and potential ability of their clients, particularly if further education is contemplated. Access to tests implies the ability to utilize such information in an ethical and accurate manner. Questions about any test can usually be cleared up by consultation with a school counselor or psychologist.

Tests administered in schools are generally of two types: intelligence and achievement tests (an extended discussion of vocational and clinical tests is provided in Chapter 19). Both types of tests are *optimum effort* tests. This means that an assumption is made that the test result reflects the best efforts of the test-taker. If such was not the case, some notation should be made that the results should only be interpreted as "minimum results," and appropriate corrections made when using that test score. Such precautions are not always taken during school testing. Group tests are the worst offenders, since each student is not always closely observed during testing. Other factors such as illness, test anxiety, poor administration, inaccurate test scoring, language difficulties, cultural bias, or test rebellion are not uncommon, and test administrators often fail to note scores as a "minimum result." As a consequence, painful errors are often made in student placement.

Intelligence Tests. Tests of intelligence yield a score called an *Intelligence Quotient (IQ),* which is believed to reflect the ability of that person to perform intellectual tasks. Each score is derived by measuring the subject against a nationally representative sample of persons in the same age group taking the same test. The IQ score can be used to assign each person to a standard *classification* which corresponds to a certain percentage of persons in his age group who share that classification. The Wechsler classification (1944) is shown below, since other test classifications have only minor differences from the Wechsler (for example, Stanford-Binet, Otis, Kuhlman-Anderson, Revised Beta, etc.):

Intelligence Classification According to IQ Scores

Classification	IQ Scores	Percent of population included in category
Defective	65 and below	2.2
Borderline	66-79	6.7
Dull Normal	80-90	16.1
Average	91-110	50.0
Bright Normal	111-119	16.1
Superior	120-127	6.7
Very Superior	128 and over	2.2

The distribution of IQ scores forms a symmetrical "bell-shaped curve." The Wechsler chart may be used to locate any person and classify his intellectual ability as compared to his own age group. If there is any reason to question the validity of an offender's score, or if the test is more than a few years old, it is probably wise to retest if decisions about school or vocational placement are to be made using the score. Normally, IQ scores have a tendency to remain constant throughout one's life.

Approximate guidelines for anticipating school and work achievement are associated with IQ classification, and are provided below for cautious use by the officer:

"Defective" (65 and below) — Special education and training are necessary, with constant supervision in a protected work setting; such individuals require protection against criminal exploitation, and can be easily led into prostitution, etc. by unscrupulous persons.

"Borderline" (66-79) — Slow learner classes are necessary, with emphasis upon practical skills and routine work tasks. They can function independently in a supervised work setting.

"Dull Normal" (80-90) — Usually unable to complete high school. Industrial training or a trade enables them to function independently.

"Average" (91-110) — Usually complete high school, some may attempt community college programs. No limits on occupation, except those imposed by educational degrees.

"Bright Normal" (111-119) — Able to complete baccalaureate programs, limited success in graduate studies.

"Superior" or "Very Superior" (120 and up) — Can complete graduate studies, or any type of professional work.

Since "under-achieving" has almost the status of a national disease, the corrections worker should be alert for any discrepancies between IQ scores and school achievement that may signify untapped potentials in his clients.

Achievement Tests. Achievements tests provide a measure of how much school-related material has been mastered. The student achieves a score which is compared to a national sample of persons at the same grade level. Local school system norms can also be devised. Achievement tests deal in basic skills, such as reading, mathematics computation, language, etc. The tests are a measure of student acquisition of knowledge, but are also used as a measure of teaching efficiency in a school system. Since a variety of achievement tests exist at all grade levels, a typical test, the *Metropolitan Achievement Test*, will be the only one discussed.

The Metropolitan Achievement Test measures Word Knowledge, Reading, Language, Mathematics Computation, Mathematics Concepts, Mathematics Problem-Solving, and Scholastic Aptitude (a general measure of abstract reasoning). Scores are converted to *stanines*, a standard statistical measure that enables test scores to be divided into 9 categories of achievement as follows:

Stanines

1 — Low

2 or 3 — Low Average Range

4, 5, or 6 — Average Range

7 or 8 — High Average Range

9 — High

Thus, a simple measure of progress in specified basic school skills is obtained, against the background of a national sample of persons who have taken the same test. Again, when the school achievement scores are discrepant with actual school performance, the corrections worker may wish to inquire about the motivation and true potential of his clients.

PRACTICE CASE 11

Instructions: Write an evaluative summary and recommendations for Judge O'Flaherty in the case of Chester Chandler, who pleaded guilty to a charge of *Illegal Sale of Hallucinogen.* Pay particular attention to the home, neighborhood, and education of this defendant in your report. You may wish to review Chapter 5 on the preparation of an evaluative summary and recommendations.

Pre-Sentence Investigation

Name: Chester Chandler	Plea: Guilty
Aliases: C.C.	Date of Conviction: 10/18/78
Co-Defendants: None	Date Report Due: 11/18/78
P.O.: Joseph T. Heller	Judge: O'Flaherty

OFFENSE AND COLLATERAL INFORMATION THERETO:

On 9/5/78 at 10 PM, Ptn. David Hennings of the Regional Enforcement Narcotics Unit met with the defendant, Chester Chandler, at his residence located at 1233 Locust Street. Following a brief conversation, Chandler stated he would sell Ptn. Hennings an ounce of marijuana for $15. Subsequently, the arresting officer and Chandler discussed the possibility of returning the next day to purchase a pound of marijuana. Hennings returned the next day, and at this time the defendant became very evasive, and the arresting officer thought that the defendant was suspicious of him. At this time, Chandler was placed under arrest. The complainant, Ptn. Hennings, states that Chandler has a poor attitude, and was belligerent; he does not believe probation would do him any good, and feels that Chandler should be sentenced.

PRIOR OFFENSES:

None

CULTURAL AND FAMILIAL BACKGROUND:

Chester Chandler is a 23 year-old single male Caucasian who was born in West Chester, Pennsylvania on 8/28/55. He is the 3rd of 5 children born to Dr. and Mrs. Arthur Chandler. Presently the defendant's parents reside at 3 Appian Way in Upper Darby, an exclusive suburb outside Philadelphia. Chester attended local private schools in the Philadelphia area, and received a high school diploma from St. Ignatius High School in the college preparatory program. According to the Lorge-Thorndike Intelligence Test, he was in the "superior" range with an IQ score of 121. School records indicate he was an honor roll student. Subsequently, he attended the University of Pennsylvania, where he majored in mathematics. Mr. Chandler indicated he dropped out of college after completing two years, stating he was "bored with college." The defendant's father, Dr. Arthur Chandler, was born in Philadelphia. He attended Harvard University, obtained his medical degree from Cornell Medical College, and is presently a practicing psychiatrist in Philadelphia. Hazel (Larkin) Chandler, the defendant's mother, was also born in Philadelphia. She graduated from the University of Cleveland School of Law, and is presently practicing in a local law firm.

The parents were married in Philadelphia, and of this union five children were born. At this time, only one child remains in the household, attending a private school. The remaining three siblings, except for the defendant, are all college graduates, and employed out of the city.

Mrs. Chandler was contacted, who stated that she and her husband were very perturbed about the arrest, since nothing of this kind had ever occurred in their family. She said that the family stood ready to help in any way possible, but that Chester "always knew his own mind" and had refused to let the family intervene in his life. She said that the family was very disappointed that Chester had dropped out of college, apparently believing that he was rebelling against his father's aspirations for him. The defendant is presently residing with Dorothy Kennedy, age 20, at 1233 Locust Street, Apt. 5. This is a two-room apartment located in a below-average income area with a high incidence of crime. Chester indicated he was splitting the rent with Dorothy, who is a junior at the University of Philadelphia. She is also a native of Upper Darby, Pa.

ECONOMIC AND MILITARY ADJUSTMENT:

The defendant is an apprentice plumber in the West Chester Valley District Plumber's Union, Local #67. He is completing his second year as an apprentice. Presently he is installing plumbing at a job site at the University of Philadelphia Medical School. He has been employed by the university for about six months, and earns $8.98 per hour. His work history is rated as satisfactory.

He states that he has never served in the U.S. armed forces.

PHYSICAL AND MENTAL:

Chester Chandler is a 23 year-old single male Caucasian who stands 6 feet in height, and weighs 180 pounds. He appears to be in excellent physical condition.

CHARACTER AND CONDUCT:

This is Chester's first contact with local court authorities. He indicated that he never drinks alcoholic beverages, nor experiments with gambling. He admits to smoking marijuana on occasion, and has also experimented with LSD. When questioned why he sold the drugs, he was very evasive. Initially, Chester stated that this was the only occasion that he had sold drugs; however, upon further questioning he admitted to sale of marijuana on other occasions.

Ptn. Hennings stated that when he purchased the marijuana, he observed the defendant weigh out one ounce from a plastic bag, and then place the purchase in a smaller bag.

Probation Officer Heller comments on the Chandler Case:

"Frankly, I never thought much of this case from the time I was assigned to it. I think (Ptn.) Hennings was miffed because he didn't make the big bust he was hoping for, and wanted to take it out on Chandler for being so uncooperative. But Judge O'Flaherty is tough on drug cases, so I got the investigation anyway. He was put on three year's probation, and I put him on a minimal reporting basis. He finally married that girl he was shacked up with, and they seemed to do all right. They bought a house together out in Upper Darby. He kept working regular, and got on with a plumbing outfit, so I had no beefs with him. I talked with him often about how he would really mess up his life if he was ever caught selling drugs again, and I hope he got the point."

"Chester always gave me the impression he was a little overwhelmed with his parents, particularly his father. That is a very high-powered family. I always thought that was why he dropped out of college, and took up plumbing . . . almost like he wanted to rub his father's nose in it. Since he has reported in so regular, I talked to the Judge about discharging him early from probation, and the Judge is considering it."

PRACTICE CASE 12

Instructions: You are to write an evaluative summary and recommendations for Judge O'Flaherty based on this PSI, paying particular attention to the home, neighborhood, and education of the defendant. You should then answer the discussion questions at the end of the chapter. In order to achieve the best results from this exercise, you should refrain from reading the probation officer's and case commentaries until you have completed your own analysis of the cases.

Pre-Sentence Investigation

Name: Joseph Jacuzzi	**Plea:** Guilty
Aliases: None	**Date of Conviction:** 3/3/79
Co-Defendants: None	**Judge:** O'Flaherty
Date Report Due: 4/3/79	**Prosecutor:** Coors
P.O.: William Raspberry	**Defense Counsel:** Public Defender
Offense: Maiming	

CURRENT OFFENSE:

On 3/1/79 Ptn. Shane, on routine patrol in Eden Park, observed a Cadillac 2-door sedan reported as missing by the Hertz car rental agency in Boone County, Kentucky. Ptn. Shane stopped the car and placed its driver, Joseph Jacuzzi, under arrest. While attempting to handcuff the defendant, Ptn. Shane was struck in the head with the defendant's elbow; the pair wrestled to the ground; the defendant produced a plastic container from his rear pocket and squirted the contents at Ptn. Shane's head. The officer pulled his revolver, ordering the defendant to stop, and summoned assistance. However, the defendant escaped due to the burning effect of the substance. Laboratory analysis revealed that the fluid was a highly caustic substance. Subsequently the officer signed a complaint against the defendant for *Maiming*. Ptn. Shane and another officer, Ptn. Frank Jones, having traced the identity of the defendant through the Hertz rental agency, went to the defendant's home to make the arrest. The defendant answered the door. When informed he was under arrest, he started to back away. The officers seized him, and retrieved a loaded .38 revolver from his pocket. On 3/3/79 the defendant, upon advice of counsel, entered a plea of guilty and was referred for investigation.

PRIOR RECORD: 8/5/73   *Breaking & Entering*   Westport, Connecticut
Disposition Unknown
A charge of *Taking An Auto Without the Owner's Consent* is pending in the Boone County Circuit Court

ATTITUDE OF COMPLAINANT: Ptn. Shane will be in complete accord with the Court's disposition of the case. However, he does not condone the offense. Although it has not been proven, the officer believes the defendant was "playing the queers" who tend to frequent that section of Eden Park. He feels the situation did not justify the viciousness of the attack. Had the caustic solution found its way into his eyes, he would have been blinded. His medical bills amounted to $145, and he is considering a civil suit against the defendant.

EDUCATION AND EARLY LIFE: The defendant was born in Boston, Mass. on January 8, 1938. He was reared in the Roman Catholic faith, attending Our Lady of Fatima Elementary School and Resurrection Catholic High School, from which he graduated in 1955. His record from that institution reveals him to have been a good student whose academic achievement was very good, with regular attendance. His intelligence was measured at 115, denoting accelerated intelligence. The defendant enrolled at Catholic University in Washington, D.C. in Sept. 1955; he left in June, 1959. His record from that institution reveals him to be below average in academic achievement. Despite the defendant's contention that he was awarded a baccalaureate in Religious Philosophy in 1959, his university record specifically states that no degree was awarded. In this instance, the defendant was untruthful with the investigator. The same discrepancy appears on the psychiatric report.

FAMILY AND NEIGHBORHOOD: The defendant's father, Giacomo Jacuzzi, was born in Boston on 8/26/1898. A college graduate, he was said to have worked as an engineer for the Boston Electric Company until his retirement at age 65. The defendant's mother, Dolores (Reilly) Jacuzzi, was born in Boston on 5/24/1898. She graduated from high school prior to her marriage to the defendant's father on 6/17/24. Both parents are alive, and reside in Boston. While this information could not be verified, the defendant states that his parents provided him with a stable home life, and that the family got along well together. The defendant is the youngest of three children; his two older sisters are married and living in Boston. The defendant has never married, and lives alone in an apartment in Mt. Adams, an area of the city known for its singles bars and "arty" living style.

EMPLOYMENT HISTORY: Currently the defendant is employed as a personnel technician with the Chaste Lady Cosmetic Company in Cincinnati, Ohio, where he has been employed for the past five years. At his request, this employer was not contacted in order to avoid jeopardy to his position. Prior to this position, he was personnel interviewer with Wetherby Personnel Services in Cincinnati, Ohio for three years. He also reported he was a boy's counselor at a private academy in Exeter, New Hampshire. Although inquiries have been directed to several out-of-town former employers, no replies have been received. Taken at face value, his work history is deemed satisfactory.

MILITARY RECORD: The defendant states that his draft classification is 4-F due to a curvature of the spine for which he sometimes wears a back brace. Thus, he has seen no military service.

PHYSICAL AND MENTAL: The defendant is a 41-year-old white single male, 5′5″ tall, weighing 180 pounds; he is rather obese, wears corrective glasses, and gives a rather "soft" appearance. Aside from the spinal deformity claimed by the defendant, he is in average health except for a hypersensitive condition for which he was briefly hospitalized in Boston recently. He was referred to the Court psychiatrist, Dr. Henry Kuykendall, who was unable to establish a psychiatric diagnosis, stating: "This man is found to be not mentally ill, not mentally deficient, and not a psychopathic offender." In describing his findings, Dr. Kuykendall reported:

"It becomes evident that Mr. Jacuzzi has always been a shy and solitary person. He has not dated at all since being in Cincinnati. He does his own cooking. He does not frequent bars as he does not like the atmosphere, but does take a drink before dinner.

"He has always been an anxious person, and is subject to hypertension. He recently returned to Boston to be evaluated for this condition after receiving urgent medical advice from a local physician to treat his high blood pressure of 210/60. He consulted this physician because of loose bowels and an odd taste in his mouth, and feared he might have contracted some disease.

CHARACTER AND CONDUCT:

"He believes himself to be not at all successful in life, even though he graduated successfully from Catholic University in 1959. He can be believed when he states that he has always been law-abiding, never aggressive, obedient to his parent's wishes, and always wanting to do the right thing. He carried the caustic solution with him for protection, fearing attack in the park at night. He states that he was in a panic state when arrested, and did not mean to injure the officer. He said he was thinking at that time, 'I knew life as I have been living it is coming to an end.' He is believed to be somewhat of a schizoid personality." The defendant was arrested for breaking and entering in Westport, Connecticut on 8/5/75. Disposition of that charge could not be determined, and the defendant is evasive about any knowledge of the charge, claiming it was a misunderstanding with a former roommate. The defendant also claims that a misunderstanding with the Hertz Rental agency in Boone County, Kentucky resulted in the pending charge of *Taking an Auto Without Owner's Consent*. He had kept the rental auto for a two-month period without informing the rental agency of his intentions.

The defendant claims to be a life member of the National Rifle Association. His personal gun collection constitutes quite an arsenal, consisting of 14 shotguns and rifles, and 6 pistols. The defendant has been informed that, as a convicted felon, he is not permitted to possess such weapons. Obviously, the defendant's penchant to use force of arms against police officers engaged in the performance of their duties somewhat tarnishes the carefully constructed public image of the National Rifle Association. While no intent exists to degrade that organization, it is difficult, if not impossible, to visualize the defendant as a typical "American Sportsman."

Probation Officer Raspberry Comments on this Case:

"I was never really sure I understood this character and, frankly, not sure I really wanted to. Just when you seemed about to corner him on something, he would slip and slide away from you. There was something a little eerie about him, ya know? Kind of a cold fish, his handshake was like grabbing hold of a wet noodle. Shane was convinced he was up in that park looking for queers . . . I had trouble seeing that. My impression was that Jacuzzi was more of an observer, who seemed to get enjoyment, if that is the word, hanging around in the park looking at people, but not getting involved. If you can imagine just standing around and watching homosexuals do their thing . . . that's why I said he makes me feel eerie. Judge O'Flaherty put him on three year's probation, with the condition that he satisfy all of the officer's medical bills and sell his gun collection, and go into psychiatric treatment.

"Well, he sold the guns, I saw to that. Then he asked to return to Boston to live with his parents. I gave him permission after he had straightened out that mess with Hertz across the river. We transferred his supervision to Boston through the Interstate Compact, and so far he hasn't caused any problems. We have no record that he ever went into psychiatric treatment."

Discussion Questions

1. To what extent do you believe that the education, home backgrounds, and employment record of these two offenders mitigated their sentence? Do you believe that two similar cases, without the benefits of college education and Class III background, would have resulted in the same judicial decisions? If not, could you justify a different handling of Class V cases like these?

2. What is the correct way to report the IQ score described in Practice Case 12 as "accelerated intelligence"?

3. In Practice Case 12, how do you account for the desperate resistance to arrest by Mr. Jacuzzi, a usually reticent person? Is there any justification for believing he might become dangerous, and under what conditions?

4. Is the home environment adequately described in these two cases? What information might you have added?

5. Did P.O. Raspberry act correctly when he apparently failed to insist that Mr. Jacuzzi undergo psychiatric treatment? What do you believe the goals and benefits of such enforced treatment might be with this client, as he is described in the report?

Case Commentary

There seems to be no quicker way to start an argument among corrections workers than to claim that possessing a college degree, a stable middle-class background, or a high-level job might justify a less severe sentence for a particular offense. The sense of justice of some officers (and students) is outraged by the suggestion that an already privileged class should get preferential treatment in sentencing. In fact, the argument is commonly heard that the white-collar offender should be punished more severely "because he is supposed to know better."

It seems that there is no perfect wisdom on these sensitive questions of social class privilege. A lot of rhetoric and much hypocrisy abound in regard to these issues. The probation officer who may be just a few jumps away from poverty himself often loudly defends the idea of equal justice for the downtrodden masses, but if that same officer happens to get caught driving while drunk, he will be quick to exploit whatever edge he believes his middle-class respectability may give him with the court.

Most middle-class citizens have a healthy fear of jails, and the threat of a jail sentence (or a brief stay in jail) often acts as a salutary deterrent for them. The middle-class person will readily pay a money fine to avoid a jail term. The lower-class offender, perhaps lacking the luxury of an option, may choose the jail term, and the deterrent effect of jail often seems minimal. The sanctions provided by law do not fall evenly upon everyone, and there are social class differences, as well as personal differences, in the reactions to punishments.

If the capacity for *self-correction* has any merit as a guide to severity of sentence, then it seems that such qualities are more likely to be associated with what are called "middle-class virtues." The habit of meeting financial and social responsibilities in a socially conforming manner is often part of the indoctrination contained in a stable family background, regardless of social class. In the same way, high-level job skills or a college degree usually signify meeting of responsibility, postponement of gratification for long-range goals, and perhaps patience. Obviously, such qualities are not automatically conferred upon every person identified as middle class, nor are they denied to lower-class persons. But in cases where investigation reveals such personal achievement and implies the capacity for self-correction, do we serve the interests of justice by ignoring such potentials in sentencing? Isn't that what the concept of probation is all about?

Social class hostility and conflict will continue to exist and continue to produce differences in sentencing policies along class lines, although the biases are usually inadvertent and unrecognized. The larger issues are beyond the scope of this Casebook, but the problems are reflected in the judgments made by every officer in his investigations. The purpose here is not to resolve the issues, but to keep them before the corrections student.

In the Jacuzzi case, Officer Raspberry seemed to be violating the Judge's instructions when he failed to insist that this client start psychiatric treatment. Mr. Raspberry may have been acting on some subtle cues he picked up in working with this client. He may have perceived correctly that this man's social adjustment was rather fragile, and that the type of repressive defenses and social isolation which characterize him are probably necessary to that fragile adjustment. Mr. Jacuzzi seems to be the type of person who lives within himself by choice or necessity, and the unravelling of such defenses through an uncovering type of psychotherapy might worsen his condition. Dr. Kuykendall's evaluation indicated a chronic schizoid adjustment, and it seemed that he pointedly omitted a recommendation for treatment. The type of externalized supervision that dealt very lightly with more intimate aspects of Jacuzzi's personality is probably as much as this man can tolerate. Schizoid personalities are usually very unrewarding treatment cases, in that such persons are not motivated to change their defenses, and can become quite anxious under active intervention. The episode in the park with the police officer, in which this man went into a panic, illustrates his tendency to violence when threatened too strongly. A kind of vigilant but impersonal supervision by the probation officer is most likely to be effective, and should keep him out of further trouble.

Supplementary Reading

Glaser, D., Lander, B., & Abbott, W. Opiate-addicted and nonaddicted siblings in a slum area. *Social Problems, 18,* 1971, 510-521.

Healy, William & Healy, Mary Tenney. *Pathological Lying, Accusation and Swindling.* Boston: Little, Brown and Co., 1915.

Hollingshead, August B. & Redlich, Frederic. *Social Class and Mental Illness.* New York: Wiley, 1958.

Hodges, Harold M. *Social Stratification.* Cambridge, Mass.: Schenkman Publishing Co., Inc., 1964

Langner, Thomas A. & Michael, Stanley T. *Life Stress and Mental Health.* New York: Free Press, 1963.

Mowrer, Hobart D. *The New Group Therapy*. Princeton, New Jersey: D. Van Nostrand Co., 1964.

Neiderhoffer, Arthur. *Behind The Shield: The Police In Urban Society*. Garden City, N.Y.: Doubleday, 1967.

Reissman, Leonard. *Class In American Society*. New York: The Free Press, 1959.

Salisbury, Harrison E. *The Shook-Up Generation*. New York: Harper & Bros., 1958.

Shaw, Clifford R. & McKay, Henry D. Social factors in juvenile delinquency. In National Commission of Law Observance and Law Enforcement, *Report on the Causes of Crime* (Vol. 2), 1931, 195-201.

Thrasher, Frederic M. *The Gang*. Chicago: Univ. of Chicago Press, 1927 (re-issued, 1963).

Warner, Wm. Lloyd. *Yankee City*. New Haven: Yale University Press, 1963.

Wechsler, David. *The Measurement of Adult Intelligence* (3rd Ed.). Baltimore: The Williams & Wilkins Co., 1944.

Chapter 12
Employment

A systematic and verified work history is one of the most crucial contributions to an investigative report. Under most circumstances, a steady history of employment is not compatible with extensive criminal involvement (unless pilferage or embezzlement from an employer is at issue). On the other hand, chronic underemployment or a chaotic work history can be a powerful incentive toward illegal acts and should be a warning signal for an investigating officer, assuming the defendant is physically able to work.

When an offender claims lack of employment as mitigation for an offense, particularly close attention should be paid to the specific connection between the offense(s) and his economic circumstances to determine whether a logical cause-and-effect relationship can be justified. General statements about "hard times" are seldom an adequate justification; documentation of an offender's efforts to find employment, his state of mind about employment prospects, and his subsequent criminal acts should form a logical sequence, if such statements of mitigation are to be convincing to a court. The integrity of an investigator can be severely compromised if illegal sources of income, such as burglary, shoplifting, prostitution, or drug sales, continue to flow while the offender is released on bond and under investigation, or even while under probation supervision!

Generally, the most useful procedure is to start with current employment, if any, and work backward systematically toward early work history.

Current Employment. Information to be obtained through interview and verification may include the following:

> *Name, address, and telephone number of current employer.*
>
> *Name of immediate supervisor, and relationship with this person.*
>
> *How long employed there?*
>
> *Any layoffs, or other gaps in employment?*
>
> *Description of job responsibilities, and characterization of type of work, such as "clerk," "warehouseman," "general laborer," etc.*
>
> *How was job obtained?*
>
> *Take-home pay, including overtime, if any.*
>
> *Union memberships, if any.*
>
> *Promotions, disciplinary actions, or other events on the job.*
>
> *Hours of work, and arrangements for commuting.*
>
> *Friends or team members on job, if any.*
>
> *Prospects for advancement, if any.*
>
> *Attitude toward present job, or line of work.*
>
> *Is bonding necessary for employee? If so, is employee bonded?*

Are special licenses required for job?

Do current or past offenses place employee in job jeopardy?

Does employer know about current or past offenses? If so, what is attitude of employer? Are ex-offenders hired?

Does employer have programs for alcoholism, drug abuse, stress, or other employment-related problems?

Since verification of current employment is essential, the investigator must determine whether the employer is aware of the current offense. He must be prepared to use judgment in verifying employment so that needless jeopardy to the offender's employment is avoided. In some cases, company identification badges, pay vouchers, W-2 forms, or other documents may be sufficient to verify employment. With the permission of his client, the officer may be able to contact the Personnel Department of a firm on a confidential basis to obtain the needed information.

If the offender is in custody, the officer may be able to use his influence to negotiate return of the offender to his employment. In some cases, the officer may be able to arrange reemployment on a work-release or parole basis, if such options are available.

If the offender is currently unemployed (or has been discharged as a result of arrest), the officer should determine what period of unemployment is involved, and determine what means of support has been utilized during unemployment. The officer should determine whether unemployment compensation, welfare payments, private charities, savings, relatives, girl-friends, illegal sale of drugs, or some other criminal activity have furnished support.

If client claims to be using unemployment compensation, the officer should inquire about job seeking methods which have been used; for example, classified ads, placement agencies, civil service applications, or public service employment, for example. The client should be able to list employers contacted, and describe the results of each contact in order to substantiate efforts to find employment.

The investigating officer must recognize that current unemployment may increase the temptation for a sentencing judge to impose a jail sentence, unless legitimate efforts to seek work can be documented.

Past Work History.   Proceeding in reverse chronological order, attempt to obtain the following information:

Names, addresses, and telephone numbers of previous employers, where possible.

How long on each job?

Rate of pay.

Names of immediate supervisors, and relations with supervisors.

Promotions, disciplinary actions, or other events on the job.

Description of duties, and characterization of type of work.

Attitude toward job.

Reason for leaving.

Since verification of past employment is essential, the officer should obtain the permission of the client to contact employers to verify periods of employment, and the employer's opinion of the reliability and work habits of the offender. A useful question is, "If you had the opportunity, would you hire this person back?" Finally, the officer must attempt to resolve any discrepancies between the statements given in interview and the information obtained from past employers.

Summary Narrative of Employment History. In obtaining work histories, it is important that interviewers be persistent about unexplained gaps in employment. When such gaps appear, do they represent vacations, drinking sprees, periods of dependency upon relatives or friends, prison sentences, psychiatric hospitalizations, periods of criminal activity, or what? Vagueness or evasiveness regarding employment gaps may be extremely significant omissions.

In compiling a work summary, patterns may become apparent, and should be reported in summary form as they are identified. A "normal" employment pattern moves upward toward increased job responsibility, increased work skills, and increasing income. Job shifts may occur often in a typical work history, but such shifts usually represent career planning and upward mobility as the worker becomes older and more experienced in the job market. Ordinarily, most clients report increased job satisfaction as they mature, and may seek additional training or education for job enhancement.

Satisfactory work adjustment is seldom reported by offenders. A typical offender pattern involves frequent lateral moves from one relatively unskilled position to another, with expediency rather than planning evident. Periods of unemployment and financial hardship are common. Dissatisfaction with conditions of employment, disputes with supervisors, and walking out without notice are often seen in offender work histories. Such histories usually culminate in a discouraged and pessimistic attitude toward employment, and the employment patterns have been described as a horizontal job movement.

Horizontal movement is often seen in young workers as they test themselves in the job market, gaining experience and self-confidence. However, a prolonged pattern of such horizontal movement may indicate serious attitude problems in adjusting to work discipline, unless a real lack of opportunity can be demonstrated.

Patterns of downward mobility are also common among offenders, with increasing periods of unemployment, casual employment in positions requiring less skill than previously held positions, with frequent job changes. While an officer must use discretion in interpreting downward shifts to allow for economic conditions and the effects of discrimination, a persistent pattern of downward mobility may reflect alcoholism or drug abuse, poor mental or physical health, family pressures, or poor work adjustment due to lack of social skills in conducting one's work life. A worker may also become enmeshed in a vicious circle of negative reinforcements that sap his self-worth, so that he has difficulty presenting himself to an employer in a positive manner.

Marginal workers are disproportionately affected by periods of high unemployment in communities, may be victims of discrimination, and may require the assistance of federally supported programs of public work or job training. In addition, the working conditions of many unskilled laborers make employment less attractive, and may increase the temptation to get "easy money" through criminal activities.

The corrections investigator, himself a working person with a history of experiences in the employment market, must do the best that he can to objectively appraise the situation of his clients, and to rise above the narrow comparison of his own experiences with those of his clients. In doing so, he builds a larger social perspective on employment problems of offenders, so that he can be empathetic to the needs of these offenders and realistic in assessing their work histories.

PRACTICE CASE 13

Instructions: A pre-sentence investigation has been conducted on Millard Johnson, who has pleaded guilty to armed robbery. You are to write an evaluative summary and recommendations for sentencing to Judge O'Flaherty, justifying your recommendations, and paying particular attention to the work history of this defendant. Finally, answer the discussion questions about this case.

Pre-Sentence Investigation

Name: Millard Johnson	**Offense:** Armed Robbery (2 counts)
Aliases: None	**Plea:** Guilty
Judge: O'Flaherty	**Penalty:** 2-7 yrs. on first offense
P.O.: Manfred Hochstrasser	**Co-Defendant:** Harry G. Cowperthwaite
	Date Report Due: 11/8/78

CURRENT OFFENSE:

On 9/10/78, at approximately 3:30 AM, the Hamilton County Police received a phone report from the Hillsdale Inn, 335 East Sharon Rd., that an armed robbery had just occurred. A white male had forced the desk clerk, Joseph Grieco, to remove $110 from the cash register at gun-point, and fled. Mr. Grieco noted a second white man in a car waiting outside, and noted the license number. The car was traced to the defendant, who was arrested at 5:30 AM that same morning at his residence, 3353 Elmridge Drive, by Blue Ash Police. The co-defendant, Harry G. Cowperthwaite, was identified as the gun-man by Mr. Johnson, and arrested a short time later. On 9/3/78, one week earlier, Hamilton County Police were notified of an armed robbery which had just occurred at the Queen City Motel, I-71 and Pfeiffer Rd. The co-defendant had forced two employees at gun-point to produce the cash box, and removed $55 before fleeing the scene in a waiting car. The co-defendant implicated this defendant as the person driving the getaway car on that occasion. On 10/8/78, the defendant entered a plea of guilty to both charges upon advice of counsel, and was referred for investigation. On 10/15/78, the co-defendant, Harry G. Cowperthwaite, having pleaded guilty to both charges of armed robbery, was sentenced to the Ohio State Reformatory for 10-25 years.

DEFENDANT'S VERSION:

Mr. Johnson claims that he met the co-defendant several months ago in a bowling alley where he occasionally goes after work to bowl. The pair struck up an acquaintanceship, and went out drinking together on several occasions. Mr. Cowperthwaite talked about getting some "easy money." The defendant admits driving his car during the two robberies. After some stalling, he admitted that he knew Cowperthwaite had a gun and that they planned the robberies together. The defendant insists that he did not know his companion was on parole, and had a prior record for armed robbery. The defendant says, "I guess I used poor judgment."

PRIOR RECORD: None.

ATTITUDE OF COMPLAINANT: The cashier of the Hillsdale Inn was contacted. She stated that none of the money was recovered, and restitution may be considered for the total amount of $110. Following the policy of Hillsdale's, they prefer to leave the matter of probation or prison sentence to the discretion of the court. Mrs. Hans Leindorf, night cashier at the Queen City Motel, verified that $55 was taken, and that is the amount of restitution due. In line with the policy of the Queen City Motel, she is willing to leave judgment to the court.

EDUCATION AND EARLY LIFE: The defendant was born 1/5/48 in Evansville, Indiana, and has lived in Greenhills since 1960. He completed the 5th grade at Linwood Elementary School in Evansville, the 6th grade at Everhard School in Evansville, and enrolled at Greenhills High School in the 7th grade. He completed 11 grades at Greenhills before he withdrew to go to work. Although no test scores were available, he appears to fall within the above-average range of intelligence. High school records indicate he attained average grades, presented no disciplinary problems, and his attendance was without criticism. In 1967-68, he attended the Ohio College of Applied Science in a 2-year apprenticeship program in the field of Lithographic Specialist.

FAMILY AND NEIGHBORHOOD: The defendant's father, Sylvester Johnson, was born 56 years ago in Evansville, Indiana, earning a Bachelor of Science degree in engineering from Purdue University. The defendant's mother, Édith (Simpson) Johnson, presently age 55, was also born in Evansville, Indiana, and is a high school graduate. The couple were married in 1945, and the defendant is the third of three offspring. His older sister, Susan, is a housewife residing in New Orleans, where her husband is in the U.S. Navy. The defendant's younger brother, Chicopee, age 20, was a student at the University of Akron until his disappearance last September. His whereabouts are unknown, although the defendant believes he has joined a religious commune in Massachusetts. The defendant related that he had a happy early home environment, and states that his parent's marriage has been sound.

On 6/5/71, the defendant married Henrietta Bradley, who was 20 years of age at the time, a high school graduate, and a Greenhills native. From this union three daughters have been born, ages 1, 3, and

6. Last September he purchased a one-family dwelling in Greenhills, where he will continue to reside if granted probation.

EMPLOYMENT HISTORY:

On October 1st of this year, the defendant secured a position with the Heimenthaler Printing Company as a lithographer, earning $15,000 per year. From 6/1/78 to 10/1/78, he worked as a lithographer for the Brighton Color Company, earning $11.10 per hour. He left this position because he believed the Heimenthaler Company offered a better long-range opportunity for him. From 5/1/78 to 6/1/78, he was a driver-salesman for the Crystal Water Company, earning $3.50 per hour. The defendant states this was an interim position until he was able to find work in his trade. From 5/1/77 to 5/1/78 he was employed as a plate-maker for the Ohio Printing Company, earning $10.50 per hour. He states he was laid off from this position, and did not return. From 7/10/68 to 4/1/77, he was employed as a plate-maker and lithographer for the Hoover Lithographing Company, where he advanced from apprentice at $3.50 per hour to journeyman at $8.95 per hour. The defendant states that he left this position to make more money with the Ohio Printing Company. Prior to these positions, he was in the 2-year apprentice program at Ohio College of Applied Science, as previously reported. The defendant is currently a member in good standing of the Lithographer's and Printing Trades Union, Local #21. His work history is deemed satisfactory, inasmuch as he has progressed steadily in his trade, earning increased salary and responsibility.

MILITARY SERVICE:

None.

CHARACTER AND CONDUCT:

The defendant claims to be a moderate drinker who limits his consumption to beer, does not gamble, and enjoys good physical health. He claims to be free from addiction to drugs, narcotics, or hallucinogens. Since the current offense, the defendant is taking phenobarbital by prescription for insomnia. Mr. Johnson claims he needs this medication only when he becomes excited, nervous, and upset.

A Protestant by upbringing, he married a Roman Catholic girl, and regularly attends Our Lady of the Sorrows Church in Greenhills, although he is not a convert to that faith. It would appear that Mr. Johnson used poor judgment in his choice of associates, indicating a lack of maturity and responsibility for his family obligations. With no previous arrest record indicated, the defendant related that the current offenses were an isolated situation which he intends never to repeat again.

Officer Hochstrasser Comments on this Case:

"I had a hard time trying to understand how Johnson, who seemed like such a clean-cut fellow, ever got mixed up with Cowperthwaite, who has a long record going all the way back to grade school. I asked him that, but I never got a straight answer. I still don't know what the big attraction was. But Johnson did cooperate with the investigation, and I gave him the benefit of the doubt in my recommendation for probation. Judge O'Flaherty put him on three year's probation with me, and I figured that with Cowperthwaite sent up for a long stretch, that Johnson would get the message, and shape up.

"However, it didn't happen that way. He took off without permission, leaving his wife and three daughters hysterical. Nobody knew where he went. It was 8 months before we got a report from Sacramento that he had been arrested there on some minor charge. He was drinking heavily, was $5,000 in debt, and very defiant . . . he was living with some girl out there. I was taken off the case, and my supervisor Mr. Cyril took over. Cyril is very hard-nosed, and raised all kinds of hell with Johnson, but managed to get his probation restored. Cyril tells me he got him to declare bankruptcy, that he has gone back with his family, and we helped get him a new job. He is even paying restitution on the robberies. He lost the house in Greenhills, of course, but he seems like he's back on track again . . . it's almost as if he had some kind of delayed adolescence . . . maybe he's got it out of his system now."

Discussion Questions

1. Criticize this PSI. What is missing? Would a more detailed version of the offender's attitude have clarified the significance of the two robberies?

2. What was the relationship of Johnson to Cowperthwaite? Would you be able to justify a difference in the sentencing of these two men, based upon this report?

3. How do you account for two armed robberies in a 30 year-old married man with responsibilities, a clean record, and a good employment history?

4. Do you believe that his employment record mitigates the seriousness of the offenses? How did you justify your answer in your recommendations?

5. Is Johnson's family life a factor in his present situation? What are your speculations about his relationship with his family?

PRACTICE CASE 14

Obtain an employment history from a classmate, colleague, or friend, using the guidelines described in this chapter. Instruct the person being interviewed to "put his best foot forward" by glossing over disputes with supervisors, covering up periods of unemployment, and hiding other undesirable aspects of their work history. Having recorded the employment history during interview, immediately review that history with your "client," asking him/her to point out the weaknesses successfully hidden from you. Write up this employment history as described in this chapter, and list the points in that work history in which you were "snowed" by your client. Discuss in class the problems of obtaining accurate and complete work histories.

Case Commentary

There is nothing like perfect 20/20 hindsight, after all the action is over. Officer Hochstrasser seemed very open in commenting on this case, considering all the problems that developed. Nobody likes to lose control of a case like that, but unfortunately it happens from time to time. Our predictions about people's behavior just aren't that good yet.

In retrospect, we can only make some guesses about what was really going on inside this man which was not captured in the PSI, and ended up overturning the predictions about Johnson's behavior. The first clue is the friendship with Cowperthwaite. What was he doing running around all night with a hardened parolee like this man? What needs were satisfied in this relationship? What do you hypothesize about a 30 year-old married man with a family and a good job who develops a secret double life where he runs around all night looking for thrills? It seems that if the significance of this emotional search had been appreciated in the investigation, his flight from probation supervision might have been predicted. Perhaps the disappearance of Johnson's younger brother, Chicopee, into some religious commune might have had some influence on this defendant.

There is very little said in the report about his family life. Either Johnson didn't give it much importance, or Hochstrasser didn't ask much. In view of his subsequent flight from home and family, an extremely irresponsible and perhaps desperate act, there were probably a lot of unresolved difficulties in those family relationships. It seems that since Officer Cyril has forcibly brought this family together, a referral for family counseling should be made.

Finally, there is Johnson's employment record which, on the surface, looks impressive. It shows a decade of training and steady progress in building a trade. However, there must be a discrepancy somewhere between the appearance and the reality. Men simply do not walk away from careers they have built unless some contradictory or alienating features exist in those jobs. Officer Hochstrasser recorded the chronology of employment, but failed to appreciate the aspirations and feelings connected with that employment history.

In reconstructing these events in Johnson's life, we can see a recent change of jobs to a more ambitious and permanent kind of responsibility, a new home and mortgage, a recent 3rd addition to his family, and a younger brother running off in some kind of personal search for meaning in his life. Perhaps Johnson felt some options for freedom and excitement were foreclosed to him under the weight of all this new responsibility; as Hochstrasser said, a kind of delayed adolescence. So Johnson went underground, and found Cowperthwaite, which came perilously close to destroying everything he had built in his marriage and career.

If there is a lesson to be learned from the Johnson case, it must be that the formalities of a case history can sometimes mislead you, because they don't tell the whole story. Formalism in information-gathering gives you a kind of spurious validity which underestimates the complexity of human motivations.

Chapter 13
Religion

"Oh, brothers who live on when we are dead,
  Let not your noble hearts against us harden,
And smile not when the noose shall claim our heads.
  A silly secret smile to ease your burden.
Nor rail against us, now you see us broken,
  Nor take revenge against us like the law,
Not all of us treat virtue with such awe.

Oh, brothers, being light of heart, be shaken.
  Oh, may our fate a lesson be,
And beg of God that He will pardon me.
  And luscious girls who flaunt their treasures
  Before the eyes of easy yokels.
  And other men who wait at leisure
  To watch, and snatch their simple shekels!
  The crooks, the molls, the flash-house owners,
  The shills by day and sharks by night!
  And yes, those dogs in uniform!
May I be guiltless in their sight.
  May heavy hatchets hit their faces,
And smash them in for all to see.
  Now I forget their filthy faces,
And beg them all to pardon me."

Gallows message from MacHeath in THREE-PENNY OPERA
(lyrics by Berthold Brecht)

In this savagely mocking song, Mac the Knife prepares to go to the gallows in Kurt Weill's musical play, *Three-Penny Opera*. MacHeath parodies the conventional last-minute religious conversion of the dying criminal, and mocks the hypocrisy of such pseudo-repentance. Having strutted and pranced as a successful con-man and thief during the play, Mac's last "con" is to ask for forgiveness from his audience, who presumably "treat virtue with such awe." This powerful play has continued to challenge, if not outrage, the audiences who have witnessed it for many years.

The song illuminates the mystifying and often paradoxical presence of moral and religious values in most criminals, although such values have not usually been effective as crime deterrents in the lives of those criminals. For example, Yochelson and Samenow (1976) reported that all but one of the hard-core criminals in their study had been exposed to conventional religious training in their early years. Some even aspired to become clergymen, and were choir boys and altar boys. They remarked:

It is important to emphasize that the criminal does not rebel against the church and in fact may seek out a strict faith and adhere almost slavishly to its ritual. It is more a matter of competing excitements than disdain for religion itself that leads to the progressive moving away . . . what the criminal child wants overrides whatever he might get out of church. The strong, primitive fears of God and devil recede in the face of desires to do the forbidden.

In adult life, many criminals go through non-violating periods of religiosity between crime sprees. Particularly in prisons, criminals are sometimes subject to periods of self-doubt and guilt which result in serious and sincere religious conversion, although such conversions seldom result in long-range deterrence in the face of further criminal enticements. Religion appears to be locked into a separate mental compartment, so that when criminal excitement looms, the "cut-off" mechanism is employed to permit violations. Thus, the criminal may go to Mass at 9 o'clock, and commit a robbery at 10 o'clock.

In some cases, the criminal may pray for forgiveness at bedtime, while planning the next day's crimes. One criminal was even reported to carry a Bible with him while committing crimes around the country. Others may pray for "good luck" in their next crime spree. Many members of the Mafia are reported to be regular church-attenders and heavy contributors, even maintaining a chapel in their homes.

However, the most cynical misuse of religion probably occurs in prisons where prisoners may attempt to "score points" by participating in religious programs. Yochelson and Samenow note:

> It is a case of a criminal's effort to ingratiate himself with the clergy, who he knows may be able to help him out. Conversions occur out of expediency. . . . Phony confessions are made, because they are interpreted as evidence of change. The criminal does everything he can to impress others with his sincerity and to indicate that he is changing. In the process, he makes an errand boy out of a clergyman, by enlisting his help in getting privileges . . . the criminal may ask his minister to make a call for him, to bring him cigarettes, or to mail a letter. Most important, he wants the clergyman to use influence to help get him out of the institution.

Probably as a result of such opportunistic exploitation by offenders, religious protestations by offenders have come to be viewed with deep suspicion by many corrections officials, and are mentioned lightly in their investigative reports, if at all. The low status of religious or moral beliefs in offenders is probably not justified. The connections between criminal acts and moral or religious beliefs run very deep in most offenders, with the possible exception of the criminal sociopath. The simple listing of church membership and participation characteristic of most investigative reports hardly does justice to this subject. In fact, it has proven difficult to locate a practice case in which religious values were deemed important.

As described earlier in Chapter 9, various amounts of shame and guilt accompany the commission of many crimes. If by the term "religion" we mean not only formal membership in a religious organization, but a repository of the moral and social values that undergird society, then we can anticipate that offenders exposed to religious values may suffer some discomfort when committing crimes. To live in a predatory manner upon others takes a toll, and these psychic costs should be explored in correctional assessments.

O. Hobart Mowrer has described the origins of "neurosis" as the torments and anxieties caused by unresolved guilt over commission of deviant (antisocial) acts (1961, 1964) which have violated the conscience of the afflicted. To the extent that the conscience is undeveloped, deviant acts leave no impression, and such persons are classified as sociopathic. However, those persons with the ordinary religious and moral indoctrination become "neurotic" under the pressures of unexpressed and hidden guilt, according to Mowrer, and seek relief in confession and expiation.

Most police officers are familiar with the compulsion to confess crimes, which often leads miscreants voluntarily to admit crimes, sometimes years after their commission. Much of police and polygraph interrogation depends upon the implicit need of the offender to "get it off his chest" through confession. Both priests and psychotherapists likewise hear many such confessions, and have developed traditional methods for relieving guilt through absolution.

Mowrer came to believe that confession alone is only partially successful in its cathartic effects, and that confession to a priest, therapist, or through prayer to God could become a "cheap state of grace." Some criminals manage to lighten their conscience enough through confession to resume their predatory criminal activity, which is a corruption of the confessional.

In order to be fully effective, according to Mowrer, confession must be *shared* with one's friends and fellow-believers, and finally, acts of *restitution* are required, as in the early Christian church (or acts of *expiation,* to use the more classic terminology). In our own time, similar practices are seen in Alcoholics Anonymous, Synanon, therapeutic communities, Muslims, fundamentalist sects, and communes. Some Marxist-oriented groups, including the Chinese Communists, refer to such catharsis as "criticism and self-criticism" sessions. The corrective power of such groups in altering behavior is often quite impressive.

If Mowrer's formulations were to be translated into modern criminal justice terms, some form of public confession, as in a court-room, would be a necessary first step. The offender would then stand ready for acts of restitution, to be prescribed by the judge, which could involve punishment, repayment of damages to victims, or other "good works" of atonement either for the victims, or for society as a symbolic replacement to the victims. While such dramas are not that far from the psychological realities seen in the courts, the impact is often lost on the offender due to the formalities of criminal processing and the adversary process.

Nevertheless, the punishment-seeking offender is no novelty in our courts, and conscience-stricken offenders sometimes become depressed, self-maiming, and suicidal when their need for expiation turns upon themselves.

The difficult task of the investigating officer is to determine the depth and sincerity of religious beliefs, their relationship to the current offense (if any), and any potentials for correction which may be associated with the client's religious background.

The investigator should be able to catalog the offender's religious background and beliefs with the same sense of balance with which he checks an employment history. This is more easily said than accomplished, since the subjective quality of religious beliefs makes it difficult to describe them with accuracy. Many officers become influenced in favor of an offender if his religious background happens to be similar to their own. On the other hand, an offender who professes no religious training may be prematurely categorized by an officer, since most corrections officers are strongly motivated by a personal code, often based upon their own religious convictions. Usually, an offender with strong religious beliefs will let his beliefs become known without much prodding from an investigator.

Much of the information to be obtained can be divided into current religious status, and past religious training:

Current Religious Status.

What is the current religious affiliation of the offender (if any)?

What activities or duties are involved?

Can religious participation be verified through interviews with clergymen?

What significance does religion assume in the daily life of the offender?

How does the offender reconcile his moral/religious beliefs with the current offense? (See Chapter Nine on attitudes)

What is the attitude of the offender toward persons he may have victimized? Has restitution been offered?

What is the attitude of the offender toward undiscovered crimes/transgressions he may have committed?

Has the offender shared religious beliefs with others, including other offenders?

Does the offender recognize the hypocrisy and opportunism which may be inferred by others because of his professed beliefs at the present time (probation, parole, sentencing, etc.)?

A number of cross-checks with clergymen, parishioners, and relatives can usually be made to test the sincerity of religious beliefs, where such beliefs are claimed as an important feature of his life-style.

Past Religious Training.

Church memberships in reverse chronological order, noting gaps, discontinuities, and affiliation changes. Verify by obtaining name of church, address, phone number, and name of clergyman.

Description of activities in church organizations. Verify.

Summary of early beliefs about God, punishment, disobedience, etc.

Even the absence of current religious affiliation, if accompanied by strong church ties in early life, can suggest some potentials which could be reactivated. Many migrants to urban areas have ceased church membership, but still retain strong religious beliefs that might be revived by renewal of church membership.

Discussion Questions

1. In a study of 500 Federal offenders by Lohman, Wahl, and Carter (1966), 28 factors influencing sentencing were ranked by probation officers and District Court Judges. "Church attendance" was ranked 20th by officers and 16th by judges. "Religion" was ranked 28th by officers and 27th by judges. How do you account for the low credibility of religious participation as a decision-making aid in sentencing?

2. Assume that you are evaluating an offender who professes no religious commitment, and whose past religious training is insignificant. In an overall recommendation, would you be willing to weigh lack of religion as a *plus* factor, a *minus* factor, or of no consequence either way? Discuss the implications of your answer in terms of moral values in society, your personal religious commitments, and the possibility of personal biases in your viewpoint.

3. What do you think of the notion that criminal confession is a "cheap state of grace" that has only a minor effect on inhibiting criminal behavior?

What do you think of the idea that public (group) repentance is necessary, with convincing acts of restitution to victims or to society in general?

4. If criminal laws could be changed to include acts of restitution, what possibilities could you visualize for shoplifting, mugging, rape, and homicide?

Supplementary Reading

Lohman, Joseph D., Wahl, Albert & Carter, Robert M. *San Francisco Project* series, Report 5 (Berkeley; Feb. 1966), 68. (Cited in *Probation, Parole and Community Corrections,* edited by Carter/Wilkins. New York: John Wiley & Sons, 1976, 221-223.)

Mowrer, O. Hobart. *The New Group Therapy.* Princeton, New Jersey: D. Van Nostrand Co., 1964.

Mowrer, O. Hobart. *The Crisis in Psychiatry and Religion.* Princeton, New Jersey: D. Van Nostrand Co., 1961.

Yochelson, Samuel & Samenow, Stanton. *The Criminal Personality* (Vol. 1). New York: Jason Aronson, 1976.

Chapter 14
Military Service

The impact of military life on young offenders is sometimes paradoxical. A successful adjustment to the structured life-style of the military services is widely regarded as delinquency-preventive, and for many unstable young persons this proves to be true. However, the permissiveness of off-duty activities in strange cities where the serviceperson is not known can prove to be a serious temptation to delinquency-prone youths, who may use their military service as a shield to cover criminal activities. For example, a U.S. Army enlistee committed several arsons of industrial buildings in cities near his military stations. These crimes went undiscovered at the time.

Careful review of periods of military service should include evaluation of off-duty activities, with check of police records in cities the offender is known to have frequented. It is desirable to obtain the service record from the Military Personnel Records Center in advance of interview when possible, if serious omissions are to be avoided. The following information should be obtained:

Circumstances of Enlistment. For example, did client drop out of school to enlist at a time when school performance was poor? Was client permitted to enlist in lieu of sentence by a juvenile or adult court? Were family problems involved, pregnant girl friend, financial problems, or other personal problems from which client wished to escape?

Branch of Service, Serial Number, and Period of Service. Did enlistment occur under other names or aliases? Verify by records.

Training. What skills were mastered that may have employment value as a civilian? Was Project Transition completed prior to discharge? Was GED achieved in service, or other education?

Military Locations. What periods of foreign service? What military action was involved, and what was client's response to combat conditions?

Weapons Mastered. What was military rating on use of these weapons? Does client maintain an interest in firearms, or possess any "souvenir" weapons from service?

Disciplinary Actions. For what violations? Was client court-martialled, and with what result? Does client have "bad time" in military stockade or Federal prisons? What was client's response to disciplinary actions, and was any rehabilitative program attempted while in service?

Civilian Arrests/Crimes. In the U.S. or overseas? What was result of such arrest? What was nature of client's off-duty activities and travel, including prostitutes, girl friends, birth of children, trafficking in drugs, pilferage, etc.

Adjustment to Military Life. Did client suffer any "breakdowns" or other problems adjusting to military life, for which psychiatric treatment/evaluation was administered?

Promotions/Demotions. Did client receive honors or dishonors, and what was rank at time of discharge? Were decorations and Good Conduct medals received?

Military Discharge. What type did client receive? Verify.

Injuries or Disabilities. Was client injured, under what circumstances, and are these conditions V.A. service-connected? Verify with V.A.

V. A. Benefits. Is client receiving V.A. benefits currently? Is client eligible for disability/educational benefits which should be included in probation/parole planning?

In summarizing military history, it is important to note whether client has ever been *excluded* from military service for physical, emotional, intellectual, or criminal reasons, and to attempt to verify such exclusion.

PRACTICE CASE 15

Instructions: Prepare an evaluative summary and recommendations on Sgt. Henry Motherseal, who pleaded guilty to *Assault with a Deadly Weapon* and *Carrying a Concealed Weapon,* with particular emphasis on his military service.

Pre-Sentence Investigation

Court of General Sessions, Beaufort, South Carolina

Name: Henry Motherseal

Aliases: None

Offense: Assault with a Deadly Weapon; Carrying a Concealed Weapon

Plea: Guilty

Co-Defendants: None

Date of Conviction: 9/12/78

Date Report Due: 11/15/78

Probation & Parole Agent: Culpepper

Judge: Cuthbert

OFFICIAL VERSION:	Complainant Melba Appletree stated that on 9/1/78, defendant had come into the King-Kwik store where she worked a couple of times. When she took the trash out at midnight, she noticed defendant drinking in a 1977 Datsun parked next to her car. She got into her car. The defendant approached her, and asked whether the car was for sale. He then pulled a large knife, saying that he was getting into the back seat and going for a ride. He placed the knife at her ribs, and attempted to force her into the back seat. Complainant fought with the defendant, and witness Harry Overstreet, U.S. Marine Gunnery Sergeant, chased the defendant into the woods. Deputy Sheriffs Hensley, Jones, and Sheets arrived at the scene, and captured the defendant in the woods. The knife was recovered, and was placed in evidence.
DEFENDANT'S VERSION:	Sgt. Motherseal states that he had attended an outpost party for a platoon that had graduated. He states that he had so much to drink he doesn't know what happened, only what he was told happened.

PRIOR RECORD: No prior record could be found.

PERSONAL AND FAMILY HISTORY:

Defendant was born September 17, 1955, in Indianapolis, Indiana to white American parents, the 3rd of 6 children born to Agnes and William Motherseal. Subject was raised by his natural parents to age 17, when he graduated from high school and got married. Subject states that he could not ask for better parents. The children were treated fairly and taught responsibility. They were adequately provided for, even though they did not get all the material things they wanted.

The parents, when questioned, stated that they were shocked, and that they were a very religious family. They were concerned about their son, and stated they would stand by him all the way. However, they did not wish news of his arrest to get out, as it might hurt the family image. Family members were listed as follows:

Father: William Motherseal, age 50, lives at 5000 Meridian Drive, Indianapolis. He is a stock broker who travels in his work.

Mother: Agnes (nee Johnson) Motherseal, age 46, is a housewife living with her husband at the same address.

Sister: Mary Lou Coffee, age 28, lives in Bloomington, Indiana with her husband, Keith, who is a physician. The couple has two children.

Brother: John Motherseal, age 25, lives in Indianapolis with his wife, Helen, and their two children. He is a meat-packer.

Sister: Jill Wiggins, age 22, also lives in Indianapolis with her husband, Philip, who is a real estate broker. She is a housewife.

Sister: Sally Johnson, age 19, lives in Gnaw Bone, Indiana, with her husband, Bob, who works in a sorghum mill. She is a housewife.

Sister: Fatima Motherseal, age 17, is a student living at home with her parents.

MARITAL HISTORY:

Defendant married Crystal Chandelier in Sept. 1972. This marriage lasted one year as they were both immature, and unable to cope with responsibility. They have one daughter, now age 7, who lives with her mother in Grand Island, Nebraska. The family are still friends with Crystal, and defendant sends an allotment for support of the daughter.

Sgt. Motherseal was married a second time in February 1974 in Beaufort, South Carolina, to Trish Mahalia. This is her first marriage. She is 21, a housewife, and the couple has a son, Mark, age 2.

HOME AND NEIGHBORHOOD:

Defendant lives with his wife and son in a three-bedroom brick home in a middle-class section of Beaufort, South Carolina. Their rent payment is $186 a month.

EDUCATION: Defendant graduated from Valley H.S. in Indianapolis in 1972 at age 17. He made above-average grades, was never suspended or expelled. He played basketball and football on the H.S. team.

LEISURE TIME ACTIVITIES: Defendant likes to watch and play football. He also paints pictures. He states that he would like to make the Marine Corps his career, but if he doesn't, he would like to get into the sale of stocks and bonds, like his father.

PHYSICAL HEALTH: Defendant is presently in good physical health. He had his tonsils and appendix removed as a child. He is 6′ tall, and weighs 210 pounds, has blond hair and blue eyes. He has a scar on his cheek which is the result of a motorcycle accident when he was 16 years of age.

MENTAL HEALTH: He does not consider himself an alcoholic. However, he admits a problem when he drinks too much, claiming it causes him to lose his memory. After this offense, he was admitted to the Marine Hospital at Quantico for psychiatric examination. While hospitalized, he showed no evidence of psychiatric difficulties. He was cooperative in treatment, and showed good judgment. He decided drinking could be dangerous for him, and decided not to drink in the future. He was diagnosed as showing no evidence of psychomotor epilepsy, or other abnormality, and returned to duty.

EMPLOYMENT HISTORY: July 1972 to October, 1972. During this time, he was employed by the A & P Company in Indianapolis as a truck loader, making $2.85 per hour. He quit, since there was no chance for advancement.

November, 1972 to present. Defendant enlisted in the U. S. Marine Corps, where he presently holds the rank of Staff Sergeant. Since joining the Marine Corps, he has received no punishments, and has been awarded the National Defense Medal, the Good Conduct Medal, Meritorious Unit Citation, Certificate of Commendation, and a Meritorious Mast. These awards are reflective of superior performance on duty. He is presently an instructor at his Marine base, has seen no overseas duty, and was commended by his Commanding Officer for reliable performance on the job.

Agent Culpepper Comments on This Case:
   "Judge Cuthbert sentenced this man to 5 years in prison, then suspended the sentence in favor of 5 years on probation. I think the Judge was trying to scare the good Sergeant, and he certainly succeeded! I don't think Sgt. Motherseal has had a drink since, or at least he claims

he no longer drinks anything except a Dr. Pepper. While it's still a little early to be sure, I don't think Motherseal is going to be in any more trouble. When you meet him, and hear about his background, it's a little hard to imagine him trying to force some girl into the back seat with a knife. I don't think I ever fully understood what was going on in his head that night. It really seemed out of character for him, but I guess that is what drinking can do to some people. The Sergeant is back on the job again, and his life at home seems OK, so I have my fingers crossed for him.''

Discussion Questions

1. What conditions of probation might you recommend (if you recommend probation), in view of Motherseal's peculiar behavior while drinking?

2. What aspects of the case are not clear? What information would you seek to get a clearer picture of this defendant? Why do you think he carried a knife? What information would you seek about his relationship with his two wives?

3. Do you believe that his religious background, his military service, and his family background are mitigating factors in sentencing?

Case Commentary

From the facts that were offered, Sgt. Motherseal may suffer from a somewhat rare condition called *pathological intoxication*. Persons subject to this condition may show psychotic or dangerous behavior, sometimes after only a few drinks. During a period of psychiatric observation, without drinking, Sgt. Motherseal would be his usual sensible self, as he apparently was at the Marine Hospital at Quantico. The most critical task faced by Agent Culpepper is to make sure that Sgt. Motherseal sticks to Dr. Pepper, if future episodes are to be avoided. In view of his two marriages and the nature of the assault on Melba Appletree, a referral for family counseling would be a useful adjunct to probation supervision.

Chapter 15
Use of Leisure Time

Many persons reveal more of themselves in their leisure-time activities than in any other aspect of their lives. If working represents a frustrating process of meeting responsibilities imposed by others, then leisure time becomes a safety valve that can restore balance to one's life. Some persons, often described as workaholics, use leisure as an extension of their work life, while others may adopt an opposite viewpoint, engaging in activities that are as far removed from the work environment as possible.

Perhaps the real significance of leisure is that it represents *self-generated activity*, time in which persons can satisfy their deepest emotional, intellectual, or physical needs by their own choices. When interviewing offenders, it is quite common to find a lack of such self-generated pursuits, which may indicate their lack of satisfaction with their lives, and their difficulty in setting recreational goals. In fact, many casual offenders seem to get into trouble during their spare time, using their leisure time in a search for criminal excitement or prolonged periods of alcohol and drug abuse. The "weekend drinker" is a typical example of such use of non-working time.

Some interviewers find discussion of leisure a fairly neutral way of getting in touch with the feelings and inner lives of their clients, affording many illuminating insights into self-concepts. However, it is not uncommon to find offenders who may be deeply secretive regarding their use of leisure, and who may even regard any inquiry as an invasion of privacy; when such defensiveness is encountered, it may indicate that the offender is hiding activities that he does not wish to have scrutinized by a probation officer. For example, an offender on probation for burglary was systematically going home to his family after work, getting drunk, and then disappearing for most of the night. It was later revealed that he spent his evenings peeping in windows. He carefully maintained a secret notebook in which he recorded the most likely times and places to see women undressing, and would go through a kind of "paper route" at night in order to "see the sights." This information was revealed to his psychotherapist in a group counseling session, but his nocturnal activities were withheld from his probation officer. Areas of inquiry into leisure-time activities might include;

Sports. What sports does client follow? As a TV-watcher, spectator, or participant? Is he alone, or do friends participate? Is the family involved or excluded? What is the level of proficiency? Is the client typically an organizer or a follower in sports?

Hobbies. Is client a collector? Does he repair or construct things, such as cars, furniture, electrical or plumbing work as a hobby? What are his reading habits, if any? Does client take courses of instruction? Any types of creative work, painting, model-building, photography? Does client have skills which might be of assistance in obtaining employment? Does client play any musical instruments?

Social Organizations. Does client belong to clubs, lodges, or charitable organizations? Any volunteer work? Involved in recreational work in playgrounds or parks? Bowling leagues, veteran's organizations, PTA, or church groups?

Other Activities. Does client participate in or attend races? Is gambling involved? What are his favorite taverns? What does he do with his friends? Favorite TV programs, if any? To what extent is family involved in spare-time activities?

A summary of leisure-time activities rounds out a picture of the life-style of the offender, permitting correctional decision makers to understand and relate to typical preferred activities of the offender, and even offering clues to work-training and alternative career possibilities.

PRACTICE CASE 16

Instructions: Compose an evaluative summary and recommendations on the case of Luther Adler, charged with embezzlement by his employer, emphasizing the aspirations and life-style of this defendant, as revealed in his use of work and recreation.

Pre-Sentence Investigation
BOONE COUNTY CIRCUIT COURT

Name: Luther Adler

Aliases: None

Offense: Embezzlement

Plea: Guilty

Judge: Hefflewhite

P.O.: George D. Whitley

Co-defendants: None

Date of Conviction: 9/15/78

Date Report Due: 10/15/78

OFFENSE:

On 8/17/78 Joseph Larkin, District Supervisor of the Friendly Finance Company, 1015 Middlebelt Rd., Ft. Thomas, Kentucky, signed a warrant charging this defendant with embezzlement of a sum of $2812.49 while employed by this concern as office manager. At that time, the defendant was no longer employed by Friendly Finance, and a fugitive warrant was issued, and the defendant was arrested at his home in Ft. Thomas, Ky. on 8/20/78. He entered a plea of guilty as charged and was released on bond, pending this pre-sentence investigation.

PRIOR RECORD:

8/15/67	Drunk	Ft. Thomas, Ky.	30 days Probation
11/11/74	1) Speeding	Ft. Thomas, Ky.	1) $20 & costs
	2) Ignoring Stop Sign		2) Dismissed
	3) No driver's License		3) Dismissed

| 4/6/76 | Speeding | Ft. Thomas, Ky. | $20 & Costs |

There are no indictments pending.

ATTITUDE OF COMPLAINANT:

Mr. Larkin related that during an audit, discrepancies were discovered on various accounts which could only be explained by falsification of loans. The defendant, who was employed by Friendly Finance Company since 9/1/72, was confronted with the financial shortage and admitted that he had used the names of former customers to re-open accounts, using the proceeds to cover accounts which were delinquent in payments on loans. By the use of this subterfuge, he maintained an excellent record as loan manager, and has been cited by the home office on several occasions for efficiency in loan operations. Although only four acounts, which were falsified, were brought to the attention of authorities, Mr. Larkin relates that a complete audit indicates shortages of nearly $45,000. Since a complete audit is still in process, a claim has not been filed with the firm's bonding company concerning the total loss. Officials of the firm retain mixed emotions regarding leniency for the defendent, but will be in agreement with whatever disposition is made by the Court.

MITIGATING AND AGGRAVATING CIRCUMSTANCES:

The defendant explained that he was extremely proud of his record as loan manager, and decided to use the falsification procedure when various accounts became delinquent, and marred his record. He adamantly denies that the proceeds were diverted for his personal use, and he is not certain as to the exact amount of the accounts which were altered. When an old account was reactivated, however, he necessarily had to withdraw cash from company funds to make payments on the new account and the old delinquent customer. These customers testified that they had never applied for second loans after their former accounts had been paid, and received no proceeds. Subsequently, when manipulation of the accounts remained undiscovered, the defendant relates that financial pressures at home induced him to use part of the proceedings illegally obtained, since he could not afford any overage in the audit.

He is well aware of the notoriety which his family has suffered from his criminal involvement and lack of discretion, but observes that he is eager to make amends with everyone concerned, in order to justify the faith displayed by his family in his ability to regain his former standing in the community.

Mr. Larkin related that the defendant was hired in 1972 as a trainee, and was promoted to loan manager in 1975. Internal audits revealed that accounts were tampered with almost immediately after his promotion. When the firm became aware of the defalcation, an independent auditing firm indicated a preliminary shortage of nearly $125,000; however, a final report by the firm indicated a transfer of $70,000 by the defendant, of which $20,000 was distributed to delinquent accounts. Net loss to the firm is indicated to be $50,000, but the only provable loss totals $10,000. 200 accounts were alleged to be tampered with, although this number is denied by the defendant.

Rumors that the defendant maintained an apartment for sexual encounters with females from his office could not be substantiated. Likewise, we were unable to confirm the defendant's purchase of an hotel complex in the Bahamas.

EDUCATION AND EARLY LIFE: The defendant's father, Luther Adler, Sr., died in and was reared in a rural section of that County. He attended rural schools there until the 10th grade, achieving average grades. He terminated school in 1957 to enter the military service, and received his GED diploma in Japan in 1960. His early life and adolescence were conventional and unremarkable in that his parents supplied a normal, congenial environment with behavior limits enforced. He enjoyed participating in hunting and fishing with his friends, and during his youth was interested in model-building and handicrafts.

FAMILY AND NEIGHBORHOOD: The defendant's father, Luther Adler, Sr., died in 1950 at the age of 70 from cirrhosis of the liver. He lived all of his life in Whitley County, Ky. He apparently was a hard-working, God-fearing individual, who worked throughout his life as a carpenter.

The defendant's mother, 64 year-old Nellie Letcher, who likewise sprang from agricultural stock, presently resides in Paris, Ky., where she subsists on a pension. The defendant is the youngest of 11 children born to the couple, the majority of whom reside in northern Kentucky, and who have achieved normal social and economic adjustments.

The defendant married Henrietta Morrow, age 42, on 5/17/66, and two offspring, James and Honey, ages 10 and 6, have been born to the couple. The defendant and his family reside in a luxurious 7-room mansion at 1219 Talawanda Terrace in Ft. Thomas, a residential community. The home is well-furnished, and reflects a comfortable standard of living enjoyed by the family.

The wife, Henrietta, is employed as a legal secretary by the law firm of Gahagan and Gahagan. Although she is 10 years older than the defendant, the couple seems harmonious. The wife gives the impression of a sincere, proud, and dedicated person who is shocked by her husband's criminal offense, but is determined to maintain her loyalty to him whatever happens. They are willing to make restitution, and she is willing to sell whatever assets they may have in order to do so. The couple apparently enjoys a number of domestic pursuits together.

EMPLOYMENT HISTORY:

The defendant is presently employed by the BiLo Oil Company as a service station manager, where he has been employed since his discharge from Friendly Finance. He earns $4.50 per hour, and the owner is enthusiastic about his progress. The owner, Fred Fleece, stated that the defendant is punctual, competent, and does not mind working over-time. For example, he always insists upon staying at the service station to count up receipts, and take them to the bank for deposit.

For the past six years, he had been employed by the Friendly Finance Company, and at the time of his discharge was earning $950 a month. Previously, for a 4-year period, he had been employed by the Ohio Barge Company as a stevedore. This position could not be verified. Before that, the defendant stated he worked as a barker in a traveling carnival, and as a truck-loader in a meat-packing plant. None of these jobs could be confirmed. The defendant's work adjustment is deemed fair.

MILITARY RECORD:

The defendant enlisted in the U. S. Navy on 1/15/53 and received an honorable discharge on 1/10/57. There was no record of court-martial or difficulty in adjustment to the military discipline. His special duties consisted of being the payroll clerk for his unit.

PHYSICAL AND MENTAL:

The defendant is a 32-year-old male Caucasian, born 1/3/46. He weighs 210 lbs., and stands 5'7" tall, and reports that he is in satisfactory physical condition, with no venereal infections. He apparently enjoys satisfactory health with no physical disabilities, except for being overweight. Although no psychological tests were available, he is believed to possess above-average mental functioning. There is no record of mental or personality disorders.

CHARACTER AND CONDUCT:

Mr. Adler was arrested in Ft. Thomas on three charges, two of which were for traffic offenses involving speeding. He believes himself to be a fast but careful driver. He was also arrested for drunkenness, and received 30 days of probation. He states that he enjoys social drinking, but has no reputation as a habitual drinker. He states he never gambles, with the exception of social card games, and has never used narcotics. His sexual adjustment appears normal, and there are no homosexual overtones. He was reared in a religious setting, and attended the

Baptist church. Within the last two months, he has again become active, stating that he has become an active member of the Mt. Moriah Baptist Church in Ft. Thomas.

Avocationally, he enjoys spectator sports and, according to his neighbors, spends the majority of his spare time with his family in domestic pursuits. He maintains a workshop in his basement, and spends considerable time in woodworking and handicrafts, which he has continued to pursue since adolescence. His former high school principal, Estil Johnson, relates that he has known the defendant his entire lifetime, and believes that he deserves a chance to redeem himself in the eyes of society. Mr. Johnson states that, with the exception of this offense, the defendant has been a credit both to his family and the community.

The defendant fully realizes that he has sacrificed a promising career in the finance field, but apparently has adjusted to the situation, and plans to make amends to the best of his ability, both financially and socially. Luther does not leave the impression of a psychopathic offender, but apparently was unable to summon the necessary emotional control and strength of character to resist the temptation to illegally profit from his situation as a loan manager. Financial pressures in the home may have played a role in the offense, but his lack of discretion and judgment seem quite inconsistent with his previous behavior pattern. At any rate, whether over-enthusiasm for his reputation with the company was a factor or not, he apparently has rationalized the entire situation, and is ready to begin life anew in a different economic capacity.

P. O. Whitley is Interviewed Regarding This Offender:

Q. Mr. Whitley, what did Judge Hefflewhite do with this case?

A. The Judge put him on one year's probation, and ordered him to pay court costs and restitution to Friendly Finance Company.

Q. Did he pay?

A. Oh, yes, he's almost got the whole $2800 paid off by now. I was surprised he could come up with the money that quick, but I think his wife helped him out some. He got himself a better job a few months after he was put on probation, and he's out on the road now selling medical supplies.

Q. Was there anything about this case that might not have appeared in your report?

A. Yeah. I always wondered how much his wife, Henrietta, had to do with what happened. She seemed more shook up about it than he did, sometimes. She was a lot older than him, you know, and she came from a nice family here. I always thought she kept a lot of pressure on him, to be successful, you know . . . and I think he was trying to prove something to her. He's really a good ole boy, he comes from around where I come from, and I think he takes himself pretty serious, too.

Q. Well, how do you think his probation is working out so far?

A. I think he's gonna be all right, far as I can tell. I think he's really learned his lesson . . . you won't see him here again.

Discussion Questions

1. Are there aspects of Mr. Adler's home life, use of leisure time, and military record for which you might have sought further information? List the items for which you might want verification. (Optional: Ask a colleague or classmate to role-play Mr. Adler, and interview him regarding these matters.) What changes in your summary and recommendations might have occurred if further information had been obtained?

2. Since this offense involved behavior on the job, were you satisfied with the work history as reported? What about his present job? What verification might you attempt to find out more about his behavior on the job, both present and past?

3. Can you pinpoint statements on the PSI which might be seen as judgmental, reflecting possible bias on the part of the investigator? (Bias can be both positive and negative with regard to the offender.)

Chapter 16
Physical Health and Personal Adjustment

Our courts, probation and parole offices, and correctional institutions constitute a set of natural gateways in society through which a great deal of physical and mental anguish passes each day. While it is hardly surprising that courts and correctional apparatus keep their main focus upon criminal remedies and legal dispositions, the probation officer, to the extent that he identifies as a helping professional, may find it difficult to ignore such a flood of concentrated human misery. In practice, only the largest urban courts have even the rudiments of medical and psychiatric expertise available to them. Until recently, our short-term jails and prisons were singularly lacking in adequate medical and psychiatric care for inmates.

For more than a decade, correctional experts have advocated a substantial shift of correctional resources away from correctional institutions, and into what has become known as community-based corrections. Such a shift necessarily involves the breakdown of the traditional isolation of courts and prisons from other social agencies, and the creation of linkages with a wide variety of community services. For example, diagnostic/reception centers attached to courts have been recommended which might diagnose, divert, counsel, refer or even treat offenders with emotional disorders, educational deficiencies, work problems, addictions, medical and dental needs, and social maladjustments.

An excellent overview of the rationale and potential of community-based corrections is presented by Carter and Wilkins (1976) who state:

> Far more is required than the one-to-one contact between probation or parole officer and the offender. The offender's predicament stems from the combination of personal deficits and social malfunctions that produced a criminal event and a social status. Most personal deficits characterizing offenders are also commonly found in nonoffenders. The social malfunctions of unemployment, discrimination, economic inequity, and congested urban living affect most citizens. The offender, like other citizens, must find a way to live with his deficits and with the disorder around him. If corrections is to mitigate alienation, it must mobilize the community services that can make such an outcome possible. . . . Corrections cannot continue to be all things to the offender. The correctional structure must change from a second-class social system consisting of a correctional bureaucracy and a dependent population of offenders subject to official control and service. Although the pattern of the future is not yet clear, it seems to consist of a brokerage service in which the agency opens up to the offender community services where such services exist, or helps create new services for the entire community where none existed before.

The implications of the community-based approach are that correctional services recognize their reciprocal responsibility with social service agencies in dealing with the physical and mental health needs of offenders. The argument cuts both ways, since over-worked correctional programs are hardly in a position to treat physical and psychiatric disorders if hospitals and clinics stand aloof from the treatment needs of offenders. With the constricted resources allotted to corrections agencies in most jurisdictions, officers must continue to do their best to identify and refer offenders with physical or mental disorders, while attempting to influence the community power structure regarding this neglected area of human need.

In practice, this means that a probation officer has a dual function of *screening* and *referral*. Screening, sometimes known as "gate-keeping," is the task of identifying treatable physical and mental disorders as such conditions are discovered during his investigations. It should be obvious that the screening function practiced in corrections can cover a wide band of skills ordinarily parceled out among a diverse group of professionals, including vocational counselors, physicians, educational advisors, psychologists, family counselors, and others.

The complementary function is that of referral. An officer conducting a PSI may seek confirmation and treatment recommendations of a disorder from an acknowledged expert to be incorporated within his own diagnostic report. Later, if a decision for treatment has been made by a sentencing judge as a condition of probation, the P.O. may *implement* referral as part of his supervision of an offender. In this case, he would be acting as a "broker," negotiating treatment through preparation of the offender and a receiving clinic, for example.

In a few fortunate corrections agencies, the officer may contract for services for an offender with funds provided by his own agency for that purpose. In the vast majority of agencies, however, the officer has little more than good will and his personal influence to persuade a receiving agency to treat an offender. In many cases, the limited amount of clout that can be mustered by probation and parole officers results in frustration of too many referrals.

The experience of most lower-class persons in obtaining medical, dental, or psychiatric treatment has been fairly negative, due to long waiting lists, slow or indifferent service, and similar problems with low-cost or free clinics. Since offenders come predominantly from lower-class backgrounds, officers need to be acquainted with these problems. The officer needs to maintain contacts within agencies and clinics where he is likely to refer clients in order to have a detailed knowledge of intake policies and personnel. Likewise, he must brief the offender thoroughly on what to expect, and offer patient support through the difficult intake period. In particular, the officer should know and respect the practices of confidentiality followed there, which usually differ from those of probation and parole agencies.

When continued treatment has been made a condition of probation, arrangements for periodic feedback on progress should be made in advance as clearly as possible. In one memorable case, a supervised offender was referred for counseling of a marital problem. When months of delay occurred in accepting this offender, the P.O. inquired of the agency the reasons for the delay. The intake social worker reported that the offender had arrived for his intake interview, and was asked why he had sought out the agency's services. He replied: "I don't know. My probation officer *made me come here!*" Under the circumstances, the agency could hardly be faulted for their lack of enthusiasm for this referral.

Guidelines for Physical Health and Personal Adjustment

When interviewing offenders, the following guidelines are suggested, to be amplified whenever positive findings appear:

Physical Health. Careful observation is often very revealing. Does the client look older than his chronological age? Are there dark circles under the eyes, are the whites of the eyes reddened, do pupils of the eyes contract equally, and appear to be of normal size? Is skin pallid or excessively wrinkled? Does client limp, have any amputations, show scars from accidents? Is voice quality normal? Is hearing impairment present? Does client appear listless and lacking in energy? Is client overweight, underweight, or show signs of poor nutrition? Is breathing labored or rasping, or is coughing apparent? Is client clean and neatly groomed (sometimes a dishevelled appearance signifies a carelessness about health)? Are tremors of the hands or body present, or facial tics? Are finger nails bitten down, or well-groomed? Condition of teeth?

Ask the client to describe the current state of health. It is particularly important to link any health condition with the current offense, if a logical connection appears to exist. If a condition of drug or alcohol use was present at the time of the current offense, obtain a detailed description of dosages, circumstances, client's response to drugs or alcohol, and the mental condition of the client at the time of the offense, and subsequently. If client cannot remember offense, discern whether memory lapses and blackouts have occurred previously.

Work chronologically backward through the health history of the client, noting particularly chronic conditions which might have a psychological or physical effect upon the client. Note major surgery or accidents, and periods of loss of consciousness, if any. Were venereal diseases, tuberculosis, nutritional problems, sickle cell disease, hepatitis, circulatory problems, dental problems, diabetes, or broken bones suffered, and was adequate treatment carried out? What childhood diseases were suffered, and were there any aftereffects? Was client regarded as weak or sickly by his parents? Was prompt dental or medical care carried out in dealing with health conditions (a morbid fear of doctors and dentists has been reported as common among criminals)? Wherever appropriate, verifying records from physicians or clinics should be sought, with the permission of the client.

In summarizing health history, medical or dental referrals may be suggested as appropriate, which may include family planning information, prosthesis, dental repair, or other identified conditions. Even cosmetic improvements may be helpful in an overall supervisory/referral strategy of preparing a client for job training and placement. For example, some offenders are deeply embarrassed by prominent tattoos on their bodies that were applied in prison or during military service. It may be possible to advise removal of tattoos by laser, which is effective and almost painless.

Personal Adjustment. For some offenders, a morbid fear of mental illness seems to be more terrifying than the prospect of a prison sentence. As one offender said, "I don't mind doing my 90 days in jail, but don't tell nobody I was seen by a headshrinker!" Any attempt to determine possible mental defects or problems is perceived by some offenders as a threat to their self-image, and any attempt to calm such fears by rational discussion can become an exercise in futility. An officer should side-step the resistive mind-set of an offender who insists, "You're trying to prove I'm crazy, aren't you?" and focus on a more positive approach.

Most offenders can be encouraged to describe their work life, their social life, and their family life, and their feelings about themselves. One test of the officer's interviewing skills is the client's willingness to share his inner life, including fears, inadequacies, depressions, hostility, and problems of social adjustment.

To the extent that such information is shared, it is helpful to ask the offender what efforts have been made to cope with these problems. Any previous efforts to seek vocational guidance, family counseling, personal counseling, or psychiatric treatment should be noted, with the offender's estimate of results obtained. Confirmation should be sought from family members or records wherever possible, with the offender's permission, and included in the officer's evaluation.

PRACTICE CASE 17

Instructions: Write a set of recommendations for the sentencing Judge on the case of Charles Harris, who has been found guilty of public intoxication. Justify your recommendations.

Pre-Sentence Investigation

Name: Charles Harris	**Judge:** Beckman
Aliases: None	**P.O.:** Horace Hepplewhite
Offense: Public Intoxication, Disorderly Conduct	**Co-Defendants:** None
	Date of Conviction: 2/23/78
Plea: Guilty	**Date report due:** 2/27/78

CURRENT OFFENSE: This 34-year-old single black dry cleaner and presser pleaded guilty to public intoxication at 11:00 PM on 2/22/78 at the Greyhound Bus Station, and was referred for pre-sentence investigation. The defendant claims he was waiting for a friend from Nevada, and admits consuming a pint of wine and a glass of beer. The defendant states he was approached by two elderly white women, and was passing the time of night with them when arrested by the police following a complaint by the station manager. The defendant blames his arrest on his strange appearance, which consists of flamboyant cowboy clothing and a large Bible. Subsequently, he was also charged and pleaded guilty to disorderly conduct in the lock-up when he persisted in quoting loudly from the Bible in the middle of the night. The defendant insists that his handcuffs were too tight, and that he was treated rudely by guards in the lock-up.

PRIOR RECORD: On February 12, 1976, the defendant was charged with aggravated robbery after being picked up on the street downtown late at night, and identified by a barmaid from a Main St. cafe. He was held on $10,000 bond, and states he waited 60 days in the County Jail while awaiting trial. He says he was subjected to sadistic treatment by guards as a result of his loud Bible-reading in his cell at night. The robbery charge was dismissed at the request of the prosecutor. Mr.

Harris says that he was wrongly identified by the barmaid, although he admits he signed a false confession after three hours of police interrogation. There are no other arrests on record.

PSYCHIATRIC HISTORY:

Mr. Harris states that he has been hospitalized 4 times in the Psychiatric ward of Beechview State Hospital, along with previous admissions at Holman Psychiatric Institute on several occasions. He believes that he is regarded as a "religious nut" by others. He states that he is gradually curbing his alcoholic intake, but in the past has been a heavy drinker and "pill-head," which involved heavy use of tranquilizers, anti-depressants, and barbiturates. He has difficulty sleeping, stating that massive doses of drugs "hardly touch me" because of his extreme anxiety.

During the present interview the defendant was extremely suspicious, hostile, and threatening, demonstrating many grandiose ideas about himself and his religious beliefs. He believes himself to be exploited by his family, by the police, by doctors, the school system, and his various employers because of his race. During interview, Mr. Harris was extremely vigilant and controlling, and only after lengthy interview did he begin to relax. He appears to be oriented, his thinking processes are formally intact, and he admits that his religious beliefs, which include "talking in tongues," having continually gotten him into difficulties with his family, employers, and police.

PRESENT SITUATION:

Mr. Harris lives with his mother at 1230 Rockdale Avenue in Sacramento. He is the oldest of 8 children, most of whom reside in the mother's home. The family are all ardent church-goers, but the defendant is somewhat alienated from them because of his extreme religious views. He dropped out of school in the 7th grade at Central H.S. because of his difficulty in learning to read. He says other students ridiculed him for his illiteracy, and he eventually taught himself to read in order to read the Bible. He has worked sporadically since age 12 as a dry cleaner and presser, and states that he is extremely competent at his work, turning out more clothing than anyone else. He is resented by fellow-workers because of his speed, and believes that he will cut back to part-time work. He says, "I am too nervous to work slow."

He states that his mother demands most of his income, which includes $100 a month for board, plus other demands made upon him by other family members. His father is said to be in Detroit, address unknown. He came to Sacramento from St. Louis, Mo. at the age of 5 months with his mother. He has never married.

SUMMARY:

This 34-year-old single black dry cleaner and presser

pleaded guilty to public intoxication and disorderly conduct after creating a disturbance at the Greyhound Bus Terminal and later in the lock-up. He is an emotionally unstable, suspicious, and overly religious person whose adjustment in all areas of his life is extremely precarious due to his psychiatric condition. He believes himself to be possessed of special powers, fancies himself to be an excellent artist, and makes various claims about his religious powers. He believes himself to be exploited by his family, the police, and his doctors because of his religious beliefs and his race. He has never carried any weapons, although he states he can handle himself in fights when necessary. He has one previous arrest in 1976 for aggravated robbery, which was dismissed at the request of the prosecutor. He dresses in cowboy garb, carries a Bible with him, and is likely to "talk in tongues" and read Biblical quotations loudly in public places. He claims numerous admissions by Beechview State Hospital and Holman Psychiatric Institute. He is regarded by this examiner as a paranoid and suspicious individual whose life-style is quite chaotic. His public behavior, particularly while drinking, can become highly annoying and provocative to most people, and may lead to further arrests.

P. O. Hepplewhite Comments on Disposition of This Case:

"Judge Beckman put Harris on probation to me for a year, with the understanding that if he got out of control, I would try to get him admitted to a psychiatric ward rather than locking him up again. Going to jail just seemed to aggravate Harris, and make him more paranoid than ever. I tried to be firm with him in pointing out that he was not to "talk in tongues" or read the Bible out loud in public, and that was not because I had any personal objections to Bible-reading and all that, but only because I was trying to offer some friendly advice to keep him out of trouble. He listened, and he argued some with me, but something must have registered because there was no further problem with him. I insisted that he go to the outpatient clinic at Holman Psychiatric Institute for medication, and that he take medication regularly, and not drink on top of it, and that seemed to help a little. When he was finally released from probation, I don't think I knew him any better than the first day I met him, he was just as suspicious as ever. I expect that, sooner or later, he'll be back."

Discussion Questions

1. What alternatives did you recommend that Judge Beckman consider, in view of this defendant's long history of psychiatric treatment? What do you believe the realistic prospects are for improvement in this case?

2. What information may be missing? What additional records would be useful in assessing this case?

3. If you considered probation, what would the goals of probation be with this case?

PRACTICE CASE 18

Instructions: Construct recommendations and justify your recommendations in the case of Jeffrey Helton, who pleaded guilty to *Cutting to Kill and Wound,* and *Assault to Rob.*

Pre-Sentence Investigation

Name: Jeffrey Helton

Aliases: Jimmy Seitz

Charge: Cutting to Wound & Kill / Assault to Rob

Plea: Guilty

Judge: Beckman

P.O.: Cyril Saylor

Co-defendant: Jimmy Lee

Date of Conviction: 10/15/78

Date Report Due: 11/15/78

CURRENT OFFENSE:

On 9/2/78 at approximately 11:50 PM, the defendant and co-defendant Jimmy Lee entered Jim's Pony Keg at 3208 Midland Rd., Hamilton. The defendant drew a small caliber revolver. The defendant then pistol-whipped the complainant, knocking him backward and into a closet, causing him to lose his eye-glasses and cutting him on the arm. The defendant and Lee then ran out, and Lee got into a stolen Checker Cab which was parked nearby, while the defendant left on foot. The complainant obtained the auto license, and called police. A quadrant was set up, and the defendant was picked up crossing the RR tracks on Haley Rd. While the defendant was in transit to Detective Headquarters, he kept asking for a "fix." Upon arrival, he refused to talk or give his name until promised a "fix," whereupon he gave his name and other information.

The defendant also admitted that he and Lee committed an armed robbery at the Sohio Station on Ludlow Ave. on 8/7/78. On that occasion, the two entered the station and after threatening the attendant with a gun and knife, removed $207 from the cash box. On 10/10/78, co-defendant Jimmy Lee was given an indeterminate sentence to the Ohio State Reformatory.

PRIOR RECORD:

3/16/72 Investigation Athens, Ga. Released
3/17/72 Runaway Hamilton, O. Counseled

7/2/72	Breaking & Entering & Vandalism	Hamilton, O.	Placed on unofficial Probation
12/16/72	Susp. Auto Larceny	Richmond, Ind.	Released Outright
12/24/72	Incorrigible	Hamilton, O.	Continued on unofficial Probation
7/24/73	Assault & Battery	Hamilton, O.	$75 & Costs — Jail one night
3/11/74	Assault & Battery	Hamilton, O.	Dismissed for Want of Prosecution
3/30/74	Faulty Exhaust	Hamilton, O.	$10 & costs
4/12/74	Leaving the Scene	Hamilton, O.	$100 & costs, suspended $50 on good behavior
4/15/75	Assault & Battery	Hamilton, O.	10 days in jail; suspended $100 & costs suspended $50 & costs on good behavior
8/4/77	Driving under Revoc.	Hamilton, O.	$100 & costs, 10 days in jail, suspended
8/8/77	Leaving the Scene	Hamilton, O.	$100 & costs, 10 days in jail, suspended
5/26/78	Forgery	Hamilton, O.	5 years Probation

There are no other indictments pending.

Detainer for probation violation filed 10/15/78.

ATTITUDE OF COMPLAINANT: The complainant stated that since this offense, he has learned that the defendant "is no good and has had previous chances." In his heart, he does not feel the defendant deserves probation and would not recommend probation to the Court. The complainant is not claiming restitution.

EDUCATION AND EARLY LIFE: The defendant was born in Hazard, Ky. on 11/4/57, but has lived most of his life in Hamilton, Ohio. He attended Harding and Millard J. Fillmore Schools. He quit school in the 10th grade at age 16 after receiving a work permit. At the Harding school, his scholastic standing, behavior, leadership, and reliability were all rated "poor." Regarding attendance, cooperativeness, courtesy, and ability to get along with other students, the defendant was rated "average." The Millard J. Fillmore School stated that his scholastic standing, behavior, cooperativeness, reliability, courtesy, and ability to get along with other students were rated "poor." His attendance and leadership were "average." School reports stated that the defendant was constantly in trouble and failed all of his subjects. He was large and "sophisticated beyond his age." His IQ score in 1970 was 67, and in 1964 was 78. These scores would indicate borderline to dull-normal intellectual functioning.

FAMILY AND NEIGHBORHOOD: The defendant's father, Michael Helton, was born on 8/22/23 in Hazard, Ky. He had little education and has worked as a laborer in Breathitt County, Ky. for the past 30 years.

The defendant's mother, Hettie Lee Pigg, was born

in Possum Hollow, Ky. on 7/16/44. She married
Michael Helton on 7/21/57 at the age of 13, and the
defendant was born several months later. The couple
currently has 9 children, 2 of whom are currently on
probation for armed robbery.

On 7/2/76, the defendant married Janie Ann Saxon
in Hamilton, Ohio. She was a 10th grade dropout.
She left the defendant six months after the marriage,
giving birth to a daughter, Crystal Mabry Helton. She
stated that she left the defendant because he was
always away from home, hunting and fishing, or so he
claimed. When filing for divorce, she told the court
that he was absent every night, returned home intoxicated, and "abused me in the bed" constantly.
A divorce was granted, and she is living in Hamilton.
The defendant has made no effort to support this
daughter.

**EMPLOYMENT
HISTORY:**

The defendant worked at the Coca-Cola Bottling
Company in Hamilton from 8/15/76 to 12/20/76 at a
salary of $3.25 per hour. According to the office
manager, he would not be reconsidered for re-employ-
ment. He worked at Hard Chrome Plating in Hamilton
as a laborer from 3/21/77 to 5/2/77 at a salary of
$3.05 per hour. According to the Vice-President,
he worked hard and did an above-average job. However, he left abruptly because of "family problems,"
and never returned. The defendant also reported that
he worked at a variety of unskilled jobs, but could not
recall names of these firms. In each case, employment
did not last more than one week.

**PHYSICAL
AND MENTAL:**

Mr. Helton is a 21-year-old divorced white male who
stands 5'10" in height, and weighs 185 pounds.
He is apparently in sound physical condition despite
a recent motorcycle accident. The defendant admitted
he has been in a number of fights. He once hit a man
with a bumper jack in a dispute at a stoplight, and
also hit another man, knocking him through a door.
He bragged about fighting three men at the same
time and that he "beat all of them." His juvenile
record describes an incident where the Sheriff was
called because he broke a chair, and threw it through
a window. He states that he started on paregoric
at age 16. At this time, he was running around with
older persons who initiated him into paregoric,
yellow jackets, benzedrine, and eventually powerful
tranquilizers.

The defendant was referred for psychiatric evaluation, which is excerpted as follows:

"He presented himself as a cooperative and sincere
young man who wanted to get out of jail and do well
"for my Dad's sake." This is significant because it
points out his relative lack of drive and self-control.

In giving information about his record of illegal behavior, Mr. Helton was more or less without emotion. His history is characterized by material indulgence and emotional instability rather than severe emotional deprivation. There was serious parental conflict in which the defendant identified with his mother, and attempted to protect her. However, in his own marriage he mistreated his wife, sometimes assaulting her, and then regretted it afterward.

"This young man's anti-social behavior can be understood as a consequence of poor character formation with weak masculine identification and poor impulse control. In my opinion, Mr. Helton needs the structure and control of a closely supervised environment for a long period of time for any rehabilitative effort to be effective."

PROBATION
HISTORY:

On 5/26/78, the defendant was placed on a 5-year term of probation after entering a plea of guilty on two counts of forgery. He absconded, but was continued on probation; on 9/15/78 he absconded again, and was declared a probation absconder. Following the current offense, a detainer was filed in the Hamilton Court. His P.O. states that the defendant cannot adjust to probation, and does not recommend further probation for him.

P. O. Cyril Saylor Comments on Disposition of This Case:

"Judge Beckman remanded this offender to the Ohio State Reformatory for an indefinite sentence. Frankly, I don't see what else he could have done with him. There was nothing there to work with. We have had no further reports on his progress there."

Discussion Questions

1. Do you regard this defender as mentally ill? How would you characterize his condition as described by the psychiatrist?

2. Did Judge Beckman's decision on this case agree with your own? Discuss your agreement or disagreement. What was the extent of agreement or disagreement among your fellow-students?

3. What might you predict his probable course at Ohio State Reformatory would be? Can you think of any alternative programs for Helton?

Supplementary Reading

Carter, Robert M. & Wilkins, Leslie T. (Eds.) *Probation, Parole and Community Corrections* (2nd Edition). New York: John Wiley & Sons, Inc., 1976.

Part 3

APPLICATIONS IN INSTITUTIONS AND AFTERCARE: USE OF PSYCHIATRIC REPORTS

Chapter 17

Institutional Placement and Classification

"Classification, recognizing the interdisciplinary character of the problems of preventing recidivism is, therefore, a team process enlisting representatives of as many areas of human behavior as possible to identify and resolve the subject's problems. Classification recognizes that problems and solutions are so very much interrelated that decisions affecting a man's training and treatment must be made jointly by people possessing usable knowledge. . . . The classification process is concerned with bringing specific resources into play to help solve specific problems presented by the subject."

Alfred C. Schnur

The network of penal institutions operated by each state and nationally by the Federal Bureau of Prisons probably represents the most developed system of prisoner classification existing in our corrections system. Characterized as "a little mental health center," the process of classification ministers to the total needs of offenders during their incarceration, and guides release on parole and other aftercare programs.

Classification has deep roots in corrections. The earliest efforts date back to the late 1700s and early 1800s, when efforts were initiated to separate youthful from older offenders, first offenders from chronic offenders, males from females, and mentally disturbed or retarded offenders from the rest of prison populations. No doubt there were practical as well as humanitarian considerations involved in such classification procedures, with the result that specialized types of correctional institutions gradually evolved.

By about 1930 the notion of diagnostic screening became a standard procedure for all prisoners entering correctional institutions, and most prison systems operated a special diagnostic/reception unit for classification purposes. Classification committees or boards were maintained, in which the work of social workers, psychologists, chaplains, physicians, psychiatrists, educators, vocational specialists, and others were utilized, along with security personnel. Our contemporary era (starting in the 1950s) has witnessed the increasing use of individual treatment planning in prisons and reformatories, reflecting the trend in society toward psychological measures to combat maladjustment and defective socialization.

It has been said that if one wants to witness the true character of a society, that he should look at its prisons. The measure of the humaneness of prisoner treatment is said to reflect the aspirations and practices of the larger society. Thus, the prison systems of the U.S. are a reflection of the dominant trends taking place in the overall society, and various waves of "reform" have transformed prisons in the U.S. Unfortunately, most prison systems remain underfunded and under-staffed, so that broad social changes in the structure of prisons seldom come to full fruition. A "cultural lag" has developed. In addition, the social forces impinging on the operation of these institutions are often in conflict, so that methods operate at cross-purposes, and results are an uneven amalgam of punitive and rehabilitative techniques.

Prison administrators and staff do their best, on the whole, to accommodate to the mixed messages emanating from the outside society. The classification committees and boards, in their daily operations, will probably continue to negotiate the societal ambivalence felt toward offenders, in their attempts to provide the most appropriate services for prisoners within their respective institutions. The most common difficulty reported by classification officers is the reconciliation of the security needs for an offender with the offender's "treatment" needs. With the increasing sophistication of prison management has come the recognition that the necessity to prevent escapes and maintain order can be made compatible with education, vocational training, and various forms of counseling. An extended discussion of this complex issue is beyond the scope of this Casebook; however, it is essential to note that classification officers and others making decisions about assignment of offenders *jointly* consider both the security needs of the offender along with his program treatment needs in making determinations.

Security and Custody

The indispensable condition of any commitment to a correctional institution is that the offender be confined with the degree of security believed to be necessary to prevent escape, and to permit the orderly running of the institutions. More often than not, prisons have over-emphasized safety, which has caused unnecessary restrictions on offender movement with consequent impairment of programs. Maximum security is also expensive, so that funds needed for other programs are sometimes diverted into construction and staff to maintain prisoner security, when lesser security measures might be effective if careful classification procedures were adopted. Therefore, many classification operations have adopted the principle that offenders should be confined with the *least* level of security measures necessary to do the job

The Federal Bureau of Prisons, faced with inconsistencies in security classification of Federal prisoners, appointed a Task Force in 1977 to study this issue (Levinson & Williams, 1979). This Task Force grouped the 38 Federal institutions according to seven criteria for security level present (in some cases, subdivisions within institutions were made for different security levels existing). Six levels of institutional security were designated. The Task Force then surveyed 47 factors believed to be associated with an offender's need for security, finally reaching a high level of consensus among classification team members on the following six factors:

1. *History of escapes or attempts, involving the degree of seriousness, and how long ago they occurred.*
2. *History of violence, the seriousness of any act against persons or property, and how long ago it occurred.*
3. *Type of detainer, the degree of severity of lodged detainers, using a scale of Severity of Offense developed by the Task Force.*
4. *Severity of current offense, based on the most severe offense resulting in the present incarceration, and using the Severity of Offense Scale just mentioned.*
5. *Expected length of incarceration, the average percent of sentence actually served for the current offense.*

6. *Type of prior commitment, the seriousness of any offense which resulted in prior commitment.*

A *Security-Designation Form* was devised (Exhibit 9) in which point totals could be summarized from the six categories, the results of which would then designate the security level required for that offender.

Example: Joseph B. has been sentenced to 10 years for arson, which involved burning down a warehouse for profit. The Severity of Offense Table (not

Exhibit 9

included) rates arson as "High," so he gets 5 points. When his 10-year sentence is adjusted for average length of time served, he receives 3 points for "Expected Length of Incarceration." Since no detainers on him are current, 0 points.

Since Joseph B. has a prior sentence for arson, he gets 3 points as a serious prior offender. He gets no points for escape attempts, but because his arsons are regarded as a "past serious" history of violence, he receives 5 points. Since he was arrested and held in custody, he receives no points for pre-commitment status. His total point count is 16 points, which means that he should be assigned to a Security-level institution at the 3rd level.

The Community Programs Officer (the Federal Bureau of Prison's term for classification officer) would then proceed to match the offender to the Federal institution at the appropriate security level, unless six administrative variables intervened that could override or modify the assignment of the prisoner:

1. *Central Monitoring Case.* This turn is used to cover specific prisoners who need to be kept separated from each other.
2. *Age.* Some Federal institutions have special requirements for the age groups they serve.
3. *Judicial Recommendation.* The sentencing judge may have recommended a specific program or institution in which the sentence is to be served.
4. *Release Residence.* Where possible, newly admitted offenders may be assigned to the area closest to their home residence.
5. *Overcrowding.* Newly admitted offenders may be distributed equitably to keep populations in balance.
6. *Racial balance.* An attempt is made to keep proportions in balance throughout Federal institutions.

The Task Force further refined the Federal prison system by designing a Custody-Classification Form (Exhibit 10), which could be used periodically (at least once every year) to review security of offenders, either reducing or increasing custody according to progress made by the offender. Seven weighted factors were established in such deliberations:

1. *Percentage of time served.*
2. *Involvement with drugs and alcohol.*
3. *Mental/psychological stability.*
4. *Type of most serious disciplinary reports, using a Scale of Disciplinary Severity devised by the Task Force.*
5. *Frequency of disciplinary reports during the past year.*
6. *Responsibility demonstrated by inmate, reflecting judgment of classification team based upon program reports.*
7. *Family/community ties, a team judgment based upon marital status, family support, family stability, regularity of mail/visits, etc.*

The classification team adds the points to establish a total which corresponds to a security level, as shown in Exhibit 10. The team may then accept the custody level established by the form, or make other decisions based upon additional information, such as aggressive sex acts, violence, threats, or other considerations not included in the form. The Warden or his designee may also enter an exception to a recommended reduction of custody, in which case he would prepare a memo outlining his objections.

The methods just described are now in use throughout the Federal prison system. They represent a rather sophisticated attempt to deal with prisoner security issues through improved classification. Initial results were reported

Exhibit 10

CUSTODY — CLASSIFICATION											

1. INSTITUTION — INSTITUTION / CODE — **2. UNIT** — **3. DATE** MONTH-DAY-YEAR — — —

4. NAME — LAST / FIRST / INITIAL — **5. REGISTER NUMBER** —

6. SENTENCE LIMITATIONS — 0=NONE / 1=MISDEMEANOR / 2=FJDA / 3=YCA / 4=STUDY / 5=SPLIT SENTENCE / 6=NARA

7. ADDITIONAL CONSIDERATIONS — 0=NONE / 1=MEDICAL / 2=PSYCHIATRIC / 3=AGGRESSIVE SEXUAL BEHAVIOR / 4=THREATS TO GOVERNMENT OFFICIAL

SECTION A — SECURITY SCORING

1. TYPE OF DETAINER — 0=NONE / 1=LOWEST/LOW MODERATE / 3=MODERATE / 5=HIGH / 7=GREATEST

2. SEVERITY OF CURRENT OFFENSE — 0=LOWEST / 1=LOW MODERATE / 3=MODERATE / 5=HIGH / 7=GREATEST

3. PROJECTED LENGTH OF INCARCERATION — 0=0 — 12 MONTHS / 1=13 — 59 MONTHS / 3=60 — 83 MONTHS / 5=84 PLUS MONTHS

4. TYPE OF PRIOR COMMITMENTS — 0=NONE / 1=MINOR / 3=SERIOUS

5. HISTORY OF ESCAPES OR ATTEMPTS — 0=NONE / 1=PAST MINOR / 3=RECENT MINOR / 5=PAST SERIOUS / 7=RECENT SERIOUS

6. HISTORY OF VIOLENCE — 0=NONE / 1=PAST MINOR / 3=RECENT MINOR / 5=PAST SERIOUS / 7=RECENT SERIOUS

7. SUB-TOTAL — TOTAL OF ITEMS 1 THROUGH 6

8. PRE-COMMITMENT STATUS — 0=NOT APPLICABLE / 3=OWN RECOGNIZANCE / 6=SELF-COMMITMENT (VOLUNTARY SURRENDER)

9. SECURITY TOTAL — SUBTRACT ITEM 8 FROM ITEM 7; IF ITEM 8 IS GREATER THAN ITEM 7, ENTER 0.

10. SECURITY LEVEL — 1=0 — 6 POINTS / 2=7 — 9 POINTS / 3=10 — 13 POINTS / 4=14 — 22 POINTS / 5=23 — 29 POINTS / 6=30 — 36 POINTS

SECTION B — CUSTODY SCORING   * WITHIN PAST YEAR

1. PERCENTAGE OF TIME SERVED — 3= 0 THRU 25% / 4=26 THRU 75% / 5=76 THRU 90% / 6=91 PLUS %

2. INVOLVEMENT WITH DRUGS AND ALCOHOL — 2=CURRENT / 3=PAST / 4=NEVER

3. MENTAL/PSYCHOLOGICAL STABILITY* — 2=UNFAVORABLE / 4=NO REFERRAL OR FAVORABLE

4. TYPE OF MOST SERIOUS DISCIPLINARY REPORT* — 1=GREATEST / 2=HIGH / 3=MODERATE / 4=LOW MODERATE / 5=NONE

5. FREQUENCY OF DISCIPLINARY REPORTS* — 0=10 PLUS / 1= 6 THRU 9 / 2=2 THRU 5 / 3=0 THRU 1

6. RESPONSIBILITY INMATE HAS DEMONSTRATED — 2=POOR / 3=AVERAGE / 4=GOOD

7. FAMILY/COMMUNITY TIES — 3=NONE OR MINIMAL / 4=AVERAGE OR GOOD

8. IF ELIGIBLE FOR SECURITY LEVEL 1, ARE MEDICAL AND DENTAL RECORDS CLEAR? — Y=YES / N=NO   **9. CUSTODY TOTAL**

10. PRESENT SECURITY LEVEL	CONSIDER FOR CUSTODY INCREASE IF POINT RANGE	CONTINUE PRESENT CUSTODY IF POINT RANGE	CONSIDER FOR CUSTODY DECREASE IF POINT RANGE	PRESENT SECURITY LEVEL	CONSIDER FOR CUSTODY INCREASE IF POINT RANGE	CONTINUE PRESENT CUSTODY IF POINT RANGE	CONSIDER FOR CUSTODY DECREASE IF POINT RANGE
s — 1				s — 4	13 — 19	20 — 26	27 — 30
s — 2	13 — 19	20 — 22	23 — 30	s — 5	13 — 19	20 — 27	28 — 30
s — 3	13 — 19	20 — 23	24 — 30	s — 6	13 — 19	20 — 27	28 — 30
	13 — 19	20 — 24	25 — 30				

SECTION C — INSTITUTION ACTION

1. TYPE OF REVIEW — E=EXCEPTION / R=REGULAR — **2. CURRENT CUSTODY** M=MAX O=OUT I=IN C=COMMUNITY — **3. NEW CUSTODY** M=MAX O=OUT I=IN C=COMMUNITY

4. DATE OF NEXT REVIEW MONTH-DAY-YEAR — — — **6. ACTION** APPROVE / DISAPPROVE

5. CHAIRPERSON — A. NAME (CHAIRPERSON) — **7. WARDEN OR DESIGNEE** NECESSARY ONLY FOR EXCEPTION REVIEW CASES / A. NAME (WARDEN OR DESIGNEE)

B. SIGNATURE (CHAIRPERSON) — 8. SIGNATURE (WARDEN OR DESIGNEE)

U. S. DEPARTMENT OF JUSTICE
FEDERAL PRISON SYSTEM   BP-15 (MANUAL) OCTOBER 1978

to be "encouraging." Such formal efforts to make explicit the criteria for security decisions may be important to the individual offender in promoting a sense of fairness and predictability to his tenure in correctional institutions, and reducing the number of arbitrary and capricious decisions. More importantly, gains in efficiency of the overall system are possible, unnecessary transfers between prisons can be reduced, and a "model" offered to state corrections systems.

The Institutional Classification Process

The three major goals of institutional classification can be delineated as follows:

Security and Custody. A primary goal of classification is to prescribe the degree of physical security believed to be necessary to prevent escape, and to maintain order within the institution. Unless administrative considerations are involved, the inmate is assigned to the least degree of security believed to be required for carrying out his/her sentence.

Program Assignment. An attempt is made to match the inmate with the institutional programs of education, vocational training, or job assignments believed to be most compatible with his needs.

Treatment. Where a need for medical or dental treatment, for individual or group counseling, or for drug or alcoholism treatment has been identified, the inmate is assigned to an institution where such services are available.

As can be seen, the task of classification necessitates a balancing of these three needs, since a full range of services is not usually available at each institution in the network of institutions within a state or Federal jurisdiction.

The classification process, as described here (Department of Corrections, State of Ohio), is fairly typical of most state systems. Classification proceeds in four stages:

1. Following sentencing in court, the inmate is conveyed to a central reception and diagnostic facility for a period of 6-8 weeks, with a temporary assignment of maximum security. At this facility, the inmate undergoes a period of orientation and adjustment to incarceration under the observation of the staff. A battery of personality, vocational, and educational tests is administered by psychologists, a social and work history is obtained by the social service staff, and a medical/dental examination is conducted. When available, the pre-sentence investigation is the floor of data from which further recommendations for institutionalization can be made. A classification committee made up of specialists from each of the disciplines involved holds a conference in which the inmate usually participates. Recommendations by the sentencing judge are sometimes included in this initial process, which results in the assignment of the inmate to the most appropriate correctional institution.

2. Accompanied by the findings from the reception and diagnostic center, the inmate arrives at the designated institution for a one-week period of orientation. The institutional classification committee interviews the inmate, reviews the work of the reception and diagnostic center, and may modify or reaffirm the program recommended, subject to approval by the superintendent of that institution, and final approval of classification by a central bureau of classification of the state. The work sheet used by the classification committee for summarizing the status of the inmate is shown as Exhibit 11 (Lebanon Correctional Institution, State of Ohio).

3. After a period of about six weeks, a conference of the classification committee of that institution is held to determine final classification, based upon progress reports.

4. Periodic reviews of classification are conducted by the classification committee as needed, but at least annually, to determine whether custody status should be increased or reduced, whether program changes are indicated (based upon progress reports), and whether any treatment programs should be initiated. Re-classification planning may include initial planning for release or parole, and consideration of family furloughs, halfway house placement, educational release, or work release programs as indicated.

Exhibit 11

INITIAL CLASSIFICATION AND RECLASSIFICATION WORK SHEET

NAME   DATE ASSIGNED

ALIAS   NUMBER

OFFENSE   RACE

SENTENCE   PAROLE BOARD DATE

OSR DATE   LeCI DATE

MEDICAL STATUS:

SOCIAL SERVICES:

PSYCHOLOGICAL SERVICES

EDUCATIONAL SERVICES

READING SCORE   OVERALL SCORE   HIGHEST GRADE COMPLETED

VOCATIONAL SERVICES   PRIOR TRAINING

JOB SKILLS:

CUSTODY COMMENTS:

SECURITY CLASSIFICATION: MIN._____   MED._____   MAX._____

JOB CLASSIFICATION:

cc: TRANSFER OFFICE   (White)
     RECORD OFFICE   (Green)
     ASSOC. SUPT. CUSTODY   (Pink)   _____
     SOCIAL SERVICES   (Canary)   Classification Committee
     PSYCHOLOGICAL SERVICES   (Blue)

Any inmate who believes himself to be adversely affected by a classification committee decision has a right to appeal such decisions in writing within five days to a central bureau of classification which reviews the decision. In general, the inmate is expected to take the initiative in participating in planning, particularly as he reaches minimum levels of custody and approaches a release date.

Institutional Programs

In order to proceed with sensible recommendations for an offender, the classification officer needs a detailed knowledge of the workings of the full range of program opportunities available to offenders within each institution, and some acquaintance with the personnel operating special programs. This Casebook can supply only a general knowledge of typical programs behind the walls. Such programs have their counterparts in the community, but within the institutions are geared toward the special needs of the offender under the constraints imposed by custody requirements. However, many institutional programs attempt to meet the same standards of equipment and personnel as their counterparts in the community, and some are actually operated in conjunction with community programs; for example, most prison schools are licensed and issue diplomas on the same basis as "outside" educational institutions. The extension of community organizations into the prisons is a tremendous aid in reintegrating offenders back into their communities. Typical institutional programs are as follows:

Education. The great majority of offenders are characterized by school rejection and low levels of educational achievement. Therefore, most modern institutions place a heavy emphasis upon remedial education. Basic reading, writing, and mathematics skills are provided in small classroom groups, with tutoring and other special aids as needed. In addition to high school equivalency diplomas by examination, college-level coursework and degrees through extension courses is becoming common.

Vocational Training. A low level of work skills and work discipline is characteristic of a large proportion of offenders. The teaching of trade skills is common in prisons, and shops may include carpentry, masonry, electrical work, plumbing, computer programming, clerical skills, printing, light manufacturing, farming, welding, weaving, or other skills-building programs. A chronic difficulty has been work activities conducted for the convenience (and profit) of the institution v. vocational training for use outside in the community; the gains in skill made by inmates may be lost if not translated into gainful skilled employment in the community after release.

Social Services. Caseworkers perform many personal services in making referrals to institutional programs, maintaining family and agency ties with the community, and preparing the inmate for reintegration back into the community. Along with psychologists, caseworkers often conduct crisis intervention counseling and adjustment, group counseling, and other personal development programs.

Treatment Services. The "right to treatment" has become the focus of many legal suits initiated by inmates in recent years (as well as the right to refrain from treatment). Courts have held that if specialized treatment is implied as the justification for incarceration, and the institution provides only custodial management, then the offender is improperly detained. To the extent that chronic maladjustment, social incompetence, drug or alcohol addiction, or sexual problems, etc., have contributed to the criminal behavior of offenders, the controlled setting of the institution may provide the opportunity for voluntary participation in remedial therapeutic or resocialization programming. Caseworkers, psychologists, and psychiatrists (or lay counselors in some cases) participate in a variety of therapeutic measures, from individual psychotherapy or group counseling to a therapeutic community.

Religious Services. Religious instruction, moral counseling, and organized religious services are almost universally provided in correctional institutions through chaplains and outside clergymen. In addition to providing a degree of comfort and reassurance for some lonely offenders, clergymen provide a link to the "normal" outside community, and a humanizing influence on prison life.

The above categorization is meant only as a curtain-raiser on the numerous activities that have been organized in various institutions, which may include prisoner self-help organizations, black culture groups, self-governance attempts, musical groups, recreational teams, and arrangements for conjugal visits.

PRACTICE CASE 19

Instructions: Assume that you are a classification officer in a reception and diagnostic facility. Your responsibility is to write the recommendations on an offender about to be assigned to an institution. Your basic responsibilities, as head of the classification team, is to decide level of security (maximum, medium, or minimum), types of institutional programs (as described), and treatment plan (as you see fit). Assume you have a wide variety of options, so that you can recommend an "ideal" institutional program for this offender. Answer the questions following the case, but do not read the commentary by the classification officer until you have written your recommendations to the assigned institution. Use both the data from your team members and the PSI.

Reception and Diagnostic Center
Summary

Name of case: Seymour Hennessey   **Date of Report:** 7/2/78

Alias: None   **Age:** 21

Offense: Burglary   **Race:** White

Sentence: 2 - 15 years   **Parole Board Date:** 7/1/79

MEDICAL REPORT: This is a well-nourished 21-year-old with no medical abnormalities noted. He stands 5'7", weighs 150 pounds. Usual childhood diseases, no sequelae. Denies VD. Chronic drug-abuser, including marijuana, alcohol, glue-sniffing, amphetamines. No needle marks or tattoos.

SOCIAL SERVICES REPORT: Expects family to visit. Claims to be single with no children. Many casual sexual contacts, but no abnormalities. Reared in lower-class rural family in Missouri, both parents weak disciplinarians and alcoholics, father died when he was 16 years of age, 4th of five children. Family moved to Mishawaka, Ohio when offender was 10 years of age, often on Welfare. No military history. This information by interview with offender, not verified except by PSI.

PSYCHOLOGICAL REPORT: Revised Beta IQ test, score of 93. Results of Wechsler Adult Intelligence Scale taken in 1974 reported to be 88. This subject is functioning in the low average range of intelligence. MMPI test indicates potential for acting out, high impulsivity, some depression, and high level of defensiveness. He scores on a reading test at the 5.7 grade level, arithmetic score at 4.3 grade level, overall achievement score 5.1 grade level, he is considered educationally retarded. Previous scores from PSI similar. During interview, he showed low drive and motivation level, denied previous counseling or any interest in treatment whatsoever.

EDUCATIONAL SERVICES REPORT: Client is far below educational level indicated by intelligence tests, he dropped out of school during the 9th grade, repeated two grades, and experienced school failure due to lack of application. He states that he did not like school, and did not show much interest following orientation to our program.

VOCATIONAL SERVICES: At the time of the current offense, offender was employed at the Good Times Cafe in Mishawaka for four months as a dishwasher, earning $2.65 per hour. During the past five years, he reports only part-time occasional work as a restaurant helper. While incarcerated in the Fontana Boy's Center, he claims to have completed a machinist course. I was unable to make a recommendation, since this young man demonstrates few work skills and no work discipline.

CUSTODY REPORT: I noted that Hennessey has been charged with crimes on 30 previous occasions, mostly related to theft of property. His juvenile record includes two escapes from custody, four probation violations, and the possession of dangerous drugs.

RECOMMENDATIONS: (deleted)

_____
Chairman, Classification Committee

*   *   *   *

Court of Common Pleas
Department of Probation
Hammond County

Pre-sentence Investigation Report

Name: Seymour Hennessey	**Judge:** Wickett
Alias: None	**Date of Report:** 5/15/78
Address: 215 Homestead Ave.	**Docket No.:** AF 20945
Mishawaka, Ohio	**Offense:** Burglary
Age: 21	**Penalty:** 1-15 years
Race: Caucasian	**Plea:** Guilty
Co-defendants: James Hargett	**Custody:** Bond
enrolled 4/30/78 Jail time credit — 62 days served	**Prosecutor:** Ronald Gray
	Defense Counsel: Public Defender

CURRENT OFFENSE: *Official Version* — On 2/25/78, around 8 A.M. the apartment of Sherry Doggett was broken into at 342 S. Main St., Mishawaka. Two store-keepers observed the defendant carrying property to an auto parked outside the apartment at that address. They asked the defendant if the property belonged to him, and he responded that it did. Police were summoned, and the car sped away, leaving the defendant standing outside on the street. Investigation by police showed that property belonging to Ms. Doggett was found in his possession, and he was identified by the two witnesses as the person who was observed removing said property from the apartment. Recovered was a leather coat, a color TV, several rings, a watch, and a tape recorder, valued at $850. Later the auto was identified through its license number, and co-defendant James Hargett was also arrested. The defendant entered a plea of guilty to burglary on advice of counsel, and was released on bond supplied by his mother. Co-defendant Hargett was nolled at the request of the prosecutor.

Victim's Statement: Ms. Sherry Doggett stated that she had met the defendant at a bar a few months prior to the burglary, and that he had stayed at her apartment a few times. She stated that she told the defendant not to come to her apartment anymore, but that he continued to do so, bringing in other men, and that he tried to force his way into her apartment. She told him several times not to return. Her $850 loss is not covered by insurance, and she requested restitution. She stated that she has no feelings about the sentence, and would leave sentencing to the court.

Defendant's Version: Defendant stated that he had been drinking all day with the co-defendant in a bar, and that the couple decided to go around to the victim's apartment "to get some dope from her." Finding Ms. Doggett not at home, they decided to break in to help themselves. They were unable to find any "dope," so they decided to steal her belongings. The defendant admits he was quite intoxicated when he committed the offense. He claims he wants to quit breaking the law because "I'm tired of going to jail. I just can't beat it." He added in a written statement: "I'm sorry I broke into this lady's house now. I had been drinking all day and didn't know what I was doing. I'm trying to get into the AA now."

PRIOR RECORD: Starting at age 10, defendant was arrested 22 times before he reached the age of 18 for offenses which started with truanting from home and school (2 times) and curfew violations (3 times) to malicious destruction of property, incorrigibility (4 times), and violation of probation (4 times). In addition, he was convicted of burglary, receiving stolen property (3 times), endangering morals (2 times, which involved glue-sniffing), and escape from custody (2 times). He has been repeatedly released to the care of his mother, who apparently was unable to control her son. He was committed to Loyalty House, a drug treatment center, but went AWOL and did not return. He was committed to Fontana Boy's Center, and was finally committed permanently to the Ohio Youth Commission, from which he was released at age 18. He has been institutionalized for approximately 4 years as a juvenile.

As an adult, he has been fined costs of court three times for disorderly conduct, had two possession of dangerous drugs charges dismissed, received a 6-month jail term for receiving stolen property (on two occasions), and had a burglary and grand theft dismissed for lack of evidence. The defendant and his brother, Sigmund, were found to have stolen firearms in their possession consisting of 9 shotguns, a .357 magnum revolver, a rifle, and two pistols stolen from the home of a local physician, resulting in the receiving stolen property charges mentioned. Thus, the defendant shows a recent trend toward possible use of firearms in his behavior. In the past three years, he was arrested 8 times as an adult.

SOCIAL SUMMARY: This defendant was born in Mingo Junction, Missouri, was the fourth of five children born to Rudolph and Ruby (Jones) Hennessey. The father was employed irregularly as a farmer's helper and laborer, and migrated to Mishawaka, Ohio when the defendant was 10 years of age to obtain employment as a janitor in a local dry goods store. However, both he and the mother continued to drink heavily, and Mr. Hennessey died when the defendant was 16 years of age. The family is known to the Hammond County Welfare Department and the Juvenile Court. The defendant lives with his mother, older brother and 3 sisters above the Good Times Cafe in that community in a rather run-down apartment and neighborhood.

An evaluation conducted by the Social Services Department of Juvenile Court in 1973 characterized the defendant as "immature, easily led, with delinquent associations, having a low level of aspirations, and involved with heavy drug usage." A psychological report from the Fontana Boy's Center during that same period showed Seymour to be "remarkably flat. He is not disturbed by his prior behavior, his present situation, or his future possibilities. There are no signs of guilt with respect to his misbehavior, and he shows clear signs of potential for manipulation." Other evaluations performed by the Ohio Youth Commission differ little from this account.

He reported that he has completed the 9th grade, but his school records indicate that he dropped out soon after completing the 8th grade. He had numerous absences, disciplinary reports, and was placed on probation 7 times for misbehavior. The Wechsler Adult Intelligence Scale, taken in 1974, report him to be functioning in the "dull normal" range with a Full-Scale IQ of 88. The Wide Range Achievement Test showed a reading level of 5.2 grades and an arithmetic grade level of 4.0.

The defendant rates his health as excellent, and states he has no physical problems. He admits he started using drugs at age 9. He insists that he has never been addicted to drugs, although he has experimented with several. These assertions are in conflict with Juvenile Court reports. He failed to complete his stay in the Loyalty House drug center program, which considered him to be drug-dependent with heavy usage of amphetamines, glue-sniffing, and alcohol. No military service was claimed. He lists no financial assets or liabilities.

EMPLOYMENT HISTORY:

10/2/77 to present: Defendant has been employed as a dishwasher at the Good Times Cafe in Mishawaka for $2.65 per hour. His employer reports that his work is acceptable, but that his absences are sometimes excessive, so that his mother must occasionally "fill in" for him.

No other full-time employment was claimed, although the defendant says that he has no difficulty in obtaining part-time work at Kentucky Fried Chicken, Pizza Hut, and other local restaurants as a bus-boy. He also stated that he was about to start work with a construction firm (J. P. Donnelly Construction Company) when he was arrested. This claim could not be verified.

Discussion Questions

1. How would you characterize the nature of Hennessey's crimes? Does he plan his criminal operations well, and carry out his crimes efficiently? Can you describe any trends in his criminal career?

2. Does this man's abuse of alcohol and other drugs contribute to his criminality? If his use of drugs were controlled, what would be the likely impact upon his criminal behavior?

3. What were your conclusions regarding the long-range effect of remedial education on this offender?

4. Is Hennessey a candidate for vocational training, and what goals would you set for such training?

Commentary by Jay Chidlaw, Head of Classification at _____ Correctional Institution Regarding the Seymour Hennessey Case:

"Yes, I know Si Hennessey. In fact, we are getting our reports together now for his first hearing before the Parole Board. I have one of our social workers who is working on a plan to parole him to a halfway house for drug offenders, and unless he screws up here, I think he's got a fair chance to make parole. We've interviewed Si's mother, and we don't think he ought to go back into that home, or even into Mishawaka at all. The mother is kind of overwhelmed trying to cope with him and four other kids, and we think Si needs a whole new life for himself, so we're talking about trying to find him a job in _____, so that he can live at the drug center.

"Si is the kind of kid that needs a lot of structure to survive. He's never been able to plan. 'Snatch and grab' was about all he ever learned, and whenever he's drunk or high, and that's most of the time, he usually gets caught. You know, when he got here from the Reception Center, he was kind of pitiful . . . this is the first time he ever got a long sentence in a big joint like _____, and he didn't show much interest in anything, so we put him on a work detail mopping floors. We heard that he spent most of his time standing around asking about drugs, but he really didn't cause any problems. That stuff in his record about escapes was more of a walkaway from some of those juvenile institutions. That doesn't happen here, not with him on medium security status.

"Well, anyway, after Hennessey stood around with his mop bucket for a few months, he asked one of the guards one day how he could get into that shop work he had heard about, and the guard put him in touch with our Vocational Training section. He ended up in the machine shop, where our instructor pointed out to Hennessey that he needed to know how to read blueprints, measure things, and stuff like that. Hennessey was placed in a remedial class and did pretty well . . . I suppose because school finally made some sense to him. He's working on a GED, and spends part of the day in our machine shop learning a trade.

"The way he's coming along, he should be ready for a machinst's job outside by the time he makes parole . . . like I said, if he doesn't screw up again."

Supplementary Reading

Hippchen, Leonard J. (Ed.) *Handbook on Correctional Classification*. Cincinnati, Ohio: Anderson Publishing Company, 1978. This extremely useful Handbook was prepared by the Committee on Classification and Treatment of The American Correctional Association. Especially noteworthy is the down-to-earth description of the process of classification by Alfred C. Schnur and the discussion of the goals of classification by Thomas G. Eynon.

Levinson, Robert B. & Williams, J.D. Inmate classification: Security/custody considerations. *Federal Probation, 43,* March 1979, 37-43.

Morris, Norval. *The Future of Imprisonment.* Chicago: The University of Chicago Press, 1974.

Chapter 18
Parole Planning and Aftercare

"Statistical predictions can be helpful in giving guidelines to parole board members as to general categories into which particular inmates fit. . . . But most experts are convinced that the optimum system is one in which both statistical and individual case methods are used in making decisions about individuals."

National Advisory Commission on
Criminal Justice Standards and Goals

Aftercare parole programs for offenders returning to their communities from correctional institutions have existed in every state of the United States since 1930. Within recent decades, the number and variety of private and public aftercare programs have proliferated, such as halfway houses, reintegration centers, prisoner self-aid programs, and the like. The old stereotyped image of the ex-prisoner arriving home in a cheap prison-made suit with $10 in his pockets and a pale prison pallor is rarely seen today. The vast majority of prisoners return home under a graduated release which is pre-planned and approved by parole authorities, who retain supervision of the offender for specified periods of time.

Mandatory Release

Mandatory release occurs when the offender's sentence has been served, minus whatever "good time" has been earned in the institutions. (For some exotic reason, "maxing out" upon expiration of sentence is often termed "conditional" release.) However, a few states, including New York and Florida, still require that all offenders who are conditionally released must remain under supervision of parole officers.

Early Release

Some prisoners qualify for early release prior to the expiration of sentences. Depending upon the jurisdiction, various options include family furlough, work release, educational release, medical release, or release into reintegration centers or halfway houses. Frequently, such releases occur within 30 to 90 days of an approved parole date, so that the offender has a tightly supervised transitional experience in the community prior to parole. During this transitional period, the offender is technically considered to be still serving his sentence, so that violations of this limited freedom can quickly result in the offender being returned to a secure institution, normally without any hearing. Early release provides a period of acquaintanceship with the parole officer, and a period of time to become stabilized in the community again, before the formal period of parole supervision.

Parole

Most prisoners move directly from the institutions into the community with a fixed term of supervision by parole officers, in accordance with a parole plan worked out within the institution with the aid of institutional parole officers (case managers or other titles may be in use at some institutions), and approved by a board of parole. Thus, in practice, it is the parole board that determines the length of time actually served by an offender, within the limits prescribed by the sentencing judge. Except for original sentencing, the parole boards control the most important decision point in the corrections system.

The discretion exercised by parole boards and the methods used in determining parole have come under considerable criticism in recent years, with some advocates calling for abolition of parole in favor of fixed terms of sentence. Certainly the problems faced by parole boards in developing a rational program of early release are formidable. First, there appears to be little relationship between the length of time served in a prison and subsequent criminality (recidivism). A study by Beck and Hoffman (1976) of 1546 adult male Federal prisoners whose post-institutional criminal behavior was monitored for two years after release concluded that, after background factors were equalized *(Salient Factor Scores),* the length of incarceration had an insignificant effect upon later criminality or rehabilitation. Of course, imprisoned offenders were incapacitated for offenses in the community while in custody, but long-term effects on recidivism appeared to be minimal.

A perennial issue in parole decisions is *equity;* offenders in custody are very concerned that, in the interests of justice, fairness should exist. This means that the criteria for parole decisions from person to person should be comparable, and should be explicit, so that comparisons between offenders can be made. Equity is a statistical concept, implying some sort of measurement criteria; therefore, "actuarial" decisions of some type are required to promote equity (this familiar issue was reviewed in Chapter One). In practice, statistical tables of parole experience have never been popular with parole boards, although they originated almost 50 years ago.

Very few offenders regard themselves as typical, as just one of the masses. Concomitantly, most offenders are inclined to think of themselves as an exception to the "percentages" and therefore as deserving more than "computer justice." Likewise, the parole board decision-maker tends to believe that human judgment, with all of its fallibility, is somehow superior to formula answers. Thus, the demand for equity tends to generate its own antithesis in practice since each prisoner tends to regard himself as an exception to any uniform guidelines. Still, the demand for a structured and explicit set of guidelines has persisted, and holds the promise of more predictable parole decisions.

A very promising system for improvement of parole decisions is now in use with the United States Parole Commission as a result of the pioneering research of Gottfredson *et al.* (1975). Rather than attempting to deal with parole *outcomes,* parole board members were asked to specify the criteria upon which their *decisions* were made, finally resulting in an 11-item *Salient Factor Score* believed to predict parole success or failure which was validated against a sample of parolees (See Exhibit 12). Based upon the Salient Factor Scores, prospective parolees were then classified "Very High," "High," "Fair," and "Low" in terms of parole prognosis. The various offenses for which inmates were serving time were then classified into six levels of severity, and median length of actual sentences served for each type of offense computed.

Exhibit 12

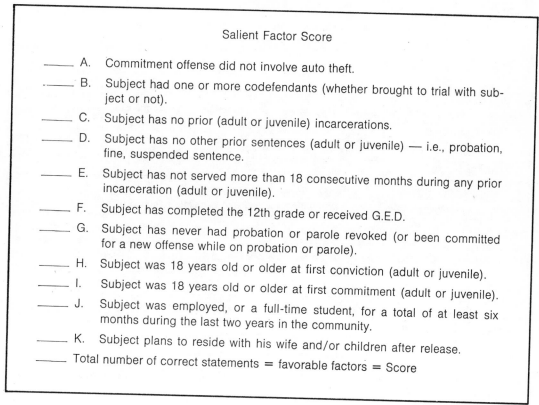

Salient Factor Score

_____ A.   Commitment offense did not involve auto theft.

_____ B.   Subject had one or more codefendants (whether brought to trial with subject or not).

_____ C.   Subject has no prior (adult or juvenile) incarcerations.

_____ D.   Subject has no other prior sentences (adult or juvenile) — i.e., probation, fine, suspended sentence.

_____ E.   Subject has not served more than 18 consecutive months during any prior incarceration (adult or juvenile).

_____ F.   Subject has completed the 12th grade or received G.E.D.

_____ G.   Subject has never had probation or parole revoked (or been committed for a new offense while on probation or parole).

_____ H.   Subject was 18 years old or older at first conviction (adult or juvenile).

_____ I.   Subject was 18 years old or older at first commitment (adult or juvenile).

_____ J.   Subject was employed, or a full-time student, for a total of at least six months during the last two years in the community.

_____ K.   Subject plans to reside with his wife and/or children after release.

_____ Total number of correct statements = favorable factors = Score

For example, minor thefts or violations of alcohol laws were rated as "low severity," with sentences ranging from 6-16 months; armed robbery or a sexual act using force and producing injury was rated "very high severity," with sentences ranging from 16-38 months.

A two-way grid was then constructed in which the severity of offense was measured against the parole prognosis from Salient Factor Score and ranges of time to be served established for each cell (See Exhibit 13). This grid became the guidelines within which parole decisions were made. Thus, a person sentenced for sale of marijuana ("moderate severity" offense) who was rated 10 on the Salient Factor Score ("Very High") might expect to serve 12-16 months before parole, using the table of guidelines. Provisions were made by the U.S. Parole Commission for what was termed a "clinical override," in which the sentence to be served before parole was either reduced or increased outside the guidelines to allow for poor institutional conduct, aggravating or mitigating offense factors, or other aspects of clinical judgment. All cases decided outside the guidelines must be justified in writing, with a copy to the offender. In practice, about 20% of cases appear to deviate from the guidelines.

The practical significance of the U.S. Parole Commission system is that parole decisions become more predictable, and that the criteria used in decision making become more visible. Parole decisions can be established early in the institutionalization process by use of the guidelines. However, it can be seen that the length of sentence is virtually determined by the Parole Commission, which restricts the sentencing options of Federal judges, although administrative procedures are established to negotiate this issue.

Certain advantages are claimed in those jurisdictions which have adopted

Exhibit 13

Average Total Time (Including Jail Time) to be Served Before Release
U. S. Parole Commission, Guidelines for Decision Making

Offense Categories*	Salient Factor Score (Probability of Favorable Parole Outcome)			
	9-11 (Very High) 6-10 months	6-8 (High) 8-12 months	4-5 (Fair) 10-14 months	0-3 (Low) 12-16 months
A. Low Severitya				
B. Low/Moderate Severityb	8-12 ''	12-16 ''	16-20 ''	20-25 ''
C. Moderate Severityc	12-16 ''	16-20 ''	20-24 ''	24-30 ''
D. High Severityd	16-20 ''	20-26 ''	26-32 ''	32-38 ''
E. Very High Severitye	26-36 ''	36-45 ''	45-55 ''	55-65 ''
F. Highest Severityf	Information not available because of limited number of cases			

*NOTES: (1) If an offense can be classified in more than one category, the most serious applicable category is to be used. If an offense involved two or more separate offenses, the severity level may be increased. (2) If an offense is not listed above, the proper category may be obtained by comparing the offense with similar offenses listed. (3) If a continuance is to be recommended, subtract one month to allow for provision of release program.

a. Minor theft; walkaway (escape without use of force); immigration law; alcohol law.

b. Possess marijuana; possess heavy narcotics, less than $50; theft, unplanned; forgery or counterfeiting, less than $50; burglary, daytime.

c. Vehicle theft; forgery or counterfeiting, more than $500; sale of marijuana; planned theft; possess heavy narcotics, more than $50; escape; Mann Act, no force; Selective Service.

d. Sell heavy narcotics; burglary, weapon or nighttime; violence, "spur of the moment;" sexual act, force.

e. Armed robbery; criminal act, weapon; sexual act, force and injury; assault, serious bodily harm; Mann Act, force.

f. Willful homicide; kidnapping; armed robbery, weapon fired or serious injury.

the strategy of setting a presumptive parole date in the early stages of incarceration. Such parole boards believe that by reducing the uncertainty in length of sentence to be served inmate anxiety can be lessened, institutional programs can be planned more rationally, and that "game-playing" with the parole boards can be reduced. Correctional administrators, on the other hand, are often inclined to believe that presumptive parole dates are capable of limiting the amount of leverage over control of inmate behavior unless the release dates are made contingent upon good behavior. In other words, many administrators feel that a predetermined parole date jeopardizes the offender's motivation to perform well in prison programs.

The issue of motivating prisoners to greater efforts toward completing institutional programs has recently been addressed creatively by the Minnesota Corrections Board (Parent and Mulcrone, 1978, reported in *Classification for Parole Decision Policy*). Having set an "upper limit" maximum parole date soon after incarceration, the Corrections Board invites selected inmates to sign a contract for a "lower limit" minimum parole date by completing educational, vocational, or work programs in their respective institutions. This legally binding contract for a *Mutual Assistance Program* (MAP) is signed by the inmate, the institution, and the Corrections Board, specifying mutual responsibilities to be completed. Average reduction of sentence through MAP contracts is 6-10 months. However, the MAP program is not available to certain categories of offenders sentenced for aggravated offenses.

Pre-Parole Planning

In preparation for parole board hearings, a comprehensive file of evaluative reports are assembled for consideration by parole board examiners. An institutional parole officer (or the equivalent, depending upon jurisdiction) assembles these reports, working with the offender on a practical release plan. While considerable variation exists in various state corrections systems, typical reports compiled by the institutional parole officer might include the following:

Presentence Investigation Report (if available)
FBI and other conviction records, including dispositions
Previous reviews on probation and parole supervision, including violations (if applicable)
Institutional reports, including disciplinary reports, work reports, education reports, counseling and guidance reports, and other relevant institutional reports (See Exhibits 14 & 15 for examples, Adult Parole Authority, State of Ohio)
Reception and Diagnostic Center report, or equivalent
Parole prognosis ratings (if actuarial tables are used)
Medical/psychiatric evaluations (if applicable)
Previous parole board summaries (if applicable)
Field reports from parole officers in offender's target community, including employment, home, family, treatment, or halfway house commitments to offender (procedures may vary in some jurisdictions)

The institutional parole officer, having gathered the required information and interviewed the offender and relatives, integrates such information into a parole plan on the forms prescribed by the parole board. Two typical parole planning forms are shown as Exhibits 16 and 17 (Adult Parole Authority, State of Ohio and Division of Corrections, State of Wisconsin respectively).

The advisory function to the boards of parole by institutional parole officers (IPO) is very similar to the functions served by the probation officers in consulting with sentencing judges. In fact, the information base used by both types of officers is the same, except that the IPO is expected to be familiar with the progress of the offender during incarceration, and to use such information in making recommendations. Both the probation officer and the IPO are concerned with the same set of issues; i.e., to balance the safety of the community against the needs of the offender, and to make predictions about the future behavior of offenders under various alternative supervisory plans to be implemented in the community.

As discussed earlier, the parole officer is guided in his assessment of offenders by the same standards of accuracy and thoroughness as probation officers. A prevalent problem with officers based in correctional institutions is to become familiar with facilities for supervision and treatment in specific communities. This is the obverse of the difficulties experienced by probation officers in maintaining familiarity with prison programs (not to mention sentencing judges!). To successfully master the transition back to the community, the offender needs the wisdom of parole officers familiar with helping programs in his home community. Therefore, extensive liaison with community-based parole officers (and others) is essential in making field investigations of the offender's intended employment, family, home, and financial prospects.

A chronic deficiency observed in parole planning (which also exists in probation evaluations) is the scant attention paid to deeply ingrained personal problems which can continue to feed criminality. The crude, formalized programs and strategies which characterize most of the corrections system are often wide of the mark in addressing the pathological methods developed by offenders to satisfy their sexual and material needs. Thus, vocational train-.

Exhibit 14

F-251-A EVALUATION FOR _____

NAME: _____

NUMBER: _____

DEPARTMENT: _____

Type of work performed by resident: _____

_____

Circle Appropriate Number

1. Quality of Work (accuracy, neatness, thoroughness)

Inferior Work		Rather Careless		Meets Requirements		Highly Accurate		Exceptional	
0	1	2	3	4	5	6	7	8	9	10	11	12	13	14	15

2. Quantity of Work (volume, amount, speed)

Very Slow		Insufficient Work		Moderate		Rapid Worker		Highly Productive	
0	1	2	3	4	5	6	7	8	9	10	11	12	13	14	15

3. Knowledge of Work

Almost None		Limited		Adequate		Good Understanding		Excellent Comprehension	
0	1	2	3	4	5	6	7	8	9	10

4. Adaptability (adjustment to change, ability to learn)

Unable To Adapt		Slow in Learning		Satisfactory		Adapts Readily		Rapid Learner	
0	1	2	3	4	5	6	7	8	9	10

5. Dependability (reliability)

Needs Constant Supervision		Needs Frequent Checking		Usually Dependable		Seldom Needs Checking		Highly Reliable	
0	1	2	3	4	5	6	7	8	9	10

6. Cooperation (working with other residents)

Troublemaker		Has Difficulty		Generally Cooperative		Gets Along Well		Excellent Relations	
0	1	2	3	4	5	6	7	8	9	10

7. Judgment (ability to make decisions, plan work)

Disorganized Illogical		Limited Judgment		Plans Well		Logical Thinker		Creative	
0	1	2	3	4	5	6	7	8	9	10

8. Initiative (motivation, interest in work)

Lazy Indifferent		Needs Pushing		Adequate		Considerable		Highly Motivated	
0	1	2	3	4	5	6	7	8	9	10

9. Personality (courtesy, appearance)

Rude Slovenly		Indifferent		Adequate for Job		Polite Courteous		Exceptional	
0	1	2	3	4	5	6	7	8	9	10

Do you endorse this man? ☐ Yes. ☐ No. State why this man was endorsed or rejected.

Supervisor's Signature _____ Date _____

ing in welding in prison may be highly desirable to an offender interested in job skills, but if welding skills are later to be used in cracking safes, then that effort has been grossly distorted.

If prisons and parole are to correct, a more direct type of focussed intervention is going to become necessary in professional corrections. The "problems" of the individual offender should be described more fully both at the point of sentencing and in parole planning, and an effort made to evaluate

Exhibit 15

Form: 452-B, Revised

ACADEMIC AND VOCATIONAL SCHOOL EVALUATION for _____

INMATE'S NAME _____ NUMBER: _____

SCHOOL LEVEL OR COURSE: _____

1. To what extent is he interested in school work? _____
    _____
    _____

2. Is he working to capacity? _____
    _____
    _____

3. Does he volunteer or ask for extra work? _____
    _____
    _____

4. Is he benefitting from the school program? _____
    _____
    _____

5. To what extent does he participate in class discussion? _____
    _____
    _____

6. Does he cause disruptions in class? _____
    _____
    _____

7. Does he waste time? _____
    _____
    _____

8. What is your overall evaluation of this student? _____
    _____
    _____

TEACHER'S SIGNATURE: _____ DATE: _____

_____
_____

---

progress in resolving those problems. Without such an effort, offender assessment can become a sterile institutional exercise in fact-gathering. Some attempt to describe problems of an offender is seen in Items 5 and 6 of Exhibit 16; however, if a full-scale effort were mounted to deal with a proclivity for sexual assaultiveness, for example, more would be required than a simple check list of problems. A more detailed plan for treatment, re-socialization, behavior modification, and referral would indicate the primacy of that problem in the life of the offender, and the necessary conditions for its control.

Exhibit 16

```
..........................                              DATE ....................
TYPE OF REPORT

                              STATE OF OHIO
                         ADULT PAROLE AUTHORITY
                         1050 Freeway Drive North
                           Columbus, Ohio 43229

CLASSIFICATION ...........                    FOLLOW-UP ...............

Name ........................................ No. ............. Admitted ..............

Address ............................................................ Paroled ............

Crime & Sentence ........................... D.O.B. .............. SS No. .............
```

1. HOME & FAMILY: Single ( ), Married ( ), Divorced ( ), Separated ( ), Dependents ( ).

   Residing With .... Renting $......... R & B $........ Since ....

2. EDUCATION, EMPLOYMENT, FINANCES: Education ...... yrs. Voc. Tr. ...... yrs.
   Handicap Yes ( ), No ( ),

   Employed .... Support Yes ( ), No ( ), Amount $...........
   　　　　　　　(Date, Name, Address)

   Type of Work .... Hours .... Wages .... Debts ....

   Financial Assistance: AFD .... ADC .... ADCU .... Pension ....

3. SUPERVISION CONTACTS: ....
   ....
   ....

4. SPECIAL CONDITIONS OF PAROLE: Yes ( ), No ( ), Explain ....
   ....

5. PROBLEMS: Significant Arrest Record ( ), Immature, Impulsive ( ), Employment ( ), Physical Disability ( ), Sociopath ( ), Attitude ( ), Criminal Inclination ( ), Poor Relationships ( ), Associates ( ), Alcohol ( ), Narcotics ( ), Borderline IQ ( ), Emotional ( ), Assaultive ( ), Sexual ( ),
   Family ( ), Other (Explain) ....
   ....

6. CLIENT'S IMMEDIATE NEEDS: Employment ...... Housing ...... Medical ...... Psychiatric .....

   Relationships .... Adjustments .... Other (Explain) ....

   Action Taken By Parole Officer: Date ...... Job Dev. .... Agency Referral ....

   Employer/Agency .... Result ....

7. CASEWORK PLAN OR SUMMARY FOR F.R. ....
   ....
   ....
   ....
   ....
   ....

Parole Officer .... Supervisor .... Date ....

APA-SR-1 30 Pads 73-650 CCIP (D-243)

Parole Violations

Having agreed to conform to the conditions of parole, offenders, released conditionally by a parole board, return to their communities under the supervision of parole officers to carry out the authorized parole plan. Exhibit 18 illustrates a typical parole agreement used in the State of Ohio. Special conditions may be added to the basic parole agreement to cover treatment of drug or alcohol problems, family counseling, financial debts, operation of a

Exhibit 17

PAROLE PLANNING INFORMATION SHEET					
NAME		NO.	INST.	DIST./CODE	HEARING
DATE SENTENCED	DATE RECEIVED	TIME SERVED	M.R. DATE		MAX. DIS. DATE
			TO M.R.		TO MAXIMUM
			PREVIOUS ACTION		PAROLE ELIG. DATE
DETAINERS					
OFFENSE AND TERM					
☐ NOTICE OF PAROLE HEARING (C-1) PREPARED			☐ NOTICE OF PAROLE HEARING NOT REQ.		
☐ PRE-PAROLE REQ.	REASON FOR PRE-PAROLE				
PLACEMENT PLAN					
CITY	EMPLOYMENT				
RESIDENCE					
FINANCIAL — INCLUDING ASSETS AND LIABILITIES					
PHYSICAL LIMITATIONS					
MARITAL — INCLUDING DEPENDENTS AND OBLIGATIONS					
SUPPLEMENTAL INFORMATION OR ALTERNATE PLAN					
SOCIAL WORKER'S APPRAISAL OF PLAN					
PREPARED BY:			DATE		

motor vehicle, medical problems, or association with specific persons. A list of special conditions is seen in Exhibit 19.

In the event that the parole officer has reason to believe that the parolee has violated the conditions of parole, he may request that the offender be detained in custody for further investigation. Alleged violations may include failure to follow the instructions of the parole officer in obtaining employment or treatment, although the typical violation involves participation in new crimes. The officer may then request a hearing before the parole board for revocation of parole. If the revocation is upheld, the offender is subject to return to a correctional institution to serve the balance of his sentence, although continuation of parole may also be considered.

In order to protect the rights of the offender, revocation hearings have become increasingly formalized in most jurisdictions, permitting the parolee to be represented by counsel, disclosure of certain reports, and the right of appeal. The task of the parole officer is to summarize evidence of parole violations, to review progress of supervision/treatment, and to review the parole plan authorized by the parole board. In effect, a parole revocation hearing is somewhat similar to the original parole hearing, with the offender normally in custody during the investigation prior to the hearing.

Exhibit 18

STATE OF OHIO
Department of Rehabilitation and Correction
ADULT PAROLE AUTHORITY
STATEMENT OF PAROLE AGREEMENT

The Members of the Parole Board have agreed that you have earned the opportunity of parole and eventually a final release from your present conviction. The Parole Board is therefore ordering a Parole Release in your case.

Parole Status has a two-fold meaning: One is a trust status in which the Parole Board accepts your word you will do your best to abide by the Conditions of Parole that are set down in your case; the other, by Ohio law, means the Adult Parole Authority has the legal duty to enforce the Conditions of Parole even to the extent of arrest and return to the institution should that become necessary.

The following Conditions of Parole are in effect in your Parole Release:

1. Upon release from the institution, report as instructed to your Parole Officer (or any other person designated) and thereafter report as often as directed.

2. Secure written permission of the Adult Parole Authority before leaving the State of Ohio.

3. Obey all municipal ordinances, state and federal laws, and at all times conduct yourself as a responsible law-abiding citizen.

4. Never purchase, own, possess, use or have under your control, a deadly weapon or firearm.

5. Follow all instructions given you by your Parole Officer or other officials of the Adult Parole Authority and abide by any special conditions imposed by the Adult Parole Authority.

6. If you feel any of the Conditions, or instructions are causing problems, you may request a meeting with your parole officer's supervisor. The request stating your reasons for the conference should be in writing when possible.

7. Special Conditions:

I have read, or have had read to me, the foregoing Conditions of my Parole. I fully understand them and I agree to observe and abide by my Parole Conditions.

Witness: . . . .   Parole Candidate: . . . .

Date: . . . .

Exhibit 19

SPECIAL CONDITIONS OF PAROLE

_____ a. Secure written permission of the Probation and Parole Officer before changing employment.

_____ b. Secure written permission of the Probation and Parole Officer before changing residence.

_____ c. Consult with Probation and Parole Officer regularly and always before making any change in employment or residence.

_____ d. Secure written permission of the Probation and Parole Officer before leaving the county of residence.

_____ e. Secure written permission of the Probation and Parole Officer before leaving geographic area prescribed by Parole Officer.

_____ f. At no time have under control any firearms or deadly weapons.

_____ g. Avoid association with persons having a criminal background and bad reputation.

_____ h. Avoid association with (Specific individual(s)).

_____ i. At no time enter _____ County until further order of the Board.

_____ j. At no time enter _____ County unless given written permission by the Probation and Parole Officer.

_____ k. At no time communicate with an inmate of a correctional institution nor visit any such institution without written authorization from the Probation and Parole Officer.

_____ l. Secure the written permission of the Probation and Parole Officer before entering into marriage.

_____ m. Secure the written permission of the Probation and Parole Officer before purchasing an automobile.

_____ n. Secure the written permission of the Probation and Parole Officer before operating an automobile.

_____ o. Secure the written permission of the Probation and Parole Officer before entering into a contract which requires installment payments.

_____ p. Secure the written permission of the Probation and Parole Officer before entering into any type of contractual relationship.

_____ q. At no time consume any intoxicating liquors to excess.

_____ r At no time consume any intoxicating liquors.

_____ s. Will (seek to) participate in (1)_____ through (2)_____ _____ concerning (3) _____ under guidance of (4) _____ for a period of (5) _____
(Optional) - Removal, elimination, or termination from this program for any reason other than successful completion of the program, is considered a violation of this condition of parole.

(1) (a) Rehabilitative program
   (b) Treatment program
   (c) Counseling program
   (d) Out-patient program
   (e) In-patient program
   (f) Group therapy program
   (g) Community health program
   (h) Vocational rehabilitation program
   (i) Alcoholics Anonymous program
   (j) Narcotics Anonymous program

(2) (a) Veteran's Hospital
   (b) State Hospital
   (c) Dept. of Voc. Rehab.
   (d) Dept. of Employment Security
   (e) Halfway House
   (f) Own resources
   (g) Parole Officer

(3) (a) Marital problems
   (b) Sex problems
   (c) Employment problems
   (d) Medical problems
   (e) Drinking problems
   (f) Narcotics problems
   (g) Financial problems

(4) (a) Parole Officer
   (b) Sponsor
   (c) Psychiatrist
   (d) Social Worker
   (e) Family
   (f) Priest, Minister

(5) (a) While on active parole supervision
   (b) Until further order of the Board
   (c) As directed by the Parole Officer
   (d) Until no further need is felt

The parole officer completes a written revocation report on the forms prescribed by the parole board, concluding with a recommendation. In general, the options recommended by the parole officer would include revoking parole to permit the offender to serve the remainder of his sentence, imposing special conditions of parole to permit continuation, or restoring parolee to supervision. In the event that revocation was caused by the commission of a new crime for which the offender is convicted, sentences may run concurrently or in addition to the sentence imposed for the fresh crime, or a "Special Term" of parole may be imposed following completion of any new sentence.

Termination

The discharge of an offender from the corrections system, as in other social agencies, usually requires a concluding summary of the case. This summary may include a brief review from the time the offender entered the corrections system, but its main emphasis is to update the case file by reviewing the main events occurring during parole supervision. The concluding summary enables future investigators to appraise the most recent experiences with an offender, in the event of additional crimes.

Corrections systems also desire a systematic method for evaluating their achievements for budgetary and research purposes. A good example of client assessment at the point of termination is seen in Exhibit 20, which represents a rating scale used by the Division of Corrections in the State of Wisconsin.

PRACTICE CASE 20

Instructions: Parole Officer James Washington has filed a report for parole revocation against Roy Whitten following an escapade with the Ohio Highway Patrol by this parolee. This report will be reviewed by the parole board at a revocation hearing with Mr. Whitten. You are to write a recommendation on this case to the parole board, justifying your recommendation in terms of his alleged violations, his progress in supervision, and his background. Answer the questions following his case.

State of Ohio
ADULT PAROLE AUTHORITY
1050 Freeway Drive
Columbus, Ohio 43229

Nature of Report: Alleged Parole Violation

Parolee: Roy Whitten

Present address: Tuscarawas County Jail

Admitted: 9/4/77

Paroled: 10/5/79

Date: 12/15/79

Institution: Ohio State Reformatory

Race: White

Crime and Sentence: Aggravated Robbery

4-25 years

Exhibit 20

ASSESSMENT OF CLIENT NEEDS
AT TERMINATION

Wis. Dept. of Health and Social Services
Form C-503

Client Name _____   Client Number _____
　　　　　　　　　　Last　　　　　　　First　　　　　MI

Date of Termination _____ Agent Last Name _____ Area Number _____
　　　　　　　　Month, Day, Year

Select the appropriate answer and enter the associated weight in the score column. Higher numbers indicate more serious problems. Total all scores.

SCORE

ACADEMIC/VOCATIONAL SKILLS

| **-1** High school or above skill level | **0** Adequate skills; able to handle every-day requirements | **2** Low skill level causing minor adjustment problems | **4** Minimal skill level causing serious adjustment problems | _____ |

EMPLOYMENT

| **-1** Satisfactory employment for one year or longer | **0** Secure employment; no difficulties reported; or homemaker, student or retired | **3** Unsatisfactory employment; or unemployed but has adequate job skills | **6** Unemployed and virtually unemployable; needs training | _____ |

FINANCIAL MANAGEMENT

| **-1** Long-standing pattern of self-sufficiency; e.g., good credit rating | **0** No current difficulties | **3** Situational or minor difficulties | **5** Severe difficulties; may include garnishment, bad checks or bankruptcy | _____ |

MARITAL/FAMILY RELATIONSHIPS

| **-1** Relationships and support exceptionally strong | **0** Relatively stable relationships | **3** Some disorganization or stress but potential for improvement | **5** Major disorganization or stress | _____ |

COMPANIONS

| **-1** Good support and influence | **0** No adverse relationships | **2** Associations with occasional negative results | **4** Associations almost completely negative | _____ |

EMOTIONAL STABILITY

| **-2** Exceptionally well adjusted; accepts responsibility for actions | **0** No symptoms of emotional instability; appropriate emotional responses | **4** Symptoms limit but do not prohibit adequate functioning; e.g., excessive anxiety | **7** Symptoms prohibit adequate functioning; e.g., lashes out or retreats into self | _____ |

ALCOHOL USAGE

| | **0** No interference with functioning | **3** Occasional abuse; some disruption of functioning | **6** Frequent abuse; serious disruption; needs treatment | _____ |

OTHER DRUG USAGE

| | **0** No interference with functioning | **3** Occasional substance abuse; some disruption of functioning | **5** Frequent substance abuse; serious disruption; needs treatment | _____ |

MENTAL ABILITY

| | **0** Able to function independently | **3** Some need for assistance; potential for adequate adjustment | **6** Deficiencies severely limit independent functioning | _____ |

HEALTH

| | **0** Sound physical health; seldom ill | **1** Handicap or illness interferes with functioning on a recurring basis | **2** Serious handicap or chronic illness; needs frequent medical care | _____ |

SEXUAL BEHAVIOR

| | **0** No apparent dysfunction | **3** Real or perceived situational or minor problems | **5** Real or perceived chronic or severe problems | _____ |

AGENT'S IMPRESSION OF CLIENT'S NEEDS

| **-1** Minimum | **0** Low | **3** Medium | **5** Maximum | _____ |

TOTAL _____

INTRODUCTION:　　At approximately 2:00 AM on 12/8/79, Ptn. John Weingarten of the Ohio Highway Patrol advised this officer that he had arrested Roy Whitten at approximately 1:00 AM this date after a high speed chase and charged Whitten with Operating a Motor Vehicle While Intoxicated, Fleeing a Police Officer, and Resisting Arrest. He is presently in custody at the Tuscarawas County Jail.

ALLEGED VIOLATIONS:

1. Violation of Rule #3: Obey all municipal ordinances, state and federal laws, and at all times conduct yourself as a responsible law-abiding citizen. To wit, fleeing from the Highway Patrol.
2. Violation of Rule #3: To wit, by resisting arrest by the Highway Patrol.
3. Violation of Rule #3: To wit, by driving an automobile while under the influence of alcohol.
4. Violation of Rule #3: To wit, by driving a 1968 Dodge pickup truck not belonging to you and without the owner's consent.
5. Violation of Rule #7 (Special Condition): To wit, by changing your address without notifying your parole officer.
6. Violation of Rule #7 (Special Condition): To wit, by not attending the Tuscarawas County Mental Health Center for counseling as directed by your parole officer.

CORROBORATING STATEMENT:

The following statement was obtained from Ptn. John Weingarten of the Ohio Highway Patrol: "At approximately 1:00 AM on 12/8/79, I observed a 1968 Dodge pickup truck on Hwy. 39 proceeding at a high rate of speed and weaving in traffic. When I attempted to intercept the driver, who was alone, a high speed chase ensued in which the subject exceeded speeds of 100 MPH, passed several cars over the double yellow line, and traveled through the village of Dover, posted at 25 MPH, at speeds exceeding 90 MPH. He eluded a road block set up to intercept him, and lost control of the truck, hitting a bridge abutment. After impact with the bridge, subject lay on the ground beside the truck, which was a total loss. Damage to the bridge was estimated at $15.

Subject, identified as Roy Whitten, age 22, was placed under arrest, and a wrestling match ensued. After arrival of four other officers, Whitten was subdued, after scratching and punching three officers. He was conveyed to the Dover General Hospital, and continued to curse, kick, and spit on the arresting officers. Doctors and nurses at the Hospital were also subjected to the same treatment while bruises on his right arm were treated. Following treatment, he was conveyed to the Tuscarawas County Jail, and was sedated by the jail physician. Mr. Whitten appeared to be intoxicated, and admitted he had been drinking, along with some unidentified drugs, but we were unable to conduct a breathalyzer test because of his uncooperativeness."

Statement from Mr. Jeb Whitten (Parolee's uncle):
Mr. Whitten, who resides on State Route #39 near Dover, stated that he had returned home from work

at about 5:00 PM on 12/7/79 to find a 1968 Dodge pickup truck missing which he had borrowed from his employer to haul manure. He notified police of the apparent theft of the vehicle. Later that evening he was informed that the truck was parked at the Bide-A-Wee Tavern and, upon going there, found that his nephew, Roy Whitten, had taken the vehicle without permission. The nephew screamed and cursed at his uncle, insisting that he needed transportation, and "just took it." He then jumped into the truck and sped away, narrowly avoiding striking his uncle, who noted that the truck had already been damaged partially.

The uncle further stated that, during the two months his nephew has been on parole, he has never lived at the uncle's home as was required by the conditions of his parole. Mr. Whitten stated that his nephew is no longer welcome there. During this period his whereabouts was unknown.

Statement from Mr. Howard Eastwood, Tuscarwaras County Mental Health Center:

Mr. Eastwood initiated counseling while Whitten was still an inmate at the Ohio State Reformatory, and it was made a special condition of parole that this counseling relationship be continued. Mr. Eastwood was surprised that Whitten did not follow up counseling, since he had appeared to be so eager at the time of parole planning.

Parolee's statement:

The undersigned officer contacted Whitten in his jail cell on 12/9/79 for the purpose of obtaining the following statements:

Whitten stated that he started drinking about 1:00 PM the day of his arrest, and that he was by himself. He was drinking vodka in large amounts, stating that he felt depressed. He also took an unknown quantity of THC and marijuana. He insists that he does not remember anything after 10 PM, until he woke up in the County Jail the next morning. He does not deny that he resisted arrest and fled from the police, saying, "I was so bombed I could have done anything."

He further stated that earlier in the day he was in need of medical attention, and was looking for someone to take him to the Belleview Hospital. He said that his head was messed up with drugs and dope, and he couldn't find any transportation, so he took the truck from his uncle's yard without permission. He doesn't remember anything except parking it at the Bide-A-Wee Tavern. He said he didn't think about calling his parole officer for help because his head was so messed up.

Whitten said he didn't know why he agreed to live with his uncle when he was paroled because he had no intention of living there. He said he had been staying with his girl friend's parents instead, until they had split up last week.

He further stated that he did not pursue counseling with Mr. Eastwood because he did not know how to get in touch with him. He said that he forgot the counselor's name, that he did not make any effort to contact him since his release on parole.

CRIMINAL HISTORY:

Whitten pleaded guilty to aggravated robbery on 9/1/77 after he had severely injured a service station attendant by running his motorcycle over him in the commission of a robbery. He said that he had been drinking at the time, and had not intended to hurt anybody. The robbery was for the purpose of getting money. The subject has no other record of arrests, except for several traffic charges of reckless driving, drunken driving, driving without a license, and operating an unsafe vehicle.

History of Supervision:

During his first visit with the undersigned officer, he was extremely pleasant and cooperative, showing deep remorse for his behavior, and stating that he had no intention of ever getting into trouble again. He went to work as a warehouseman with the Kroger Company, but that position was terminated three weeks later for excessive absenteeism. While he appeared to have a good attitude and reported regularly, it was discovered later that he was not living with his uncle or working regularly. After lengthy investigation he was discovered living at the home of Anthony and Mary Black in Dover, where he was seriously involved with their daughter, Ruby, age 16. He was ordered to remove himself from the Black household or be charged with contributing to the delinquency of a minor. He promised to return to his uncle's home. However, his attitude was very poor, and he subsequently appeared to be drinking heavily. At one time he threatened to take his own life and asked to return to the institution because "things are just not working out for me." On 12/3 he called the County Sheriff's Department, and asked to be returned to the institution. The undersigned officer was contacted, and he managed to have a counselor from the Tuscawaras County Mental Health Center visit with Whitten to ascertain his mental state. He was reported to be rational and well-behaved during the interview, and counseling around his drinking was arranged. However, he did not keep his appointments with the Center. He was severely admonished by this officer to seek counseling, and to return to his uncle's home, but apparently did not do so.

James Washington
Parole Officer

Discussion Questions

1. What alternatives did you consider to deal with Whitten's alcoholic abuse and drug-taking?

2. On the basis of this information provided, to what degree did you conclude that a structured environment might be necessary?

3. What aspects of the case would you have liked more information about?

4. Do you have any concerns about his behavior if he is returned to the reformatory for an additional sentence?

Parole Officer James Washington Comments on the Whitten Case:
"The parole board bought my recommendation, and sent Whitten back to the reformatory for the rest of his sentence. I really don't know what else they could have done, since he absolutely refused to follow any of my suggestions to him. Whitten would smile at you, promise to shape up, but the minute your back was turned and he got a few drinks in him, all hell would break loose. I don't think any officer has to put up with that kind of behavior. To tell you the truth, if the parole board had sent him back to me, I'd have done my best to get him committed for observation at a state hospital.

"Whitten just wasn't able to listen to anybody. He was slippery, you couldn't get a hold on him, and he was just bound and determined to drink and have his own way, whatever happened. He could have killed somebody in that chase, you know, including himself. It's too dangerous to let him run around loose in that condition. If there were somebody in his family who might have given him a little stability, but the parents are divorced and living in Florida, and his uncle was tired of his shenanigans. He wanted to marry that 16-year-old girl, you know. He figured she would straighten him out . . . that's typical alcoholic logic, and her parents were just dumb enough to go along with it until I broke *that* up. No, he's better off where he is . . . back in the joint."

Supplementary Reading

Beck, James L. & Hoffman, Peter B. Time served and release performance: a research note. *Journal of Research in Crime and Delinquency*, 1976, *13*, No. 2, 127-132. (Reprinted in *Federal Parole Decision-Making*, see below.)

Gottfredson, Donald M. *et al. Classification for Parole Decision Policy*. Washington, D. C.: National Institute of Law Enforcement and Criminal Justice, U. S. Department of Justice, July 1978 (U. S. Government Printing Office, Washington, D. C. 20402, Stock Number 027-000-00688-4). An excellent discussion of an action research project to assist seven states in the development of guidelines for parole decision making by their paroling authorities.

Gottfredson, Don M., Hoffman, Peter B., Sigler, Maurice H., & Wilkins, Leslie T. Making paroling policy explicit. *Crime and Delinquency*, 1975, *21*, No. 1, 34-44. (Reprinted in Federal Parole Decision-making, see below).

U. S. Parole Commission Research Unit. *Federal Parole Decision-Making: Selected Reprints.* Washington, D.C.: U.S. Government Printing Office, 1978 (Stock Number 281-379/1455)
A collection of 16 previously published articles on issues of parole decision-making from 1974-77.

Chapter 19
Evaluation of Psychiatric/ Psychological Reports

There are few resources available to the corrections specialist that show greater promise than the increasing collaboration with the mental health professions. Whether such collaboration occurs in the court, institutional, or parole setting, there are many benefits for correctional agencies in seeking links with the network of community mental health centers and mental hospitals in their vicinity. In some states and in many metropolitan areas, a forensic psychology unit or court psychiatric center may exist with formal responsibilities to courts, agencies, and institutions. In other instances, consultation contracts with mental health agencies or private practitioners may be in effect. In either instance, the corrections investigator must be in a position to utilize, or in some cases, interpret the diagnostic work of the psychiatrists and psychologists. This implies a working knowledge of the professional work of the psychiatrist, clinical psychologist, and psychiatric social worker.

Basically, the expertise of such workers lies in the diagnosis and treatment of mental deviance, or *psychopathology*. Obviously, there are areas of overlap between criminality and psychopathology. Criminal acts are committed by persons as a result of mental problems, and the interaction of these two systems of *social control,* the criminal justice and mental health systems, is frequent (and occasionally acrimonious!). Consider, for example, the sexual offender, the alcoholic or drug-addicted person, or the self-destructive and depressed person. The ultimate responsibility for handling such behavior may depend upon circumstances, or the relative availability of psychiatric alternatives.

One of the most surprising findings of the Hollingshead-Redlich study in New Haven (1958) was that 52% of the Class V (lower-class) residents of that community had their first psychiatric hospitalization effected through the police and courts. It appeared that these criminal justice agencies, recognizing a serious mental condition, were acting on behalf of clients whose condition would ordinarily have been handled through families and private physicians in the other social classes.

While it is not possible to delineate the full range of possible involvements of the mental health professionals with probation/parole officers, some of the primary relationships may be described as follows:

1. *Competency to Stand Trial* — Under our system of law, it is necessary for the defendant to understand the proceedings against him, and to be able to prepare a defense. If the defendant is not believed to be in a mental condition to meet these requirements, it is customary for the Court to retain a psychiatrist or clinical psychologist to evaluate the ability of the defendant

to stand trial. The probation officer's involvement with such proceedings is usually minimal.

2. *Referral for hospitalization or other treatment as a sentencing alternative* — In some cases, the mental condition of the defendant, in relation to his offense(s), warrants a diagnostic evaluation for possible psychiatric treatment. Such an evaluation can be made a condition of probation, or the judge may place the implementation of the referral in the hands of a probation officer without specifying probation. Such action is usually initiated by the judge.

3. *Psychiatric/psychological consultation is requested by the probation officer as a part of the pre-sentence investigation* — This is probably the most common use of psychiatric/psychological resources. The probation officer, confronted with a family counseling situation, a sexual perversion, a drug addiction, or some other problem for which referral to a community service agency seems indicated, requests an evaluation for the purpose of verifying diagnostic and treatment recommendations and sometimes providing an intake report to a prescribed agency. In this case, the psychiatric report would be incorporated as a part of his PSI to the Court.

4. *Psychiatric/psychological consultation is requested by the probation/ parole officer on an ongoing case, for clarification of supervision strategies or referral purposes* — If supervision problems are encountered, or if referral to a treatment agency is being considered, a consultation with a mental health specialist may be considered, in order to facilitate handling of the case. Specialized treatment of alcoholism or drug problems, or of family relationships, might be a typical reason for such consultation.

5. *Evaluation of "outside" psychiatric evaluations for the sentencing judge, when such evaluations are offered to the court by defense attorneys* — While it may appear presumptuous for a probation officer to get involved in "second-guessing" mental health professionals, it is certainly within a judge's discretion to request clarification on psychiatric formulations through consultation with the officers of his court. Where courts maintain their own psychiatric staff, consultation or re-examination of the defendant by the internal staff members would be preferable. However, the probation officer's familiarity with the network of mental health agencies and with treatment methods make him a valuable resource to judges, especially in those instances when the court does not employ its own internal treatment staff.

6. *A sentencing judge desires a prediction of an offender's probable response to incarceration* — There are offenders whose adjustment is so precarious that the imposition of a jail sentence may precipitate a negative outcome which exceeds the requirements of justice. For example, a depressed defendant could become a suicidal risk. In another instance, a frail-looking 18 year-old was diverted to a halfway house for sentence because of the likelihood of homosexual attack in a jail where adequate safeguards against such attacks were not deemed sufficient. While the common practice has been for jails and prisons to deal with such contingencies "after the fact," the effort to prevent such unwarranted outcomes adds to the humanizing of sentences, and the overall efficiency of correctional efforts.

7. *Psychiatric/psychological evaluation to aid classification and assignment within correctional institutions, or to evaluate impact of correctional programs within institutions* — Such evaluation for the purpose of classification is commonly performed for all offenders entering many correctional institutions. Within recent years a Federal judge required the state of Alabama to perform

individual re-evaluations on all inmates to determine program adequacy. Such judicial intervention has become more common in the last decade, which represents a reversal of the "hands off" policy of courts in the administration of correctional institutions which had previously obtained.

Requesting Psychiatric/Psychological Evaluation

Whatever the setting in which the corrections investigator may make his/her request for advice, it is always helpful to be as specific as possible about the information wanted. An open-ended evaluation request invites a diffuse and possibly irrelevant response from the specialist. The most typical psychiatric referrals request diagnostic impressions from the clinician for the purpose of justifying treatment recommendations. The presence of aberrant thinking or behavior, predisposition toward violence, intellectual deficits, brain damage, alcoholic or drug addictions, emotional instability, or self-destructive tendencies are common reasons for referral. A typical referral form is shown in Exhibit 21 (Court Psychiatric Center, Hamilton County, Ohio).

In requesting such evaluations, an assumption is made that the mental health professional possesses greater expertise than the probation officer (or judge) in the areas of inquiry; otherwise, no reason would exist for the referral. However, the amount of sophistication possessed by clinicians in the workings of the corrections system varies greatly, so that recommendations proposed by psychiatrists and psychologists in their reports are not always necessarily realistic; their expertise can be considerably diluted as these professionals move away from their familiar treatment settings, and onto the "turf" of the corrections worker (and sentencing judge).

Thus, considerable grounds for misunderstanding and debate can occur when psychiatry and the judiciary fail to respect the boundaries of each other's expertise. Such differences are probably inevitable from time to time, considering the differences in philosophy and practice of the mental health and criminal justice systems. The most prominent exceptions to the above are the forensic psychiatrists and psychologists with a career interest in criminal corrections. Such persons have earned the right by their efforts to speak with authority to both law and the helping professions, and exert an important "bridging" function between these two systems.

"Clinical" Methods

In order to utilize diagnostic evaluations most effectively, the corrections worker should have a working knowledge of the vocabulary and methods of the psychiatrist and psychologist. In addition to sheer experience, courses and workshops in abnormal psychology are recommended as a minimum standard for corrections workers.

Psychiatry

Psychiatry is a medical specialty that deals with the diagnosis and treatment of mental disorders. Practitioners in psychiatry are physicians with advanced academic and practical training in the treatment and management of conditions of mental abnormality, such as psychoses, brain disorders, schizophrenia, severe maladjustment, and substance addictions.

The psychiatrist's main tools are sharp and well-trained eyes and ears to pick up subtle nuances of thinking and behavior that signify mental aberrations. Like the social worker and corrections workers, he is experienced in discerning patterns of abnormality in social histories of his clients. He often

Exhibit 21

PSYCHIATRIC REFERRAL FORM

FROM:

☐ Court of Common Pleas   Date Referred: _____

☐ Municipal Court   Case/Docket No.: _____

☐ Adult Parole Authority   Date of Birth: _____

TO: Central Psychiatric Clinic — Court Psychiatric Center

1. _____ , having been charged with _____

   _____ and (please circle) convicted of/plead guilty to

   _____ before the Honorable _____

   is:

    a. Presently located at:

        1) Address _____ Phone _____

        2) Incarcerated at _____

    b. Sentence _____ (If applicable)

    c. Continued to _____ (Date & Room No.)

2. The above individual is referred to the Court Psychiatric Center for evaluation to determine:
   (Check as many as applicable)

   ( ) Competency to Stand Trial   ( ) Advisability of Treatment
   ( ) Commitment under the Ascherman Act   ( ) Psychological effects of
   ( ) Necessity for Hospitalization   Incarceration
   ( ) Potential Dangerousness to self or   ( ) Other (see below)
        others

        Please check if this is non-probationable offense

3. Report to be forwarded to:

   ☐ Judge   Date Due: ☐ Urgent — Date _____

   ☐ Probation Department   ☐ Not Urgent —

   ☐ Parole Authority   Date _____

4. Other Instructions: _____
   _____
   _____
   _____
   _____
   _____

   _____
                              (Judge)

administers a mental status examination that deals with orientation, memory, and thinking ability. For example, he may ask a patient to count backwards by 7s from 100, or ask the meaning of common proverbs, like "No use crying over spilt milk."

The psychiatrist then determines through observation and interview whether a pattern of symptoms exists that justifies a diagnosis of mental disorder. He may refer to the *Diagnostic and Statistical Manual of Mental Disorders,* published by the American Psychiatric Association. After consultation with psychiatric social workers, clinical psychologists (or others), the psychiatrist may conclude with a set of treatment recommendations to ameliorate the conditions which have been diagnosed.

Clinical Psychology

Psychologists are behavior specialists who deal with a wide range of behavior problems in families, schools, colleges, institutions, and corporations, in addition to the traditional mental health agencies and hospitals. They are educated in graduate university programs, which include a one-year internship, and training in research methodology. The qualifying degree is the Doctor of Philosophy, although many psychologists with Master's degrees function in correctional institutions with classification and counseling responsibilities.

In their diagnostic assessments of offenders, psychologists make use of interviewing skills and social histories. However, they are best known for their use of psychological tests which are commonly (though not universally) utilized in their evaluations. (The development and use of intelligence and achievement tests has been described in Chapter 11.) At this point, we are concerned with tests of personality.

A psychological test should be regarded as a standard set of stimuli which, when applied to an individual, results in a pattern of responses that can be compared to various groups in a quantified fashion. The power of a test is its ability to measure the tested person against the background of a known group. Personality tests generally fall into two types, *objective* and *projective*.

Objective Personality Tests

The best known of the objective tests of personality is the *Minnesota Multiphasic Personality Inventory (MMPI)*. This 566-item true-false scale results in 10 clinical scales, on which the subject is measured against known groups on traits such as *hypochondriasis, depression, psychopathic deviate, schizophrenia*, etc., and three validity scales. The MMPI is empirically derived, which means that the subject's score is obtained by counting the number of items which were answered the same way as the various deviant groups used to standardize the test. The MMPI has been heavily used for screening and classification in correctional institutions. The profiles derived from MMPI use must be interpreted by an experienced psychologist, who may consult an atlas of personality descriptions associated with various test profiles, or use a computer scoring service which performs the same function.

Other "objective" personality tests include the *California Personality Inventory, Cattell 16PF, Edwards Personal Preference Schedule (EPPS)*, and numerous others. Vocational aptitude tests are also constructed on the same principle of the similarity of the subject's answers to established occupational groups; examples are the *Kuder Preference Record* and the *Strong Vocational Interest Blank*. The use of objective-type tests is well-established, and in the hands of skilled examiners who understand their limitations, can provide an accurate and inexpensive method for evaluating large groups as well as single individuals.

Projective Tests

Projective tests of personality are based upon the idea that when subjects are confronted with an ambiguous stimulus, they must use their imagination to respond, and thus "project" their personalities into those responses. Whatever problems or distortions of thinking exist in the subject are believed to be delineated in such projections. For example, an offender convicted of making obscene telephone calls to strange women from the back of a dry-cleaning shop stubbornly denied the facts, and continued to insist he was a victim of mistaken identity, and to deny the existence of any personal problems whatsoever. When asked to "draw a person" on a blank sheet of paper, he proceeded to draw a sweetly smiling, bland male figure; then, to the astonishment of the psychologist, he added a grotesquely enlarged penis to the drawing! Then, asked to draw a figure of the opposite sex, he produced a very buxom female. During the inquiry into the meaning of the drawings, this offender gradually revealed a great deal of sexually obsessed thinking, which had included sexual exhibition, window-peeping, and obscene phone calls.

Projective personality tests illustrate a rather oblique approach to uncovering significant problems. Best known of the projective tests are the *Rorschach* ink-blots; also used often are the *Thematic Apperception Test (TAT)* cards, in which the subject is instructed to tell a story about each card. The *House-Tree-Person* is another drawing test. *Word Association* and *Incomplete Sentences* are semi-structured tests in which the subject responds to words in a rapid-fire fashion, or completes sentences, such as "My father . . ." or "When I see a policeman, I . . ."

Projective tests can be a powerful tool in the hands of an experienced clinician; however, their use is limited to persons with extensive training in their interpretation. Responses to projective test items are, by definition, highly individualized, so that their proper interpretation is somewhat subjective. Reliability and validity of projective tests have proven difficult to establish through research.

Role of the Clinician in Corrections

The intervention of mental health professionals into the field of corrections has not been without its detractors. Some writers have argued that in "psychiatrizing" the offender we have provided him with another set of justifications for continued criminality, and have failed to assist him in change (Cohn, 1979). Holland (1979) has noted the differences in diagnostic styles and recommendations between three psychologists and a psychiatrist working in a prison diagnostic unit making pre-sentence investigations. Classifying diagnoses into categories of *normal, personality trait disturbance, sociopathic personality,* and *psychiatric disturbance* for 560 Federal offenders, Holland found wide differences in utilization of information, diagnoses, and recommendations for sentencing between these four clinicians. He recommended a combined statistical/clinical approach to promote greater uniformity and accuracy in offender assessment.

Thomas Szasz, on the other hand, concludes that clinicians serve as a definite detriment rather than as an asset to fairness in courts and prisons. He states (1979):

> I maintain that lawyers and judges should not be able to call on psychiatrists and psychologists to testify about the mental condition of persons accused of crime; and that judges should be unable to sentence criminals to imprisonment in institutions run by clinicians. Nothing short of such a seemingly radical — but actually conservative — policy would suffice to eliminate the now rampant abuses of coercive and deceptive psychiatric and psychological interventions imposed on persons caught up in the criminal justice system.

This author would insist that, in the real world of corrections, it is possible to improve sentencing, to make institutional placement more efficient, and to humanize the field of corrections through the judicious use of clinicians, without necessarily weakening the interests of justice, as envisioned by Cohn and Szasz. Further, the vagaries of diagnosis and recommendations cited by Holland also exist at every level of decision making by judges and corrections personnel.

Finally, Szasz's words are animated by his concern for arbitrary and capricious use of institutional "treatment" by clinicians without the civil liberties guarantees provided by law, which he finds hypocritical and unfair to offenders. Surely adequate checks and balances against coerced treatment are being introduced through law to counter such deceptions without depriving the entire corrections system of the services of mental health professionals, as he suggests should be done.

As someone has said, "Criminal justice is too important to be left to judges!"

PRACTICE CASE 21

Instructions: Read the PSI and psychiatric evaluation on this 18 year-old single man who has pleaded guilty to Burglary, then write an evaluative summary and recommendation to Judge Underwood which incorporates the information from the psychiatric evaluation.

Pre-Sentence Investigation

Name: Joseph Levy

Address: 34 Pursewood Drive
Cincinnati, Ohio

Age: 18

Education: 8th grade

Race: Caucasian

Judge: Underwood

P.O.: Summers

Charge: Burglary

Penalty: 1-5 yrs.

Plea: Guilty 11/30/75

Custody: County Jail

Report due: 12/20/75

Prosecutor: Redfern

Defense Counsel: Dinwiddy

CURRENT OFFENSE: On 10/7/75 at approximately 3:30 AM, the defendant and three accomplices broke a door-glass, reached in and unlocked the door, and entered the premises of the Sunlight Food Company, a catering firm, at 4021 East Imprint Lane in Forest Hills, a suburban community. A son of the owner was working in a rear room when they entered and shouted at the burglars to stop. The other three ran out the door. The defendant approached the owner's son, who knocked him flat and subdued him until Forest Hills Police arrived. There are no co-defendants in this case, since two accomplices have been referred to Juvenile Court and the third is still at large.

PREVIOUS OFFENSES:

6/24/71	Dependency Hearing	Juvenile Court	Sent to the Welfare Children's Home
8/26/74	Malicious Destruction of Property	Juvenile Court	Returned to the Welfare Children's Home
9/30/74	Runaway	Juvenile Court	Returned to the Welfare Children's Home
11/3/74	Incorrigible and Runaway	Juvenile Court	Dismissed—Committed to Greenacre Sanitarium (private)
9/20/75	Disorderly Conduct	Municipal Court	$25 and costs

ATTITUDE OF COMPLAINANT:

The complainant, James Jones, states that nothing was stolen since the the defendant was immediately apprehended. He repaired the broken window himself. He will abide by the Court's decision.

EDUCATION AND EARLY LIFE:

The defendant was born in Tar Flats, Ohio, and attended six different schools before dropping out after the 8th grade, at age 17. His attendance record was poor, and he was failing all subjects at the time. The defendant was born to Greenslee and Helen Hensley as one of three children in Tar Flats. Both parents were alcoholics and had other undesirable characteristics, and the Logan County Welfare Department removed the children from the parental home. After placement in several foster homes, the defendant was adopted by Jacob Levy when he was seven years of age. The adoptive father is a college graduate who is a former social worker and is presently a researcher and planner with a public agency. He is 60 years of age. The defendant's adoptive mother, Dolores Levy, is 51 years of age, and is employed as a school teacher. There is also a 14-year-old Vietnamese girl adopted in this family, who has presented no behavior problems to the family.

Mrs. Levy has been in treatment with a psychiatrist, Dr. _____, for several years, ostensibly because of menopausal adjustment problems, but also mentions a history of past neurotic problems. Mr. Levy is also in treatment; he presents himself as a compulsive talker, full of complaints about his health and his career.

EMPLOYMENT HISTORY:

The defendant's only jobs have been very sporadic as a part-time gas station attendant.

MILITARY RECORD:

The defendant enlisted in the U. S. Navy on April 12, 1975 and was discharged for medical reasons on June 5, 1975, classified "unadjustable."

PHYSICAL AND MENTAL:

The defendant is an 18-year-old single Caucasian man who is 5'10" in height and weighs 175 lbs.

No intelligence tests were given, but he was estimated to be of below average intelligence. Joseph was a school behavior problem, and was placed in the Children's Welfare Home by his adoptive parents at the age of 14 because his parents could not handle him. After repeated runaways from the Children's Welfare Home, he was finally committed to Greenacre Sanitarium, a private mental hospital, under the care of Dr. _____. Joseph was referred to Dr. Green, a psychiatrist, for evaluation at the Court's request, and was examined in the County Jail. Dr. Green diagnosed the defendant as suffering from "chronic undifferentiated schizophrenia," and recommended for institutionalization.

CHARACTER AND CONDUCT:

The defendant is a very dependent, easily led person who just cannot function independently. His employers state that he worked hard, and would stay around the service stations after hours to help because he was lonely. This state of mind, even without his schizophrenic condition, would tend to lead him into all sorts of situations which would get him into trouble. The defendant has a Juvenile Court record which resulted mainly from striking his parents when they attempted to discipline him. This defendant, if he had been blessed with strong, stable, and concerned parents, might have been able to overcome his handicaps.

Psychiatric Evaluation

From: Horace Green, M.D.

To: Hon. Christopher Underwood

Re: Joseph Levy

Dear Judge Underwood:

Thanks so much for the opportunity to see Mr. Levy. I performed a psychiatric evaluation on this young man in the County Jail on 12/12/75, and spoke with Drs. _____ and _____, who have been treating his parents.

Joseph stated that on the day of the burglary, he was picked up at work by "an old friend" whom he had known from the Welfare Children's Home. He described the friend fearfully, and said that he was afraid not to go with him, afraid he'd be hurt. He stated he had not wanted to commit the break-in, but went along with the others, and when the police were called, the others ran off and he gave himself up.

Joseph stated that he had been adopted when he was 7 years of age. His biological parents were both alcoholics. He denied problems with his adoptive parents, but the doctors treating his parents both report that chronic and severe adjustment problems at home exist, to such an extent that placement in the Welfare Children's Home, Juvenile Court, and Greenacre Sanitarium have been necessary.

During the time Joseph was in Greenacres, he was grossly psychotic, and was extremely paranoid. He was treated with tranquilizers, and reportedly did very well, until his parents had him discharged home. When he returned home, there was instant fighting, arguing, tension, and chaos.

Joseph felt his family was against him while at Greenacres, but denies this feeling now. He dropped out of school in the 8th grade after flunking the 4th grade, and generally making *Ds* and *Fs*. He said he couldn't concentrate, or pay attention, and his mind wandered all the time. Subsequently he enlisted in the Navy, and was medically discharged after two months following a psychotic episode. Since then he has had a few jobs at service stations, which he has held unsuccessfully.

Mental status examination shows Joseph to be of "dull normal" intelligence. He appears to have little judgment or insight. His ability for rational action and thought is impaired, as obviously is his life style. He is not delusional or dangerous to himself or others, and is oriented to time, place, person. He is also quite cautious with me, and reluctant to tell much about himself.

Diagnosis: *Chronic Undifferentiated Schizophrenia*

Recommendations: It seems that Mr. Levy does best in constantly supervised situations such as a state mental hospital. He certainly should not be at home since great turmoil develops. However, it would be important that if committed to a state hospital, that he not be discharged immediately to his parents. Prison would certainly be contraindicated for this chronically psychotic youth.

Discussion Questions

1. Do you regard Joseph Levy as a "psychiatric" or "criminal" case? How did you set about justifying your recommendations, in either case?

2. *Schizophrenic reaction, chronic undifferentiated type,* is defined as follows: (DSM I) "The chronic schizophrenic reactions exhibit a mixed symptomatology, and when the reaction cannot be classified in any of the more clearly defined types, it will be placed in this group. Patients presenting definite schizophrenic thought, affect, and behavior beyond that of the schizoid personality, but not classifiable as any other type of schizophrenic reaction, will also be placed in this group. This includes the so-called 'latent,' 'incipient,' 'pre-psychotic' schizophrenic reactions." Does this definition seem to fit the defendant?

3. What deficiencies did you detect in Officer Summer's write-up of this case? Do you find any biases in his expressed viewpoint?

Probation Officer Summers Comments on the Levy Case:
"The psychiatrists were welcome to have this case, as far as I was concerned. I really didn't see much chance of supervising this youngster. The Children's Welfare Home couldn't do it, Greenacres couldn't do it, and neither could the Navy. I don't know what Judge Underwood expected me to do with the case, and I told him that in no uncertain terms. But I got the case, anyway. Judge Underwood put him on probation for three years, with the understanding that Joseph would stay in jail until the parents committed him to the state mental hospital. They finally did that, and he stayed in the hospital for 18 months.

"The idea of probation was that when he returned home, there would be some control over him, to keep down arguments at home, and give those parents some relief. That part of it didn't work too well. He was discharged from the hospital, and there was no place for him to go, so he went home. I got him a job working in a Mobil station pumping gas, and he seemed better for a few months. Then he started hanging around Forest Hills at night again, and the police picked him up several times for curfew violation. Then he would fight and argue with his parents all the time, just like before. He just wouldn't listen to me.

"Finally, he broke into the gas station where he worked, and stole $50. He was arrested, and charged with burglary and P.V. (probation violation). Joseph claimed they had cheated him on his pay, and he only took what was coming to him, no more. He was referred for another psychiatric evaluation, this time in our Court Center. The doctors said he was 'in remission,' and that probation supervision should be continued. I told the Judge I had enough of this young man, and I didn't think it would work out. So he was sentenced to the Ohio State Reformatory for an indefinite sentence, and his probation terminated. The parents tried to get him out, but the Judge over-ruled the motion to suspend sentence when I objected, and as far as I know, he's still there. I feel sorry for the parents getting all that grief after they adopted Joseph, but they just didn't seem to be able to handle him."

Case Commentary

There are different conclusions that can be gleaned from this case. It seems that we may have been dealing with a severe *adolescent adjustment reaction* all along, and that the schizophrenic diagnosis was probably not justified by the clinical evidence, but by expediency. Perhaps Dr. Green stretched the clinical symptoms a little thin, believing that a psychiatric hospital would be more beneficial than a prison sentence, which is certainly understandable. Yet the chronic undifferentiated schizophrenia is a weak diagnosis often used in marginal situations. The subsequent examination by the Court Psychiatric Center found Joseph to be "in remission" and "functioning at a clinically normal level," which is a fine bit of hair-splitting. As a result, he was thrown back into the corrections system, and ended up with a reformatory sentence, since his probation officer considered him an unsuitable candidate for supervision.

The period of adolescent transition is extremely agonizing for many youngsters. Some actually believe they are "going crazy," and refer to themselves in such terms. The turmoil they experience is trying to everyone around them, and particularly to elderly parents. Such adolescents simply will not be contained in their frenzy by ordinary means, and flail about, testing every limit imposed upon them. As a result, many youths are shuttled around from youth shelters to jails, to military service, and to sanitariums and mental hospitals, in a frantic effort to find an environment that will offer reasonable control. This is what seems to have happened to Joseph Levy.

About the only good thing that can be said about such stormy adolescent reactions is that they gradually subside, "sanity" is restored, and most youths are appalled as they survey the ruin they have produced. Yet consider the crudeness of our social remedies. Neither mental hospitals nor reformatories are really suited for these youthful offenders, nor should the military services be viewed as a panacea for maladjusted youth. The social stigma associated with prisons and mental hospitals has to be considered as well. Perhaps the structured environments of youth camps like the Job Corps, some of the Federal institutions for youthful offenders, or a type of halfway house would be a more favorable climate for youths like Joseph Levy to develop.

Supplementary Reading

APA Task Force on Nomenclature and Statistics. *Diagnostic and Statistical Manual of Mental Disorders* (3rd Ed.). Washington, D.C.: American Psychiatric Association, 1978.

Cohn, Alvin W. The failure of correctional management — revisited. *Federal Probation, 43* (No. 1), 1979, p. 10-15.

Dalessio, Donald J. *Mental Status Examination: Practical Aspects for the Clinician.* Videocassette, 1978.

Holland, Terrill R. Diagnostic labeling: individual differences in the behavior of clinicians conducting presentence evaluations. *Criminal Justice and Behavior, 6* (No. 2), 1979, p. 187-199.

Hollingshead, August & Redlich, Frederick. *Social Class and Mental Illness,* New York, Wiley, 1958.

Page, James. *Psychopathology,* (2nd Ed.). Fairlawn, New Jersey: Aldine Publishing Co., 1975. An excellent general reference for self-study of categories of abnormal behavior and their classification.

Szasz, Thomas S. Insanity and irresponsibility: psychiatric diversion in the criminal justice system. In *Psychology of Crime and Criminal Justice* (Hans Toch, Ed.). New York: Holt, Rinehart and Winston, 1979.

Chapter 20
Trends in Criminal Assessment

The corrections student and newly appointed officer frequently have a difficult time adjusting to their role as they confront the pragmatic realities of corrections work in the field. The compassion and idealism that compelled many persons to seek a career in corrections has a way of dissipating under the pressures of bureaucracy and the rigors of assessing offenders. To the extent that academic criminal justice programs have advocated major societal changes or intensive uncovering psychotherapy as the answers to crime, such programs may contribute to the human wisdom of the student while generating unrealistic notions about the day-to-day professional work of the corrections specialist.

The most common reaction of the corrections neophyte, particularly those educated in the helping professions, is to see mitigation everywhere in an offender's background; in his low social competence level, his poor employment record, his lack of progress in education, his broken family, and his socially disadvantaged status. In identifying with the offender, the student or officer may assume a "Savior Complex," desiring to protect his client from an indifferent and punishing corrections system, as he sees it. When such special pleading is not received sympathetically, some newcomers to the field may over-react, adopting a protective cynicism with punitive overtones. Such oscillations usually settle down with more experience in the field, with the emergence of a more balanced and objective approach.

Some workers eventually find that they are unable to accommodate their ideologies and values to the pragmatic tasks of assessment and supervision. This phenomenon has acquired the fashionable name of *personnel burnout;* this type of attrition, which is accompanied by low morale and pessimism, has become an important topic for study by correctional administrators. (A surprising number of mental health professionals have worked in corrections for brief periods and, finding the work unrewarding for a variety of reasons, have abandoned this field.)

The remedy for such early adverse reactions to corrections practice is to broaden one's conceptual perspective and lengthen one's time perspective. A developed understanding of criminal assessment is a career skill which cannot be mastered in a college course or a two-week workshop in an agency. This Casebook is a framework to begin professional assessment, and a reference book from which to gain pointers. The broad spectrum of criminality has proven difficult to conceptualize with a limited set of theoretical assumptions. The specialized and fragmented nature of much correctional investigation seems to encourage limited perspectives, which can detract from an overall appreciation of the total impact of the system. The recruitment of corrections personnel from a variety of professions can add elements of confusion to a system already fragmented. For example, neither psychoanalytical therapy or client-centered counseling have been proven very effective treatment for offenders when brought wholesale from other settings without considerable translation into the requirements of correctional counseling.

Finally, the investigative reports on criminal assessment have sometimes been executed in such a narrow and perfunctory manner that their usefulness is limited; in fact, they are sometimes filed and never used. There is needless duplication of effort at each level of decision making about offenders, with little effort at coordination. Norval Morris concludes, for example (1974):

> Experienced administrators and scholars of the prison system have concluded that the reception and diagnostic centers to which most felons are first sent for what is called "classification" are largely a waste of resources. At most such centers the prisoner spends the first four to six weeks of his incarceration being subjected to physical, psychological, and sociological study and casework analysis; he is sent on to one of the very few prison placements that are in any event available to him; and the painstaking records prepared in the reception and diagnostic center or in the institution thereafter rest undisturbed in files.

Morris recommends that a more economical procedure would be a court-recommended decision to a designated institution based upon prior record, with orientation and classification taking place at the institution. He suggests that only 10-15% of prisoners really require an extended diagnostic study. Morris' recommendation for a division of diagnostic labor between courts and institutions, with a more selective policy on extensive evaluations, is probably sound as a partial solution to the duplication and discontinuity that has characterized most state-managed correctional systems.

An Integrated Model for Offender Assessment

It appears logical to predict more integration of correctional sub-systems into large state-wide networks in which probation, institutions, parole, and aftercare facilities are coordinated into a total program for the management/ supervision/treatment of offenders. A comprehensive program for improved classification of offenders would be the key to such overall planning. If such coordination of assessment efforts is to take place, what is the most appropriate location for such reception/diagnostic centers?

There are many compelling reasons for placing the major work of offender assessment at the "front end" of the correctional process at the court/community level:

1. Sentencing judges are in the most central and influential role to prescribe correctional remedies, in response to the instant offense. The most potent justification for correctional remedies of whatever type appropriately remains the current and prior record of criminal offenses, despite the benevolent intentions of many reformers in the corrections field. The initiation of overall plans for offenders should start at the court/community level, given a comprehensive diagnostic facility conveniently available to judges.

2. 95-97% of offenders who serve sentences in institutions eventually return to community settings.

3. Specialized services, such as those provided by psychologists, social workers, vocational specialists, educators and others, are more likely to be available in communities than in remote institutional settings.

4. The bulk of correctional personnel, including probation and parole officers, halfway house workers, alcoholic and drug center personnel, work

release program personnel, etc., are located in the community, which facilitates communication and referral activity.

5. The institutional behavior of inmates in prisons and reformatories has proven to be a weak predictor of future criminal behavior in the community following release. In fact, the "game-playing" of inmates in their pseudo-cooperation with institutional programs has reached such a cynical level of sophistication and manipulation that some authorities, such as Morris (1974), recommend that participation in institutional programs should be on a voluntary basis only, with minimal influence on parole decisions for release.

6. The real battle for reduction of criminality (for those criminals for whom reduction of recidivism is a realistic goal) takes place in the community where, under varying degrees of supervision, the criminal is exposed to criminal temptations. The major task of the correctional investigator is to prescribe conditions of supervision/treatment which will eliminate or reduce criminality without exposing the community to unacceptable levels of risk.

If the rationale for community/court reception and diagnostic centers should prevail, one consequence might be the rapid demise of geographically remote diagnostic centers at the state-wide level. As originally proposed by Hellervik (1974) among others, diagnostic centers of this type have come under increasing criticism in recent years because of their expense, duplication of effort, and the poor utilization of their reports by institutions.

If an overall correctional strategy is to be implemented, communication/administrative links between courts, parole agencies and correctional institutions must be greatly strengthened. Probation officers compiling a total management plan for offenders cannot afford to be out of touch with prisons and parole agencies. The occasionally myopic preoccupation of probation officers and sentencing judges with immediate disposition must yield to a long-range set of objectives for each offender. To be more specific, probation officers must be trained and knowledgeable in the security requirements recommended for their cases, the types of institutional programs deemed suitable, and the level of supervision likely to be necessary after release on parole.

An innovation which might facilitate overall offender planning would be the regular participation (in those cases where incarceration is likely) of an institutional classification officer and parole officer to the team conducting pre-sentence investigation. In this way, the issues of incarceration and aftercare could be addressed at the beginning of sentencing.

Is such long-range planning for offenders feasible? The answer may lie in the establishment of administrative and record-keeping practices to facilitate such changes. Smith (1978) has reported a Master File which is maintained by the Department of Corrections in Arizona, guided by his earlier work in the U.S. Bureau of Prisons and the California Department of Corrections. The statutory basis for establishment of a Master File in Arizona provides:

> The department of corrections shall maintain a master record file on each person committed to it, containing the following:
> 1. All information from the committing court.
> 2. The reports of the reception-diagnostic centers.
> 3. Evaluation and assignment reports and recommendations.
> 4. Reports of disciplinary infractions and disposition.
> 5. Progress reports prepared for the board of pardons and paroles.
> 6. Parole progress reports.
> 7. The date and circumstances of final discharge.
> 8. Any other pertinent data concerning the person's background, conduct, associations, and life history as may be required by the

department with a view to his reformation and to the protection of society.

The utility of such complete record-keeping promotes both sensible planning and research. If there is a hazard in such long-range programmatic planning for an offender, it may lie in the too-literal use of prediction formulas that fail to sensitively monitor changes in individuals as they progress through the corrections process. There should be many intermediate decision-points built into corrective programs in which updates and changes can be introduced as warranted. The introduction of a more scientific data base into corrections should never be an excuse for a mechanical, perfunctory handling of the criminal.

On the other hand, the keeping of systematic records to aid decision making is a counterweight against the importunings of the sociopathic criminal, who thrives on the discontinuities and lapses of memory of our corrections officials. As stated in this Casebook several times previously, there is simply no simplistic answer for the problem of clinical v. statistical prediction in correctional assessment work.

The Prediction of Dangerousness

Some states have enacted "extended" sentencing to deal with the disproportionate amount of crime caused by a minority of habitually crime-intensive individuals. The violence-prone criminal who has a history of victim injury is a particular focus of public concern. In her study of 49 armed robbers in California, Petersilia (1978) quotes one of these robbers as follows:

> There is no doubt in my mind that I would have killed any victim who tried to cross me. You have to understand, I was fighting a full-fledged war against 'them.' 'Them' was anyone — the establishment, whites, police, anyone. I did seriously hurt a couple of victims and I actually felt pretty good about it. I thought I was getting back at 'them.' At times I thought I might be winning the war. They would do something to me and I'd do something back. It was kind of a game. You see I wanted to make 'them' pay for all the shit I had to put up with. Oh yeah, there is no doubt that, especially in my earlier years, I was out to bust some heads — all you had to do was get in my way just a little bit.

Petersilia *et al.'s* study of patterns of violence in this group suggested that criminal violence spilled over from the violence in the offenders' personal lives, and that the violence tended to decline with additional maturity. Therefore, the early identification and incapacitation of chronically violent offenders through lengthy sentences were recommended. The use of extended sentences to incapacitate the violent and chronic offenders, which is usually a minority of young offenders, rests heavily upon the ability of correctional workers to discriminate meaningfully between such offenders and other run-of-the-mill criminals. The research thus far on correct prediction of dangerousness is not reassuring.

Morris (1974), for example, in analyzing the issues of prediction of dangerousness noted:

> There is a seductive appeal to drawing a distinction between the dangerous and the nondangerous and confining imprisonment to the former. It would be such a neat trick if we could perform it: prophylactic punishment — the preemptive judicial strike, scientifically justified — saving potential victims of future crimes and at the same time minimizing the use of imprisonment and reducing the time to

be served by most prisoners. But it is a trap. Social consequences
are often counter-intuitive. The concept of dangerousness is so
plastic and vague — its implementation so imprecise — that it would
do little to reduce either the present excessive use of imprisonment
or social injury from violent crime.

Morris reanalyzed a study by Kozol *et al.* (1972) in which 435 high-risk
prisoners in Massachusetts were evaluated for future dangerousness by a team
of clinicians and social workers prior to their release from incarceration and
followed over a 10-year period. Morris concluded that the cost of controlling
one violent person through imprisonment was the needless detention of two
additional "false positives" who need not have been imprisoned. Such social
trade-offs must cause the thoughtful corrections worker to reexamine his
values. How much community safety can be guaranteed, and at what price,
in terms of our conceptions of justice?

In fact, the most common practice among diagnosticians prognosticating
dangerousness is to over-predict for violence. The underlying rationale seems
to be, "If in doubt, why take a chance?" The social consequences of releas-
ing a dangerous offender who subsequently indulges in a violent crime are
much more severe, in terms of adverse publicity and criticism, than if the
diagnostician (or judge) errs on the side of heavy sentencing in marginal
cases. The social costs of excessive incarceration are hidden, borne by the
criminal and the prison system. Indeterminate forms of sentence, as well as
civil commitments to psychiatric hospitals, have fallen into some disrepute
because of the widespread tendency to over-predict future dangerousness
upon release.

The social isolation of dangerous persons is a serious public issue which
must continue to be addressed. The stakes are high, although answers are not
simple, as has been indicated. Two trends are apparent. First, more research
may yield more precise indicators of violence-prone persons, enabling correctional personnel to classify such persons with more confidence. It seems
more likely that results will take the form of rating scales based upon past
violent behavior, rather than any formulation depending upon personality
psychodynamics.

The second trend would move the decision for extended sentences and
fixed terms of release to the "front end" of the corrections system at the
point of sentencing, and permit less discretion by institutional parole boards
or other release authorities.

Participation in Decision Making by Offenders

The reversal by courts and legislative bodies of the traditional "hands off"
policy in the running of correctional institutions appears to be producing a
paradoxical effect on the options open to offenders within institutions. The
invoking of "due process" for offenders, the delineation of the rights of
offenders, and the prescription of health and treatment standards for prisoners
is certainly having a salutary effect on the general conditions within prisons
and on the improvement in equitable handling of prisoners. However, the
narrowing of discretionary options of correctional officials in the interests
of "fairness" has exacted a high price. In place of negotiated decisions involving prisoners, we now have a voluminous file of laws and administrative
regulations that prescribe conditions for most correctional decisions.

The net result is certainly less discretion in making decisions, with more
codification and standardization of the correctional process. What was intended to be a safeguard against abuse has added a degree of rigidity to

the processes of incarceration (which was probably not intended by the law-givers). The advent of fixed sentences prescribed in many states in recent years is once again overcrowding our prisons, whose populations were at a low ebb in the late 60s and early 70s. Overcrowding by itself restricts the program options available in prisons and increases the need for security measures to reduce the possibility of disorder.

The experiments in inmate self-government and self-help which were prevalent in the late 1960s appear to be on the decline. In addition, the mixed success of community corrections projects has generated pressure for more institutions, which could divert funds from community projects. The clouded crystal ball of corrections in the 1980s appears to be moving toward greater use of institutional restraints in crime control.

PRACTICE CASE 22

Instructions: You are to recommend a complete correctional program for this client, as described in this Casebook. Thus, your recommendations are to include institutional classification and release planning. Please note that Hector Benson has been convicted of a non-probationable offense.

Cuyahoga County Adult Probation Department
Pre-sentence Investigation

Name of Client: Hector Benson		**Prosecutor:** O'Shaughnessy	
Alias: None		**Defense Counsel:** Kermit Ronson	
Address: 234 McClintock Ave.		**Custody Status:** County Jail	
Cleveland, OH		**Charge:** Rape	
Finding: Guilty (jury trial)		Kidnapping (dismissed)	
Report Due: 3/24/76		**Penalty:** 4, 5, 6, 7 to 25 years	
Probation Officer: R. A. Prewitt		maximum fine of $10,000	
Judge: Kirkpatrick		**Plea:** Not guilty	

CURRENT OFFENSE:

Official Version (including victim's statements)

On December 18, 1975, Ms. Lavinia Blaze, age 18, reported to Cleveland Police that she had been kidnapped and raped by Hector Benson, age 23, the previous night at about 11:30 P.M. in a parking lot off Warehouse Drive in Cleveland. According to Ms. Blaze's account of the episode, she had gone to a movie, and was returning to her car to return to her apartment. As she was scraping ice from her car windows, a man came up behind her, placed his hand over her mouth, and pressed a sharp object into her side. She was ordered to keep quiet, and to drive her car away.

Her assailant, later identified as Hector Benson, displayed a large hunting knife, and theatened to injure her severely if she did not do as he said. He asked her if she had ever given a "head job" before (fellatio); she said no. He ordered her to drive to an isolated parking lot off Warehouse Drive, where he commanded her to remove all of her clothing. When she protested, he began slapping her repeatedly in the face, held the knife against her abdomen, and screamed many obscene epithets at her, ending up by ordering her to perform fellatio. Ms. Blaze attempted to comply, fearing great bodily injury.

The defendant appeared quite intoxicated, according to Ms. Blaze, and had difficulty sustaining an erection. He continued to scream and yell obscenities, said he would "f--k her all night," and she would never see her home again until she complied with his wishes. He attempted penetration, but was unable to complete a sex act due to his lack of erection. This event brought on a fresh round of curses and threats, and he again ordered her to fellate him, after threatening her again with use of the knife.

Eventually he ejaculated (testimony deleted here), and Ms. Blaze was permitted to put on her clothes. Benson was laughing, and she asked why. He said that he wished he had met her under other circumstances because he "liked her." Ms. Blaze responded that no one could enjoy any relationship when they were forced at the point of a knife. Benson kissed her several times, and asked if he could see her again, saying that she "gave a good head job." Ms. Blaze said she feared he might become violent again, and gave him the address of her apartment. She drove him downtown, then went to her apartment. She called her boyfriend, who attempted to calm her down. She reported the rape and abduction to the Cleveland Police the next morning. The defendant's wallet was found in the back seat of her car, and he was subsequently arrested. A polygraph examination by Cleveland Police showed that her account of events was accurate.

Defendant's Version:

Benson denies that he forced or threatened Ms. Blaze into having sex with him. He admits that they had sexual relations that night, but says that Ms. Blaze was a willing participant. He stated that he "picked her up" outside a movie theatre, that after talking with her for about 10 minutes, that she agreed to drive with him to the location where sexual relations occurred. He said that only after Ms. Blaze's boyfriend discovered the event did she accuse him of kidnapping and rape. He states that he intended to see her again for other dates, and that she had willingly given him the address of her apartment. He is dismayed by the jury verdict, and intends to appeal the case.

PRIOR RECORD: Within the past four years, the defendant has been convicted three times for driving while intoxicated. On the first offense, he failed to appear for sentencing, and was sentenced to 6 months in the County Jail, which was suspended in favor of 10 weekends. His second offense for DWI resulted in a 3-day jail sentence, $100 fine, and 30 day's driving suspension. His third DWI offense resulted in a 6-month sentence in the County Jail, and a three-year driving suspension. At the present time, he is forbidden to drive.

In addition, he was convicted of disorderly conduct on 6/4/73, which involved peeking into windows of an apartment house, receiving a fine of $25. On 5/30/73, he was charged with contributing to juvenile delinquency, which involved sexual play with a 15-year-old girl. This charge was dismissed for want of prosecution. This is his first known felony conviction, and no further charges are pending.

SOCIAL BACKGROUND: Hector is the first of four children born to Olivia (Charles) Benson, age 39, and Hardisty Benson, age 56. The couple have lived in Cleveland all of their lives, and Mr. Benson is an engineer with the Cleveland Light and Power Company. Mrs. Benson is a homemaker. Hector's younger brothers are Henry, age 21; Horace, age 19; and Jonathan, age 12. The defendant lives at home with his family, where he has his own room in a quiet, middle-class neighborhood. Mrs. Benson described him as a "popular youngster, who was always my favorite. I guess we spoiled him a little, being the first. But Hector has always been used to having his own way around the house."

Mrs. Benson noted that Hector was sometimes a disciplinary problem, and she could not persuade him to continue school, so that he eventually dropped out of high school in the 10th grade. She did not believe that Hector drinks excessively, but believes him to be "unlucky," so that when he does drink on paydays and holidays, he has ended up under arrest. Mrs. Benson showed much concern for Hector's future, saying that his conviction has left the family shocked and dismayed. His school records revealed him to be a below-average student, with an excessive number of absences and disciplinary reports.

EMPLOYMENT HISTORY: After dropping out of high school at age 16, Hector obtained a job as a foundry helper with the Haines Metal Working Company in Cleveland, earning $3.25 per hour. He worked at this position for 8 months, and left following a dispute with his supervisor. Through the intervention of his father, Hector next worked as a maintenance man with Cleveland Light and Power Company, where he was employed for $2.85 per hour for approximately one year, when he was discharged for tardiness and absenteeism. He was employed at the Johnson Iron and Metal Company as a sweeper, earning $3.10 per hour, where he was again discharged for absenteeism after working for approximately one year. He was employed by the Pepsi-Cola Bottling Company as a driver's helper, earning $2.35 per hour, but was discharged following a dispute with his supervisor. For the past three years, he has been employed by the Ajax Window Cleaning Company as a window-washer, where he has earned from $2.85 per hour to his present salary of $3.55 per hour. His supervisor, Mr. Kryluski, states that Hector is a satisfactory worker, but that he requires a good deal of supervision because of his occasional drinking on the job. His work adjustment is regarded as satisfactory. Mr. Kryluski says that he would consider taking him back on the job upon completion of his sentence.

PERSONAL HISTORY:

The defendant is 5'10" in height, and weighs 175 pounds. He has a stocky, muscular build. He had the usual childhood diseases, and reports himself to be in good health. He was the first of four sons in his family. He says "I guess I was always a little spoiled by mom." The defendant was born when his mother was 16 years of age, his father was 32 years old. Although the family is unclear on this point, it would appear that the marriage was forced by her family to avoid the scandal of an out-of-wedlock child. The relationship of the defendant seemed rather distant to his father, the father appearing to prefer the younger sons for companionship. Family life appeared to be uneventful, with no irregularities noted. The father was not available for interview.

During interview, the defendant admitted sex play with girls in his neighborhood, beginning about age 8. Masturbation began at age 12, and his first sexual experience was with a divorced woman living nearby when he was 14 years of age. This liaison continued sporadically for several years until this woman moved away. He dated occasionally in high school, noting "those girls were always so stuck up." After dropping out of high school in the 10th grade, he started patronizing bars at night, where he made a number of casual pickups. Benson said, "I never had to pay for it. I always got what I wanted." He reported contracting gonorrhea once, for which he received medical treatment. No steady or lasting relationship was reported with a female. In the last three years, his drinking pattern has increased. He became evasive about the charge of peeking in windows, saying "I just went back there to take a leak." He denied any previous rapes.

He was reared as a Roman Catholic, and attended

parochial schools. Since leaving high school, he has ceased to participate in church attendance. He denied any use of illegal drugs. He has had no military service. With regard to his use of alcohol, Benson says he can take it or leave it, and denies a drinking problem. He owns no automobile because of his driving suspension. He pays no board at home, and reports no financial obligations. No hobbies or recreational interests were noted.

Discussion Questions

1. If the current offense of rape is considered as a "problem" to be solved, what evaluation did you make of this event? How did you evaluate the attitude of the defendant with regard to the offense?

2. What remedial steps would you recommend to resolve the rape behavior? What do you believe the objectives of sentencing should be? In an ideal situation, what remedies might you suggest?

3. What recommendations did you make for Benson's institutional program? What is your rationale for these recommendations?

4. What predictions would you make following his release on parole? What type of community supervision/treatment would be most effective? Should he return home to his parents?

Parole Officer Jacob Mendoza Comments on the Benson Case

"I've only had this case a few weeks, so I really can't add much to what you already know. In my talks with him, Benson still denies he raped that girl. Mrs. Benson came in to talk with me, and she supports his story, too. He kept his nose clean at _____, (the Reformatory) and all the reports from there were that he made a good adjustment to being locked up. He completed his G.E.D. diploma in prison, and I think that impressed the Parole Board, since they let him out after he served the minimum time. With good time off, that was about three years.

"His parole plan called for him to live back at home, so that's where he's at. He managed to get a job with Ajax (Window-Cleaning Company) again, and his supervisor is supposed to make regular reports to me. Because this was a serious felony, I put a curfew on him, and told him that if he's seen hanging around any bars, that he may as well kiss his ass goodbye, because I won't put up with that. I made him promise to go to A.A., but I don't think he's very happy about that. He's to report to me once a week regular. What else do you want to know about him?"

Supplemental Reading

Hellervik, Lowell, et al. *A Model Assessment and Classification System for Men and Women in Correctional Institutions.* Minneapolis, Minn.: Personnel Decisions, Inc., 1974.

Morris, Norval. *The Future of Imprisonment.* Chicago: The University of Chicago Press, 1974.

Petersilia, Joan, et al. *Criminal Careers of Habitual Felons.* Washington, D.C.: National Institute of Law Enforcement and Criminal Justice, Law Enforcement Assistance Administration, 1978. (USGPO Stock No. 027-000-00696-5

Smith, A. LaMont. Standards for classification information systems. In *Handbook on Correctional Classification*, 137-148. Cincinnati, Ohio: Anderson Publishing Company, 1978.

Kozol, Harry L., Boucher, Richard J., & Garofalo, Ralph F. The diagnosis and treatment of dangerousness. *Crime and Delinquency, 18,* 1972, 371-392.